D1326744

REFERENCE
(K)

The Inner Temple

A COMMUNITY OF COMMUNITIES

BPP Law School
021877

5

THE INNER TEMPLE

A COMMUNITY OF COMMUNITIES

EDITED BY CLARE RIDER AND VAL HORSLER

III THIRD MILLENNIUM
PUBLISHING, LONDON

The Inner Temple: A Community of Communities

Copyright © Authors, the Inner Temple and
Third Millennium Publishing Limited

First published in 2007 by
Third Millennium Publishing Limited,
a subsidiary of Third Millennium Information Limited

2–5 Benjamin Street
London
United Kingdom
EC1M 5QL
www.tmiltd.com

ISBN: 978 1 903942 66 6

All rights reserved. No part of this publication may be reproduced or transmitted in any form or by any means, electronic or mechanical, including photocopying, recording or any information storage or retrieval system, without permission in writing from the publisher.

British Library Cataloguing in Publication Data
A CIP catalogue record for this book is available from the British Library.

Edited by Clare Rider and Val Horsler
Designed by Susan Pugsley
Production by Bonnie Murray

Reprographics by Asia Graphic Printing Ltd
Printed by 1010 Printing International Ltd
on behalf of Compass Press Ltd

Contents

Foreword

by Master HRH The Princess Royal

BUCKINGHAM PALACE

The Inner Temple means many things to many people. Its long history stretches back over 800 years to the time when the Knights Templar established their 'new Temple' here on the north bank of the Thames. Its almost equally long association with the lawyers, who came here over 600 years ago, is unbroken. Its buildings have, inevitably, changed and often suffered over the years from the perils of fire and bomb; but they still form an oasis of elegant peace within the bustle of London's busy streets. The gardens may now have to contend with the roar of traffic; but they remain a haven against the pressures of daily life, not just for the lawyers who work here but for Londoners too, who can come and enjoy their green abundance.

History and tradition exude from the very stones, and have extended their reach all over the world. There are Inner Templars to be found everywhere – and particularly in the Commonwealth, where the education and training offered by their *alma mater* to young students from the former empire over the last 200 years helped to lay the foundations of modern society. And home-grown lawyers nurtured here are to be found everywhere in the United Kingdom and at every level of the law. The Inner Temple has a lot to celebrate.

This is particularly so in 2008, the 400th anniversary of the presentation to the Societies of the Inner and Middle Temples of their Royal Charter by King James I. The Charter granted them perpetual ownership of their properties, and also laid down for all time their responsibility to practise and teach the law and to maintain and care for the ancient Temple Church – which still enjoys the status of a royal peculiar, answerable only to the crown. It is all too evident to a visitor to the Inner Temple today that the Society continues to honour the commitments they made four centuries ago, and will continue to do so.

I am proud to be a Royal Bencher of the Inner Temple, and delighted to join with the Society in celebrating this momentous anniversary.

Anne

Foundations & Traditions

IN THE BEGINNING: THE TEMPLE OF THE KNIGHTS

The Knights Templar, whose primary duty when they were founded in the early twelfth century was that of defending pilgrims to the Holy Land from infidel attack, rapidly grew into an international order of enormous wealth and influence. Early on in their existence they established a foundation in London, on a site in Holborn, and immediately attracted royal patronage, being granted land and manors in several counties. But already by the 1160s their first English home had become too small, and they moved their preceptory to a new site on the north bank of the Thames where they constructed their 'New Temple'. The consecration ceremony was conducted in 1185 by Heraclius, Patriarch of Jerusalem, and was almost certainly attended by King Henry II. Further monastic buildings were constructed on the site, including two dining halls.

The Templars quickly established a close relationship with the English monarchy, being entrusted with the guardianship of the royal treasure and wielding strong political influence. It was while he was lodging at the Temple in 1215 that King John was approached by the barons seeking a charter of liberties, and the Master of the Temple acted as one of the witnesses to the subsequent signature of the Magna Carta at Runnymede. John's son, Henry III, conferred many favours on the Templars, as well as borrowing more money from them than any other monarch, and at one time declared his wish to be buried in the Temple Church (though he later decided on Westminster Abbey instead). One of his sons who died in infancy is believed, however, to have been buried in the Temple.

Effigy in the Round.

The Temple Church, although much altered internally and heavily restored, still bears witness to the wealth and importance of the order at this time. The knights began building it as soon as they had taken possession of their new domain on the north bank of the Thames – a bank which then ran a good distance further north than it does today. A detailed account of the new building is given in *The Temple Church in London* by David Lewer and Robert Dark, from which the following summary is taken.

The distinctive round shape of the new Temple echoed that of its predecessor – as was confirmed by building work in Holborn in the late Victorian period – and was a form very much favoured by the order. It was popular all over Europe too, in the wake of the Crusades, modelled as it was on the church of the Holy Sepulchre in Jerusalem with its rotunda centred on the cave believed to have been Jesus Christ's burial place.

The period during which the new Church was being constructed, the second half of the twelfth century, was a time of architectural innovation. The introduction of the pointed arch was beginning to transform the heavy Romanesque style of building into a new heavenward-aspiring style which would become known as Gothic. The Temple Church is one of the most important surviving examples of this 'Transitional' style: the heads of the great west doorway and the windows retain the semicircular Romanesque shape, while the six arches of the main arcade, cut into the round drum supporting the roof, are pointed. The

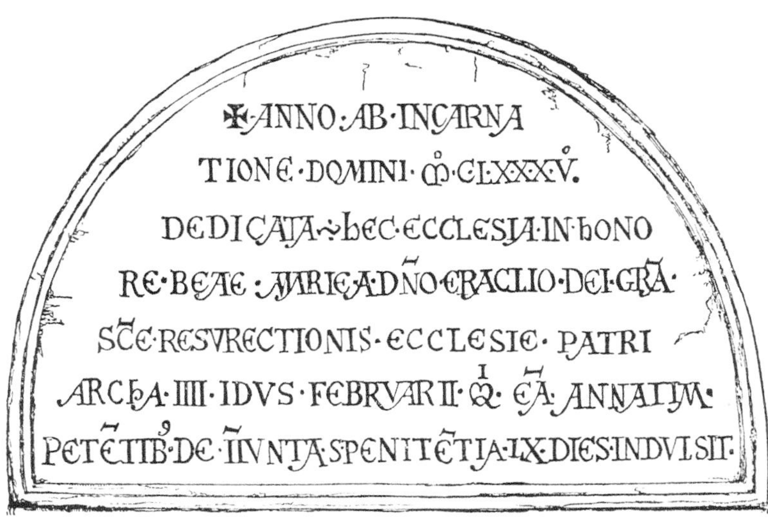

Dedication inscription, 1185, originally over the south-west door.

triforium arcading is truly Transitional: a series of interlaced semicircles resulting in pointed arches. The building was innovative in other ways too: the Purbeck marble piers and columns were arguably the first to employ that material since Roman times, possibly predating by a few years its use in Canterbury Cathedral. The contrast between this dark stone and the white Caen stone used for the main structure is striking. And the splendour of the great west doorway, with its decorated shafts and capitals and its alternate plain and high relief mouldings, is enhanced by the beautiful Norman wheel window above it.

There is evidence that the original building included a small chancel to the east, but this was soon demolished to make way for an extended chancel which was dedicated in 1240. This building too was unusual, in that the side aisles were of the same height as the soaring central aisle. Its width was the same as the diameter of the Round, and there were five bays, all stone vaulted, supported by free-standing piers and substantial external buttresses. Plenty of light was afforded by triplets of lancet windows in the walls.

The porch at the west end of the Round was added early in the Church's history, and the court to the south was enclosed by cloisters, of which only the west side can now be defined with certainty; this was reconstructed by Sir Christopher Wren in 1682 and rebuilt to his original design after the destruction of the Second World War. To the south of the Round there originally stood a two-storey building housing a chapel later known as St Ann's. It was supposedly in this building that the Templars initiated novices into the secrets of the order, and speculation further links it with Freemasonry. It was demolished in 1826 when improvements were being made to Church Court.

Little is known about the effigies of knights still to be seen in the Church, apart from the fact that three of them represent William Marshal, Earl of Pembroke, and two of his sons. Their beardlessness may indicate that they were associates of the order, rather than full members, and it is not clear whether or not the crossed legs of some of them indicate that they had been on a crusade. The repositioning of the effigies within the Round on several occasions has destroyed any relationship there might have been with the coffins found beneath the floor during excavations in 1841. These coffins were of both stone and lead, those of lead being buried more deeply and therefore presumably earlier. The skeletons found in some of them bear witness to the physique perhaps necessary for a medieval knight: one was six feet four inches tall and another six feet two inches.

The end of the Order of the Knights Templar was to come with devastating suddenness in the early years of the fourteenth century. It was perhaps inevitable that, with their original purpose gone after the loss of all Christian strongholds in the Holy Land, the wealth and influence of this powerful community would come under attack. Philip the Fair of France began the onslaught in 1307, accusing the Templars of many kinds of heresy and depraved practices as a pretext for seizing their property in France. Five years later the pope, Clement V, dependent as he was on the support and goodwill of the French king, endorsed the campaign and declared the abolition of the order.

In England, the special relationship between the Templars and the monarch initially dissuaded Edward II from joining in the persecution and obeying the pope's instruction to act against the

The south side of the Temple Church.

Above: Interior of the Round.
Left: The Round from Church Court.

order. When he eventually complied and started proceedings against them, the interrogations and trial dragged on for several years with the inquisitors seeking anything provable against them and the members of the order staunchly defending themselves and refusing to admit any wrongdoing. One of the charges was that Sir Walter le Bacheler, Grand Preceptor of Ireland, had been murdered while confined in the Penitential Cell – the notorious chamber in the thickness of the bell tower stair wall which was too small to allow a man to lie down. He had died there after eight weeks of confinement, and his body had been taken out at dawn and buried in the middle of the court between the Church and the Hall. As C G Addison wrote in his 1843 publication, *The Temple Church*, 'In this miserable cell were confined the refractory and disobedient brethren of the Temple, and those who were enjoined severe penance with solitary confinement. Its dark secrets have long since been buried in the silence of the tomb.' But this accusation too could not be proved, and eventually the only solid charge against the Templars was that the Master had believed he had the power to absolve his followers of their sins, despite being a layman.

However, even then the English knights escaped the horrors inflicted on their counterparts elsewhere, particularly in France where hundreds were threatened with torture and the last Grand Master was burnt at the stake in Paris in 1314. In England they were pardoned after making public confession, and reconciled to the church. Their property, however, had been seized by the crown, and some of it was eventually handed over by the king to the Knights Hospitaller. This gift included the consecrated part of the New Temple in London, which the Hospitallers were soon to lease to the lawyers.

The Temple Church is owned and managed jointly by the Inner Temple and the Middle Temple, an arrangement that has led at some points in its long history to disputes. One of those episodes, known as 'the Battle of the Pulpit', arose when the Mastership fell vacant in 1585. The Reader of the Temple, a staunch Calvinist, was expected to accede to the post, but instead Elizabeth I, on the advice of John Whitgift, the Archbishop of Canterbury, appointed Richard Hooker, who would become the founding father of Anglican theology. Since the Master preached at morning services and the Reader at those in the afternoon, the messages coming from the pulpit tended to contradict each other; as Izaac Walton commented, 'The forenoon sermon spake Canterbury; and the afternoon Geneva.' Eventually, Whitgift intervened to prevent the Reader from preaching and the Anglican order prevailed.

To this day, the Temple enjoys the status of a royal peculiar, another direct legacy from the Knights Templar, who were answerable only to the pope and immune from all other ecclesiastical and lay authority. This position survived Henry VIII's Reformation in the early sixteenth century, though the English monarch, as head of the Anglican church, assumed control of the Temple Church; moreover, James I's Charter of 1608 explicitly reserved to the crown the right to appoint the Master of the Temple. To this day the Temple is exempt from the jurisdiction of the Bishop of London and answerable only to the crown through the Dean of the Chapels Royal.

Removal of Sir Walter le Bacheler's body from the Penitential Cell; print from Addison's The Temple Church, *1843.*

The Temple Church and *The Da Vinci Code*

The Reverend Robin Griffith-Jones, the Master of the Temple

Mid-morning on an ordinary weekday: time for the verger to open the Church for visitors. As usual, there is a group of visitors waiting to come in. He already knows what they will ask: 'Where is the crypt? Where are the knights' effigies? Where is the tomb without a figure?' And most eagerly of all, 'Have you read the book?' He used to think they were asking about the Bible. He knows better now.

In *The Da Vinci Code*, the novel by Dan Brown, are to be found conspiracies and machinations extending over 2000 years. Here are the mysteries of the Knights Templar and the Opus Dei. Here is the most secret of all secret societies, the Priory of Sion (past Master Leonardo da Vinci) and its great mission: to preserve from all enemies – especially the Roman Catholic Church – the descendants of Sarah, daughter of Jesus and Mary Magdalen, and to protect the documents that prove the lineage of these descendants, the attendant treasure and the body of the Magdalen herself.

The verger by the west door.

Filming The Da Vinci Code.

The Temple Church is the setting for a climactic scene in the novel, when the hero, heroine and (so far unrecognised) villain come to the Church to find the next clue in their search for the Holy Grail – a knight's tomb lacking an orb. Pursuing them are the villain's servant and a giant albino monk…

At one point in the book the hero feels 'as if he were living in some kind of limbo… a bubble where the real world could not reach him.' Quite. The fantasies of *The Da Vinci Code* do not stand up to the clear light of history and theology, as I suspect Dan Brown himself knows all too well: the name he gives his villain is an anagram of the name of one of the authors of *The Holy Blood and the Holy Grail*, the ideas from which are the basis of much of his book, and the name of the villain's pawn translates from the Italian as 'red herring'.

But nothing is likely now to temper the fascination which the Temple Church holds for avid readers of the book and keen followers of the search. The film has only added fuel to the fire, and long gone are the days when I naively agreed to talk to documentary makers and, expecting to expatiate on the Templars, instead found myself fielding insistent questions on Jesus, Mary Magdalen and sacred orgies!

Opposite: Knights on the Millennium Column: sculpture by Nicola Hicks.

The Coming of the Lawyers

Master Baker

It is unlikely that the origins of the Inns of Court will ever be dated with precision. Unlike colleges at Oxford and Cambridge, they did not owe their being to founders and benefactors, they were never incorporated and they took over existing premises which were occupied under informal leases. We can, nevertheless, date at least three of them with reasonable confidence to the second quarter of the fourteenth century, and on a balance of probabilities to the 1340s. There is no evidence that collegiate societies of lawyers were in existence in the 1330s, when the king's courts and the attendant profession moved for a few years to York. Indeed, it is indicative of their absence that when an agreement was made in 1323 to provide maintenance for a law student, the terms were not that he should attend some fixed institution or location but rather that he should spend four years among the apprentices 'at our lord the king's court of Common Bench, wherever the said Bench should be in England'. Lodging arrangements were *ad hoc* and informal, and not worthy of mention in records and chronicles.

When the profession returned from York *en masse* in 1339, there must have been a serious lodging crisis, and the likelihood is that the decision was then taken to establish informal societies which could pool resources to rent substantial town-houses (*hospicia*) such as the Temple in Fleet Street and Lord Grey of Wilton's inn in Holborn. Already by March 1339 some of the 'apprentices of court' had a servant who was indicted for killing someone near the Temple and had allegedly fled into Temple Church, whence he had made his escape at night. Although the record does not explicitly link his masters with the Temple, it shows that there was a community of apprentices sufficiently organised to hire servants, and it seems a plausible inference that this particular community was located in the Temple. On a Sunday evening in the following June, four apprentices of the Bench – men from parts as distant as Somerset and Cumberland – were involved in a fatal battle with two Chancery clerks opposite the rent of Serjeant Thomas de Lincoln in Holborn, a possible first reference to Lincoln's Inn, though not to the present premises. The apprentices fled to the house of one John Davy or Tavy, which we know from Tavy's will (1348) was let to apprentices and which later became Thavies Inn. Clifford's Inn may well belong to the same decade, since we know that in 1344 it was let, perhaps for the first time, to apprentices of the Bench. Another bloodletting in Holborn, on Sunday 25 February 1341, introduces us to a John of Cornwall, 'manciple', whose house faced that of the Bishop of Lincoln and must have been close to Gray's Inn.

This word 'manciple' is of considerable evidential significance. It was an academical term, doubtless borrowed from Oxford, and indicated stewardship of a hall of residence with collegiate features. A search through legal records of this period reveals the names of other manciples frequenting the western suburbs of London, and since some of them had under-servants it is obvious that they served substantial communities. This was a whole generation before Geoffrey Chaucer's 'gentle manciple… of a temple [had] masters… more than thrice ten, that were of law expert and curious'; he at any rate was clearly employed by a well-established legal society, maybe the Inner Temple, where Chaucer is said to have been a member. Since the term was never used for private stewards, the appearance of 'manciples' in the legal quarter in the 1340s affords some of the best evidence we are likely to find for the establishment of collegiate legal communities at that period, communities perhaps consciously modelled on the colleges of Oxford and Cambridge. The previous two decades had been the most active period of college foundation at both universities, and also in Paris. And it is from the same generation that we find evidence of complex pleading exercises, and lectures on statutes, which later grew into the familiar educational routine of moots and readings. The Temple which was sacked by Wat Tyler and his rebels in 1381 was by that date firmly associated in the popular mind with the upper levels of the legal profession, the *apprenticii juris nobiliores*, who kept trunks full of their clients' papers and muniments in the Church.

The manciple from Chaucer's Canterbury Tales *(from the Ellesmere Manuscript).*

There was once a tradition that the lawyers in the Temple originally formed a single society, which then at some unknown date divided into two. This now seems highly unlikely. There were already two halls in existence in the time of the knights, and halls were the social and educational centre of a legal community. One of the Templars' halls was connected with the Church by a cloister, and was evidently on the site of the present Inner Temple Hall. The Inner Temple Hall which was demolished in 1868 was perhaps only of fourteenth- or fifteenth-century date, but it was built on the foundations of a still earlier building, some of which – or rather, foundations belonging to the same range of buildings, which included a chapel – can still be seen exposed opposite the south end of the cloisters. The original Middle Temple Hall, on the east side of Middle Temple Lane, was converted into chambers when the Elizabethan hall was built, and then demolished in 1639; but some medieval foundations apparently coeval with the Round of the Church were discovered on the site in 1735. This was very much in the 'middle' of the Temple, and would account for a name which now seems less geographically apt. The bipartite division of territory had also preceded the coming of the lawyers, the Inner Temple portion corresponding to the consecrated inner precinct, with the refectory of the priests; and this division had been preserved when the Temple was first let by the Knights Hospitaller in 1324. The rent of the consecrated portion in 1336 was £12 4s 1d, which is not far short of the customary uncertain rent of 'about' twenty marks (£13 6s 8d) paid by the Inner Temple to the landlords until the sixteenth century. There were therefore effectively two Inns to let in the Temple when the legal profession returned from York in 1339. Both parts were leased from the same landlord – the Priory of the Hospital of St John of Jerusalem, as successor in title to the Knights Templar – but separate rents were paid until the dissolution of the Priory in the time of Henry VIII. It seems inherently unlikely that this state of affairs could have come about through a partition negotiated with the landlord, given that the demarcation had occurred before the initial letting and would probably have passed into oblivion if the Temple had been let to a body of lawyers in its entirety.

The Inns were certainly separate entities in 1388, when a call of eight serjeants at law took place, all of whom (according to a manuscript note by a law reporter) came from the Temple and Gray's Inn. The greatest number, five, were from the Inner Temple (*interioris Templi*), while only one was from the Middle Temple. One of the five Inner Templars was William Gascoigne (d 1419), later Chief Justice of the King's Bench, immortalised by Shakespeare and renowned for his display of judicial independence in committing Prince Henry (later King Henry V) for contempt. There are numerous references in the fifteenth century to the 'Inner Inn' of the Temple, or more usually 'the Inn of the Inner Temple' (*hospicium interioris Templi*). Until the sixteenth century it was a larger society than the Middle Inn, which drew its members chiefly from the west country. There was also a small portion of the Temple known as the Outer Temple, which provided a new serjeant in 1425; but it seems never to have been a distinct Inn, and by the early 1500s its residents were members of the other two Inns. The Outer Temple seems, from complaints in the Inner Temple's records, to have been chiefly the responsibility of the Middle Temple; but in 1510 and 1517 it was the Inner Temple which assigned chambers in a tower there known as Le Bastelle.

The surviving records of the Inner Temple begin in 1505, though there were at one time earlier books and rolls. These show a society of substantial size governed by long-standing customs and regulations. As in the other Inns, the original constitution was independent of the degree system which grew up during the fifteenth century (and will be described below). All the members were regarded as members of the fellowship (*societas*). A barrister of two years' call in 1557 could describe himself in legal proceedings as 'one of the fellows (*socii*) of the Inner Temple', a title claimed equally by Benchers and students. As in the other Inns, the fellowship was divided into two 'companies', known as clerks' commons and masters' commons, alluding to their separate tables in Hall. Clerks were newly admitted students, who paid lower dues and had cheaper commons (food rations) in return for waiting on the masters in Hall. They remained in this station for about two

Old buildings in Inner Temple Lane, from the Illustrated London News, *1860.*

years, until they were called up to masters' commons. The masters were divided into Benchers (or masters of the Bench), utter-barristers (or masters of the utter bar) and inner-barristers (or masters of the inner bar); it was only in more recent times that the title 'Master' came to denote Benchers. Regulatory decisions were made at meetings known as 'Parliaments', the Inn's customary governing body, which were originally meetings of all the fellows. Every year, at a Parliament, a Treasurer and two or three governors were elected to carry on the daily administration. The first known holders of these offices were Thomas Welles, Richard Danvers and Richard Hall, who as *'thesaurarius ac gubernatores Interioris Templi'* sued thirteen members for dues in 1484. Two years later the governance had passed to Morgan Kidwelly, Robert Sheffield, Thomas Kebell and Richard Littleton. These were distinguished members of the legal profession. Kidwelly, later knighted, was Attorney-General to King Richard III; and it is noteworthy that Richard's Chancellor of the Exchequer (William Catesby, beheaded in 1485) and Solicitor-General (Thomas Lyneham) were also Inner Templars. Sheffield, son of a Bencher of the same name, was to become Recorder of London, knighted after the battle of Blackheath in 1497. Kebell, attorney of the Duchy of Lancaster and a famous serjeant at law, was the subject of a full-length biography in 1983. Littleton, who also practised at the Bar, was the second son of Sir Thomas Littleton (d 1481), former Bencher of the Inn and author of the *Tenures*, the standard introduction to land law for four centuries. Other fifteenth-century governors included Robert Brudenell, later Chief Justice of the Common Pleas and ancestor of the earls of Cardigan, and Richard Sutton, co-founder of Brasenose College, Oxford.

In the early sixteenth century the Masters of the Bench were considered associates of the governors, but by the time of Elizabeth I they had taken over from them the control of the Inn, as a governing body acting under the chairmanship of the Treasurer. The last recorded election of governors was in 1566. The Treasurer was of course responsible for finances, and this included control of admissions, which were a matter of careful financial negotiation: a new member could be excused the holding of offices, or permitted to be in or out of commons at his pleasure, in return for a substantial fine or a hogshead of wine. The entrants were not, as a rule, university graduates, and certainly not graduates in law. They were mostly sons of the gentry, since an exhibition of at least £10 a year was necessary in 1500 to cover expenses, and there were no endowed scholarships; but it was nevertheless possible for clever young men from obscure backgrounds to gain admittance and perhaps, through their efforts, establish their family in the gentry. The majority of members were not 'learners' bent on a legal career, and the educational system (see below) was not compulsory. The principal sanction was self-qualification. No one was obliged to join an Inn of Court, but he could not advance in the law beyond the status of an attorney unless he did so; and if he meddled in litigation without being a member of an Inn he was probably guilty of the offence of maintenance. No one who joined an Inn was obliged to attend its learning exercises, provided he was prepared to pay a fine or find a substitute; but he could not graduate as a barrister or a Bencher without doing so. And only Benchers could expect to become serjeants at law or senior legal officials. For the majority, the non-learners, the Inns provided an introduction to the metropolis and civilised culture, to the nation's institutions and to the elite who would manage them. A smattering of law, learned from elementary books such as Littleton, would serve them sufficiently in managing their own affairs.

The compulsory side of discipline was primarily directed to the payment of commons and dues, and the preservation of good order. Social order was enforced by fines or by temporary expulsion from commons (meals), the last resort of permanent expulsion being rare. All members were expected to behave like gentlemen, to treat each other with courtesy, outside the Inn as well as inside, and to wear suitable dress – which was assumed to be the ankle-length gown of a gentleman. In Tudor times the colourful parti-coloured robes of the fifteenth century gave way to the plain open gown of a dark colour, though there was no prescribed pattern until the end of the sixteenth century. The first distinctive type of Bar gown, decorated with black velvet facings and two vertical bands of black velvet on the upper arm, is seen on an effigy at Bromsgrove,

Worcestershire, representing George Littleton (d 1600), who was called to the Bar by the Inner Temple in 1583. From this period until the eighteenth century, black skull-caps were also *de rigueur*, and were worn with gowns in Hall. Benchers were allowed to wear more elaborate gowns, with black lace and tufts.

There was a Library by the early sixteenth century, and although it possessed a number of interesting manuscripts – none of which have survived – it seems to have been very modest in its holdings and facilities. Members of the Inns had to rely chiefly on private collections, containing manuscript as well as printed books, and to make good the deficiencies by loan or exchange. The only communal meeting place, apart from the Round of the Temple Church, was the little medieval hall where members took commons and attended learning exercises. Commons in the Inns were served on wooden trenchers, with green earthenware pots for beverages. A number of earthenware vessels have been found in Hare Court and elsewhere in the Temple; and a seventeenth-century green-glazed drinking jug with a Pegasus stamp, unearthed at Temple Stairs, is now in the Museum of London.

The explosion of litigation in the century before 1640 occasioned an expansion of the legal profession and of the Inns' membership. By 1634 there were around 800 members listed on the rolls of the Inner Temple (which survive for that year in the Public Record Office); the number of admissions between 1600 and 1640 alone was over 1700. This expansion required continuous enlargement of the buildings. The rebuilding of the Temple is not well recorded, because most projects for erecting chambers were carried out privately, with the Inn's leave, the investors gaining an assignable interest in the chambers for which they had paid. Hare Court, for instance, commemorates a rebuilding scheme financed by Nicholas Hare and his relations in 1567. By Hare's time there were around 100 sets of chambers in the Inn, making it the second largest (after Gray's Inn). Chambers were primarily residential at that time; but only fifteen Benchers and twenty-three barristers lived in, well outnumbered by the 151 resident students. The extensive building projects of the sixteenth and seventeenth centuries are discussed below (p 60).

A surprisingly large proportion of the entries in the Inn's earlier records relate to the courtly traditions of Christmas, which were taken very seriously in all the legal societies. Attendance was compulsory for new members. Special Christmas officers were elected from among the fellowship, though many were the defaults of those elected and heavy the fines. There were a steward, clerk of the kitchen and butler, masters of the revels and a marshal. There was probably a student 'king', as in Gray's Inn, who presided over the festive season with his mock officers of state, including a lord high constable and judges. The masters of the revels engaged the services of actors and minstrels, while the domestic officers oversaw the plentiful provision of Christmas fare. These customs died hard. Attempts to abolish them in the 1660s met with fierce resistance, and they survived at least until 1697, when the diarist John Evelyn recorded the riotous 'Bacchanalia' in the Inner Temple – followed in January by a masque performed in the presence of Peter the Great, Tsar of Russia. The heavy emphasis on Christmas in the records was a reflection of the difficulty of enforcing its traditions rather than of its relative importance. Seldom do we find any mention of the academical routine of the Inn, apart from the election of Readers, although legal education was more central to its purpose and will be considered further below (p 26).

Professor Sir John Baker QC is the Downing Professor of the Laws of England at Cambridge University, and is an Honourary Bencher of the Inn.

An eighteenth-century view from Mitre Court Buildings towards the King's Bench Office.

The Royal Charter, 1608

Clare Rider

On 13 August 1608 King James I granted to the Masters of the Bench of the Inner and Middle Temple by their personal names the freehold of 'the Inns and capital messuages known as the Inner Temple and the Middle Temple or the New Temple', by Letters Patent. There was no charge for the issue of these Letters Patent or Charter, but there were conditions attached, the most significant being the maintenance and repair of the Temple Church and the guarantee that the Inns 'shall serve for the accommodation and education of those studying and following the profession of the aforesaid laws, abiding in the same Inns for all time to come'. A further stipulation was the provision of accommodation and an annual salary of £17 6s 8d for the 'Master, Keeper or Rector of the Temple Church', whose appointment was to remain a royal one, and the payment of an annual fee-farm rent of £10 to the crown. With the exception of the fee-farm rent, which is no longer payable, these terms remain in place. Fortunately for the Master, the salary has risen with inflation, although on one occasion when a royal appointment had been made against the Inns' wishes, the angry Benchers threatened to revert to the stipulated salary. A new, more acceptable Master was rapidly selected and installed.

As a sign of their gratitude to James I, the Inns presented him with a gold cup, weighing twelve and half pounds and costing £666 13s 4d, a enormous sum in contemporary terms, paid equally by the Inner and Middle Temple, together with a second smaller cup in a velvet case. Royal finances being tight, it was not long before the cups were apparently pawned in Holland, whence they never returned. On the 400th anniversary of James I's grant, the Inner and Middle Temple can look back with pride on their long history and continuing role; but what is the significance today of their Royal Charter?

By 1608, the two Inns, probably founded in the 1340s, had been in existence for at least 250 years, leasing the Temple site and buildings from the Knights Hospitaller, as successors of the Knights Templar, and subsequently from the crown. The Letters Patent granted the Inns the freehold of the land and ownership of the Temple Church, although it did not effect any demarcation between the property interests of the two societies; the formal division of the site and buildings was agreed and then modified by later Deeds of Partition. The Patent also conferred upon the Inns an official status and a defined purpose. In the absence of a written constitution, they continue to rely on this document to prove their legitimacy. Moreover, under the terms of a Papal Bull of 1162, the Knights Templar had enjoyed freedom from outside interference, both lay and ecclesiastical. Three hundred years later, in 1608, the legal societies that had replaced them were granted similar privileges in perpetuity by James I's grant. The Temple Church's status as a royal peculiar, excluding it from the jurisdiction of the Archbishop of Canterbury and the Bishop of London and reserving the appointment of the incumbent to the monarch, was confirmed by the Charter, as was the Inns' exemption from secular authorities, including the City of London. These have not survived uncontested. However, the two Inns have retained their unique status as local authorities, acknowledged in government legislation, and the Temple Church still enjoys the privileges of a royal peculiar thanks to the generous gift of James I.

Dr Clare Rider is the Archivist of the Inner Temple.

Portrait of James I from the 1608 Charter.

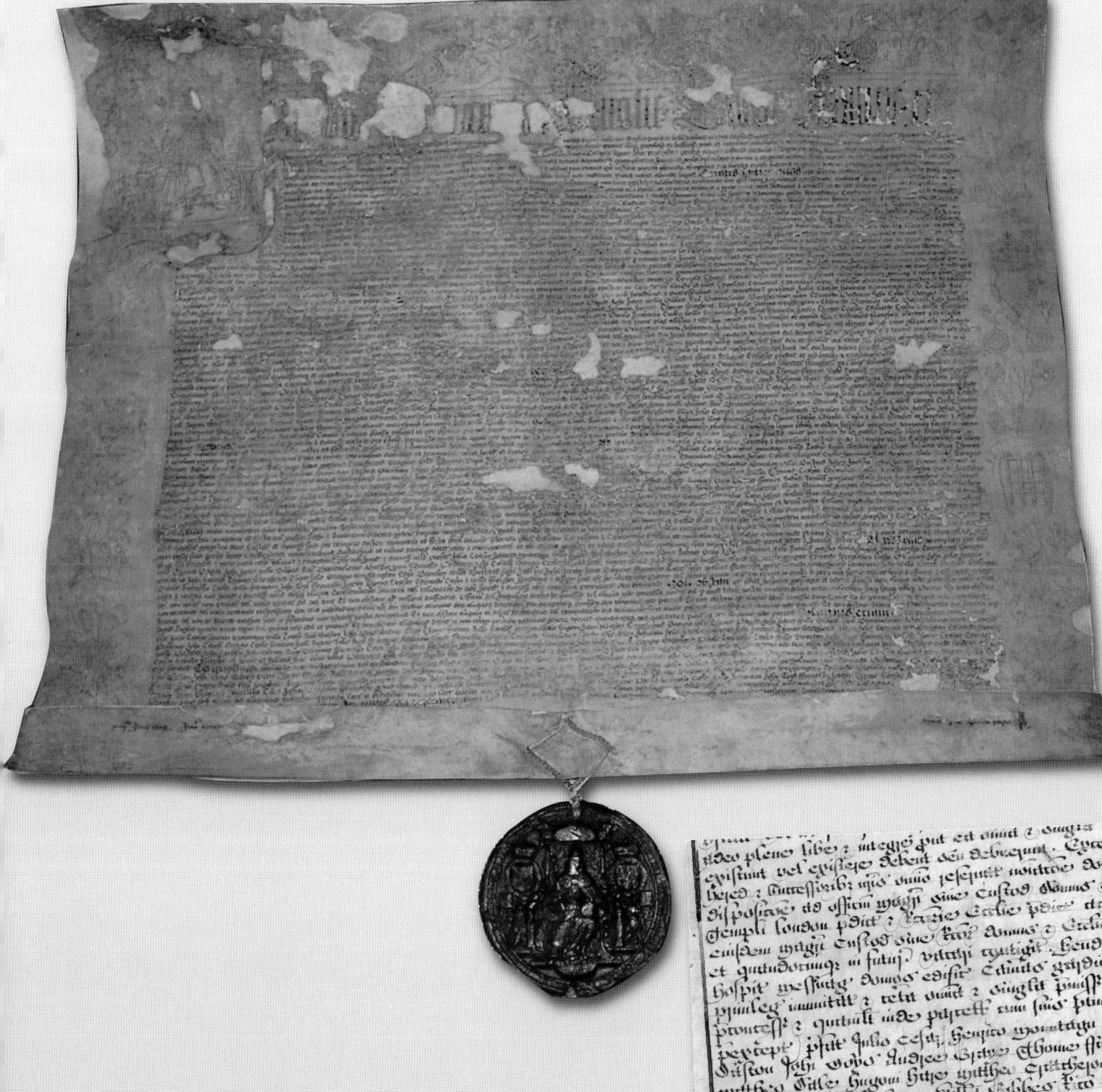

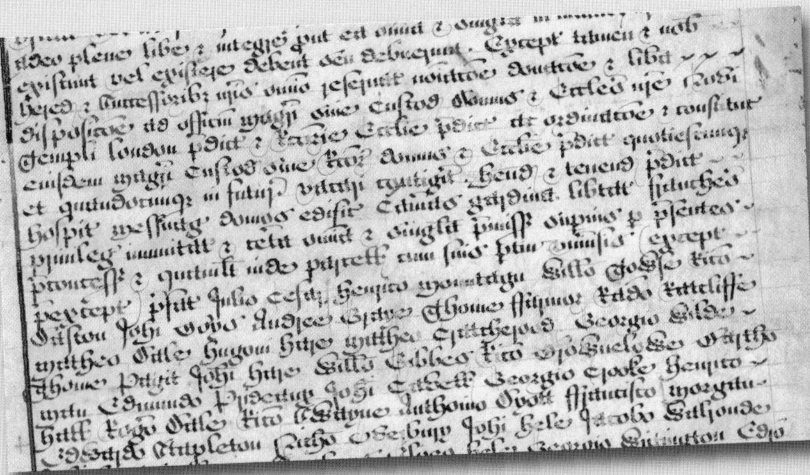

Above: Original 1608 Letters Patent or Charter held in the Middle Temple Archives.
Right: Extract from the Patent Roll copy of the Charter in the National Archives.

The Pegasus

Clare Rider

The weather vane above Crown Office Row.

> *Then who so will with virtuous deeds assay*
> *To mount to heaven, on Pegasus must ride*
> EDMUND SPENSER, 'RUINES OF TIME'

According to one version of the Greek legend, Pegasus, the winged horse, was born from the neck of the gorgon, Medusa, after Perseus had severed her head. Rising heavenward to Helicon, the home of the Muses, he became a symbol of virtue and creative inspiration. The Honourable Society of the Inner Temple reflects that sentiment in its Latin motto, originally 'Volat alta ad sidera virtus' and more recently 'Volat ad aethera virtus' ('virtue flies to the heavens'), which frequently accompanies the image of the flying horse.

Visitors to the Inner Temple, unable to miss the ubiquitous symbol of the Pegasus on buildings throughout the Inn, frequently seek the origin of the emblem. Would that we knew! Without definitive evidence, several theories have been put forward. One holds that the Inn adapted the design from one of the Knights Templars' seals, the image of two knights seated on one horse, which is reproduced in the bronze statue by Nicola Hicks on Ptolemy Dean's Millennium Column in Church Court (see p 15). It is not known whether the Templars aimed to indicate by the two knights sharing a horse the original poverty of the order or the charity and brotherly love that it embodied. Either way, it is possible that the two knights came to represent the wings of the Inner Temple's flying horse. Some credibility is lent to the hypothesis by the Middle Temple's subsequent adoption of another Templar seal image, the lamb and flag. Another interpretation assigns the origins of the flying horse to an image on the tiles in the Temple Church, which showed a single mounted knight holding a shield with bars, which might have resembled a wing. A more commonly held view is that the choice of the Pegasus emblem dates from the 1561 Christmas revels, when Lord Robert Dudley acted the part of Prince Pallaphilos, governor of the Inner Temple and patron of the fictional order of the Pegasus. As Master of the Queen's Horse in real life, it is likely that the use of the Pegasus symbol in the revels was designed in his honour (below p 150). Representations of the flying horse were widely used by the Inn thereafter, both in revelry and as an official armorial device. This ancient usage was confirmed by the College of Arms in 1967, endorsing the Inner Temple's right to use a silver Pegasus on an azure (light blue) background – *Azure a Pegasus salient argent* – as its device. Whatever its origin, the Pegasus emblem is here to stay.

Niblett Pegasus, formerly above the entrance to Niblett Hall.

Opposite: Pegasus as depicted in a stained glass window in the Inner Temple Hall.

LEARNING THE LAW

Early Forms of Legal Education and Later Developments

Master Baker

There was once a theory that the Inns of Court began as mere lodging houses, and acquired their educational routines in the fifteenth century. This is now known to be wrong. As with the colleges at Oxford and Cambridge, the Inns grew up within an existing university and were from the outset actively concerned with the continuation and improvement of an established system of education.

The fateful decision of the English university law faculties not to concern themselves with English law had led by the 1250s to the introduction of specialist training for the apprentices of 'the Bench' (the Court of Common Pleas in Westminster Hall), chiefly in the form of lectures on procedure and property law, and the disputation of imaginary cases. After the appearance of collegiate societies in the time of Edward III, the training was distributed between the Inns of Chancery, for younger students, and the Inns of Court, which provided more advanced courses. The lectures on procedure and tenures gave way to elementary books, the *Natura Brevium* and the *Old Tenures.* At both levels the exercises of learning were now divided into lectures on statutes (called 'readings') and arguments upon pleadings (called 'moots'). They obviously owed their inspiration to the university system of lectures and disputations, and the choice of statutory texts for the readings evidently reflected the medieval assumption that lecturing meant reading out and expounding written texts.

By the mid-fifteenth century there was also a graduation system resembling that in the academical schools. The Hall of the Inn was arranged after dinner to resemble a court, with a Bench and a Bar. Utter-barristers, corresponding with bachelors in the universities, were those who took part in disputations by arguing cases in Hall as if at the Bar of a court – that is, standing outside the Bar – and for centuries a barrister could only take that degree at a moot. The word 'barrister' therefore refers not to the Bar of any court of law, but to the Bar of an Inn of Court. It occurs in the Lincoln's Inn records in the 1460s, vying briefly with 'barrer' as an alternative; a 'barester' of the Inner Temple is mentioned in 1481. The process of self-graduation, by performing an exercise, was at first more significant than the 'call' which authorised it. Indeed, until the 1550s, barristers were still sometimes 'called' in vacation by the other barristers present. An order of 1556, still in force today, finally placed call in the hands of the Benchers; and from 1567 calls to the Bar were recorded. The Benchers, who by 1556 had become the governing body of the Inn, were originally conceived of as graduates holding a superior degree corresponding with that of master or doctor. Like masters, they qualified themselves by delivering a course of lectures and thereafter sat on the Bench at moots. Since the election of a Reader belonged to the whole company, it was always recorded in the Parliament books, beginning with Lent 1506. There is a slightly earlier mention of an Inner Temple Bencher by that title in a Gray's Inn moot, where Edmund Dudley makes a flattering reference to 'Baker, *bencher de interiori templo, que fuit bien erudite en la ley*'. It was another John Baker, possibly his son, who was the first Inner Templar known to have been called to the Bench without having read (in 1517): a sign that the degree was beginning to be divorced from its original *raison d'être.*

The readings were not given in term-time, when students were supposed to attend the courts in Westminster Hall, but in the two 'grand' vacations during Lent and the early autumn (August). These were the chief events in the educational cycle, and were regularly attended by those judges and serjeants who were former Benchers of the Inn. Each course originally lasted at least four weeks, though they became shorter in later centuries. Our earliest surviving Inner Temple reading is that of Thomas Welles (the first known Treasurer) in 1460, on the first six chapters of the Statute of Merton. Most of the fifteenth-century readings are now lost, but it is known that Sir Thomas Littleton and Serjeant Kebell both lectured on *De Donis* and that William Catesby lectured on Magna Carta. Richard Hall's reading (1481) on the first part of the Statute of Gloucester, and Morgan Kidwelly's reading (1483) on chapter 11 of Magna Carta, were printed by the Selden Society in 1954.

Clifford's Inn Hall.

The original custom was for Readers to work their way through the thirteenth-century statutes (the *statuta vetera*) from Magna Carta until the reign of Edward I, each Reader beginning where his predecessor left off, just as masters in the university delivered their ordinary lectures on the set texts, clause by clause, word by word. By early Tudor times we find some Readers breaking from the old cycle, perhaps in order to make a mark and impress the crown with their usefulness: the earliest known example is Edmund Dudley's reading in Gray's Inn on *Quo warranto*, around 1485. The first reading of that type which we have from the Inner Temple is Thomas Frowyk's on *Prerogativa Regis* in 1495. A notable example here was Thomas Audley's reading on Uses in 1526, a defence of feudal revenue which may well have helped him to become the Inn's first Lord Chancellor. Once Readers had a free choice, they were able to introduce an element of practical usefulness into a course which was still necessarily random in its coverage. After 1500 it was quite common to expound the recent statutes, including those concerned with technical matters or with matters of special interest to the Reader; in 1609, for instance, John Lloyd (a Bencher from Merionethshire) read on the Laws in Wales Act 1543.

The readings, like *lecturae ordinariae* in the universities, consisted of exposition followed by disputation. The Reader read out a clause of his statute each day, commented upon it and then explained its operation with the aid of a spectrum of illustrative cases. The most intellectually testing part of the reading was the disputation of cases. Each day a few of the Reader's cases were challenged for argument by the barristers, Benchers, serjeants and judges who were present; and we have reports of some of these arguments in the Inner Temple dating back to the 1480s. The disputations in the course of readings have sometimes been confused with moots, but they were a different exercise. Moots were primarily vocational pleading exercises, founded upon sets of facts provided to the students for the purpose, like examination questions. The problems were taken from moot-books, originating in the fourteenth century, and were sometimes of formidable complexity. The object was not to thrash out a contested point of law in a single sitting, but to practise the art of pleading, and only incidentally of oral argument, in an exercise divided up into a number of manageable instalments. The first task would be to draw a writ in Latin, and then suitably elaborate pleadings in law French bringing out all the questions in the case, recited orally and with argued exceptions at each stage. In 1527 one of these ancient cases is reported as occupying the Inner Temple for a whole vacation.

The Inns of Chancery

There were nine Inns of Chancery in 1500, all of different origin. They were smaller than and inferior to the Inns of Court, and associated in some obscure way with the Chancery. It is uncertain how they came to be linked to their parent Inns of Court, but by the middle of the sixteenth century the Inner Temple had acquired a special relationship with three of them: Clement's Inn (near St Clement Danes), Clifford's Inn (near St Dunstan's) and Lyon's Inn (near the Aldwych). The societies which occupied them were governed by a body of 'ancients', who were mostly attorneys, under the presidency of a principal (in Lyon's Inn, a Treasurer), who was sometimes a young man intended for the Inns of Court. The young men were generally two or three years younger than those of the superior Inns, and the minority who actually studied came to learn the rudiments of writs, pleading and tenures before admission – should they have the means and the aptitude – to the Inns of Court. The essence of the relationship between the Inns of Court and their

Lyon's Inn, 1800.

satellites was that the former provided Readers for the latter, and resolved any disputes which arose internally. It was expected that an utter-barrister would 'read in Chancery' before being called to read in his Inn of Court. This required him to lecture, not in vacation but in all four terms of the year, and to preside over moots which were not confined to the members of one Inn, but were open to all law students. We still possess notes of the lectures given in Clement's Inn in 1543–4 by John Clerk and Richard Blackwall of the Inner Temple.

Sir Heneage Finch, later Lord Nottingham (1621–82); portrait attributed to John Michael Wright, one of four 'fire judges' portraits donated to the Inner Temple by the Corporation of London in 1952 (see p 102).

Decline of the old system

The lectures underwent a qualitative decline in the Tudor and Stuart period. Sir Edward Coke (Bencher of the Inner Temple 1590–1606) complained in the 1620s that readings had become 'long, obscure and intricate, full of new conceits, liker rather to riddles than lectures, and the readers are like to lapwings, who seem to be nearest their nests when they are furthest from them.' Coke himself was one of the worst offenders: his reading on Uses, in 1592, wandered over a wide range of unconnected subjects, including the ownership of swans. Declaratory authority in the common law had by this time come to repose chiefly in the courts at Westminster, and the readings were seen as individual performances of varying quality rather than as a traditional corpus of common learning. Many members of the Inn attended only the Reader's feast, the origin of the present Grand Day, the expense of which fell on the Readers themselves.

The system was suspended in 1642, when all the Inns were temporarily vacated by reason of war. Readings ceased, and moots were revived only in an elementary form to enable barristers to graduate. There was a movement in the 1650s to reform legal education, so that lectures might be given on the common law, and especially on matters of use to students. But nothing happened until after the Restoration in 1660 – and then the decision was made to resuscitate the medieval system, albeit in a severely reduced form. The Reader's feast in the autumn of 1661, provided by Sir Heneage Finch (later Lord Nottingham, Lord Chancellor), was particularly magnificent and was graced by the presence of King Charles II. But it was the Grand Day rather than the lectures which everyone remembered. And it was to be the Grand Days rather than the lectures which survived. Readers preferred to pay the fine for not reading; the Inn doubtless found the fines more useful than the lectures; and so by collusion the antiquated system of legal education was compounded for. After the 1670s, the law student was left entirely to his own devices – as Blackstone put it, 'by a tedious and lonely process to extract the theory of law from a mass of undigested learning'. The Inns of Court survived this collapse of legal education because they alone had the power to call to the Bar. But the Inns of Chancery, having no remaining public functions, became semi-private dining clubs controlling admissions to chambers. They were eventually sold off for the benefit of the ancients, although before the last one (Clifford's Inn) was sold in 1903 the courts decided that the proceeds should be held on trust for legal education.

In the eighteenth century, self-help through reading and attendance in court was augmented by coffee-house debating societies for law students and by the nascent system of pupillage. But no formal instruction was offered until the nineteenth century. In 1828, Charles Erdman Petersdorff, a special pleader in the Inner Temple, announced a course of sixty lectures in Lyon's Inn Hall on the theory and practice of the laws of England, charging a mere six guineas for the whole. The course would also include six lectures on elocution, by a Mr Smart; and these were recommended for intending solicitors and 'chamber counsel' as well as advocates. The printed proposal and syllabus show that it was a comprehensive survey course intended for pupils and articled clerks alike. It seems from the date that it was a deliberate attempt to cash in on the recent success of University College London in resurrecting legal education; but the course was only given once. Five years later, the Inner Temple itself instituted a course of lectures, and rather bravely appointed as its lecturers Thomas Starkie, the Downing Professor at Cambridge, whose efforts had proved redundant in attracting students there, and John Austin, who had just given up teaching at University College for want of an audience. They were attended by the future Lord Justice Rolt, who was not profoundly enthused by them. Starkie, he thought, had included too much legal history, with the result that even Austin's lectures – which are said to have been timid and almost inaudible – were considered more useful. The lukewarm reception caused both of them to give up; Austin persevered into a second year but stopped when the audience fell to single figures.

In the 1840s the absence of any formal education for law students became a topic for public debate, and in 1845 the House of Commons appointed a Select Committee on Legal Education. At the last moment – galvanised, no doubt, by fear of what the Select Committee might recommend – the Inns of Court began to think hard about putting their house in order. By June, all four Inns reached agreement on establishing four lectureships: on constitutional law, real property, common law and equity. The Select Committee then published its report on 25 August 1846. It concluded that the state of legal education was 'extremely unsatisfactory and incomplete' and that 'no Legal Education, worthy of the name, of a public nature' was to be had anywhere in England. It recommended the improvement of university education in law, especially by increasing the number of professors and improving the examinations, but also by making an outline of legal history ('the history and progress of law') and the elements of jurisprudence part of the undergraduate arts course. For the purposes of vocational education, the committee suggested that it was better to adapt old institutions than erect new ones, and that the Inns of Court should 'resume anew the original objects of their institution' by providing a proper course of instruction. This would require the four Inns to cooperate in appointing professors to give lectures open to all Bar students and instituting examinations, acting thereby as a kind of 'law university' in which the several Inns were the constituent colleges. No one would be permitted to matriculate at this law university without first obtaining an academical degree – and that, once the university law schools had been reformed, should be a degree in law. The committee ended its report with the threat that, in case their 'invitation' to introduce reform was rejected or neglected, recourse should be had to a Royal Commission.

With the exception of Lincoln's Inn, which backed out of the agreement, the Inns proceeded to appoint lecturers as agreed, and the Inner Temple for its part appointed Robert Hall, a barrister of Lincoln's Inn and Recorder of Doncaster, as lecturer on common law at a salary of £300 a year. Hall gave up lecturing in 1851, when a new system was inaugurated under the auspices of the Council of Legal Education, which also introduced examinations. But little else was done to implement the recommendations of the Select Committee – some of which have still not been implemented, notably the requirement of a law degree. In 1854 the threatened Royal Commission was appointed, under the chairmanship of Vice-Chancellor Page Wood (later Lord Hatherley), and it conducted the only full survey of the Inns of Court in the many centuries of their existence. Its report is full of interesting information. The annual revenues of the Inner Temple amounted to over £21,000, although the annual surplus was nearer £5000. There were heavy expenses in maintaining about 680 sets of chambers, and funds had to be set aside for rebuilding: it was stated in evidence by the Treasurer that the seventeenth-century buildings in Fig Tree Court, Farrar's Buildings, Hare Court, Inner Temple Lane and the upper part of King's Bench Walk had all been condemned as 'hardly safe' and would have to be replaced at a cost of at least £100,000. The expenses of dining in Hall amounted in 1854 to £4248 0s 2d, for 5865 meals (854 for Benchers, 1783 for barristers and 3150 for students), whereas only 820 meals were taken in the Middle Temple. The commissioners approved strongly of the practice of dining together, but criticised the absence of any 'such security as the community is entitled to require' with respect to the intellectual qualifications and professional knowledge of members of the Bar. There was no entrance examination – the Inner Temple alone had pioneered the use of a preliminary examination (in Classics) but had abandoned it in 1847 – and the legal examination introduced by the Council of Legal Education was entirely voluntary. The commissioners pursued the suggestion of 1846 by recommending that the Inns of Court be constituted as a university, comprising 'the Chancellor, barristers at law and masters of laws', under the control of a Vice-Chancellor and Senate, which would provide courses and compulsory examinations for the two degrees of barrister and master. It seems to have been assumed that all this could be achieved without substantial new expenditure. But the idea of a professional law university met with insufficient enthusiasm to carry it through, and it seems that the Inner Temple was actively opposed to it. The course adopted instead was one of cautious improvement: to increase the efforts of the Council of Legal Education by providing more lectures and better courses, to introduce stricter entrance requirements and (in 1872) to institute a compulsory bar examination. The academic stage was left to the university law schools.

Clement's Inn sundial now in the Inner Temple garden.

Readers' Shields

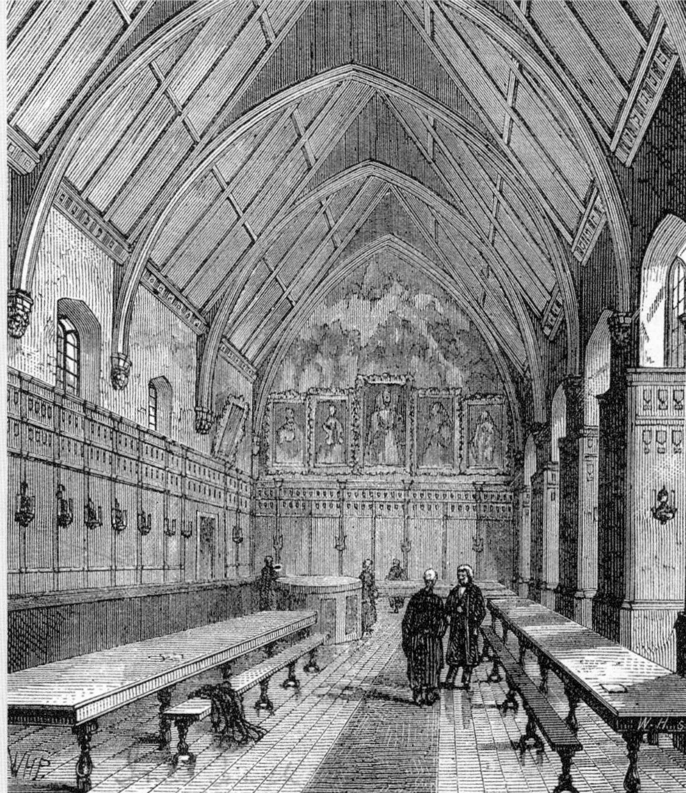

Inner Temple Hall, with Reader's shields affixed to the panelling.

Soon after the Great Fire of 1666 necessitated major rebuilding work in the Inner Temple, it was decided to commemorate the Readers by hanging painted escutcheons carrying their coats of arms and their names and the dates of their readings. The first three were commissioned in 1669–70, when £1 2s 6d was paid for the painting of three shields – those for the Lent Reader of 1667 and the Lent and Autumn Readers of 1668. It was then decided to extend the system backwards by commissioning shields for as many previous Readers as possible, a process which was completed by 1685/6. But the painters did not check their facts very well, and it was discovered that some coats of arms were not necessarily those of the named Reader but of someone else of the same name.

The shields were first hung in the Library, where they remained and were added to for over a century. Then in 1816 they were transferred first to the Parliament Chamber and then to the Hall. There they stayed until the Hall was demolished a few years later, after which a new set of shields was painted, still reproducing all the old errors. These were finally dealt with after the Second World War when the Hall was being rebuilt again; the new shields carried true coats of arms where they could be correctly ascertained or were left blank where they couldn't.

The importance of the Reader's office declined in the seventeenth century until it became a sinecure, but it remained a position of consequence because, in 1691, it was ruled that the Treasurer should be chosen from among the Readers. The two offices moved even closer when it was decided that there should be a new Treasurer each year, as well as only one Reader a year; the immediate result was that one year's Reader became the next year's Treasurer. However, the arms set up in the Hall continued to be those of the Reader not the Treasurer, so some Benchers who did not wish to be Treasurer, but did wish to have their shields displayed in the Hall, allowed themselves to be appointed Reader and then immediately resigned. The shields of these 'readers for a day' have now been removed, and a Reader's shield bears the date of the Readership but is not placed in the Hall until he or she becomes Treasurer.

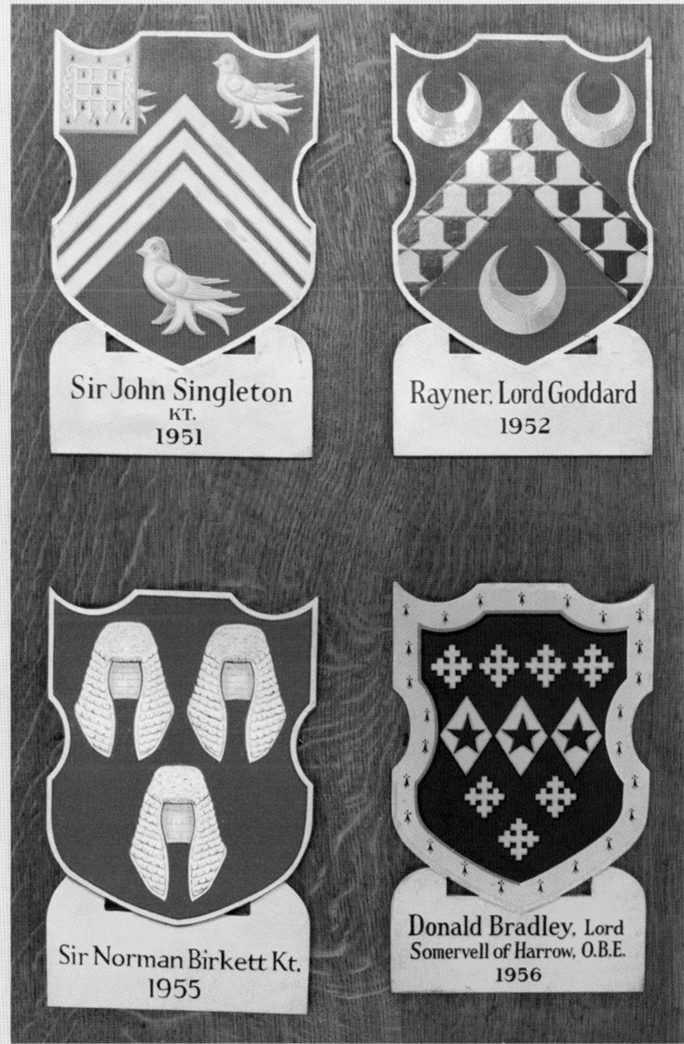

Readers' shields in the post-war Inner Temple Hall.

Opposite: Call ceremony in the Temple Church, Michaelmas 2006.

Six Centuries of Dining

Until the later seventeenth century, the status of the Inns of Court as residential law schools required students to keep a certain number of terms, as at the universities, by being physically present in the Inn. They were also required to be present for learning vacations and to participate in the revels, particularly those at Christmas. The age-old test of residence was presence at dinner in Hall on a certain number of days each term, a test that later – after residence in the true sense ceased – had to be quantified for those who wished to be called to the Bar.

There are four legal terms each year – Hilary, Easter, Trinity and Michaelmas – and in 1762, by agreement between the four Inns of Court, the number of terms a graduate student was required to keep was fixed at twelve. This number stayed the same until 1968 when it was reduced to eight. In 1798 it was agreed that attendance at three dinners a term – ie thirty-six, and then twenty-four – was the minimum required for residential qualification; the total of dinners required has since been reduced to eighteen. A dinner counts only if the student is present for grace both before and after the meal, and gowns are worn; and the element of formality used to be further preserved by the blowing of the horn to summon members to the meal, a custom that fell out of use in 1886 when the then Head Porter ran short of breath. It was revived in 1937 when a new horn was presented to the Inn, but has since lapsed again.

Mr Lakin, then Head Porter, performing the ancient ceremony of winding the horn.

Eating together in Hall performs a social as well as a residential function, helping to foster a sense of community and continuity at all levels of the society and providing a forum within which senior and junior members of the Inn can meet, mix and communicate. The continuation of the dining tradition is seen as central to this community spirit, and remains an important part of a barrister's education. Adjustments have of course had to be made as legal training has become less London-centred and outposts of the Inns have sprung up elsewhere within Britain, and it is now possible to gain in other ways some of the credits that would once have been the sole result of dining. However, the experience of enjoying civilised meals in the company of one's peers and one's masters in a splendid environment is in itself a continuation of one of the early functions of the Inns of Court as a training ground in courtliness and elegance, and is an ongoing feature of membership of the legal community.

The importance of music, dancing, theatrical performance and other courtly pursuits is well attested in the early Inner Temple records, when many young gentlemen joined the Inns of Court less to learn the law than to acquire a broad education in the manners and attributes fitting for their station within society. But even when

Old Hall in use for dining, in an acquatint of 1826.

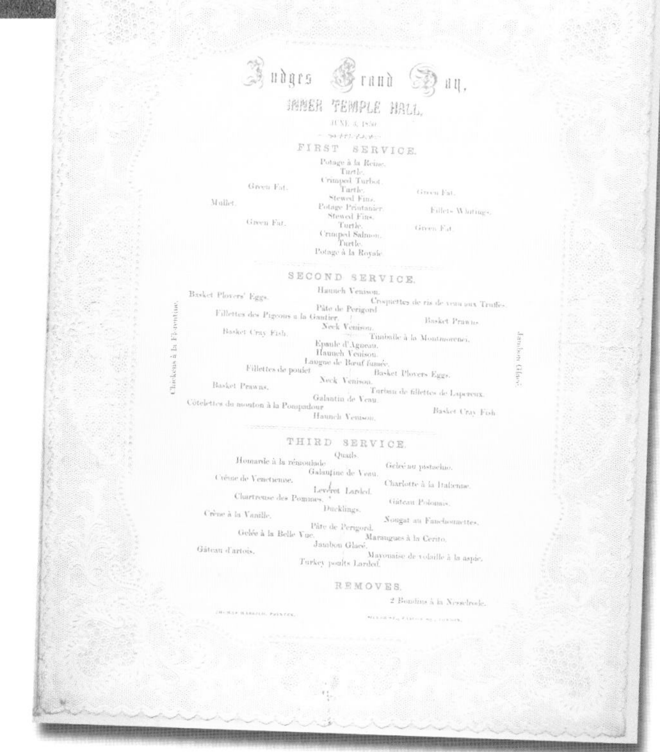

Judges Grand Day,
INNER TEMPLE HALL,
JUNE 3, 1850

FIRST SERVICE.

Potage à la Reine.
Turtle.
Crimped Turbot.
Green Fat. Turtle. Green Fat.
Mullet. Stewed Fins.
Potage Printanier. Fillets Whitings.
Stewed Fins.
Green Fat. Turtle. Green Fat.
Crimped Salmon.
Turtle.
Potage à la Royale.

SECOND SERVICE.

Chickens à la Florentine. Jambon Glacé.

Haunch Venison.
Basket Plovers' Eggs.
Croquettes de ris de veau aux Truffes.
Pâte de Perigord
Fillettes des Pigeons a la Gautier.
Basket Prawns.
Neck Venison.
Basket Cray Fish.
TimbalIe à la Montmorenci.
Epaule d'Agneau.
Haunch Venison.
Laugue de Bœuf fumée.
Fillettes de poulet
Basket Plovers Eggs.
Neck Venison.
Basket Prawns.
Turban de fillettes de Lapereux.
Galantin de Veau.
Côtelettes du mouton à la Pompadour
Basket Cray Fish
Haunch Venison.

THIRD SERVICE.

Quails.
Homarde à la rémoulade
Gelée au pistachio.
Galantine de Veau.
Créme de Venetienne.
Charlotte à la Italienne.
Leveret Larded.
Chartreuse des Pommes.
Gâteau Polonais.
Ducklings.
Crème à la Vanille.
Nougat au Fanchonnettes.
Pâte de Perigord.
Gelée à la Belle Vue.
Marangues à la Cerito.
Jambon Glacé.
Gâteau d'artois.
Mayonaise de volaille à la aspic.
Turkey poults Larded.

REMOVES.

2 Boudins à la Nesselrode.

Grand Day menu, 1850.

they were not serious students of the law, the rules of membership of an Inn of Court nevertheless required them to keep the same conventions as genuine students, among which was attendance at important events like the Christmas revels. They ate well at these times: in 1407 a record for Furnival's Inn has twenty-six members keeping commons and partaking of meat pies, mortreux (stew) of pork, baked chickens and rabbits, apples and raisins for dessert and five gallons of red wine, along with two of sweet wine, to wash it down. A hundred years later the food included venison and other meats along with a wide range of sweets, and the 'Brerewood manuscript' in the possession of the Middle Temple speaks of 'costly vyandes' and 'bountifull banquettings' in the seventeenth century.

'Lords of misrule' and a 'student king', appointed to oversee the revels, were accompanied by minstrels, players and waits, and the traditions of medieval Christmases were maintained by decking the halls with holly and eating boar and spiced delicacies. The twelve days of the celebrations were a mixture of this carefully preserved medieval tradition with officially tolerated horse-play, sometimes – as in the now lost account of a 'grand Christmas' in 1526 – involving senior as well as junior members. On that occasion, most of those appointed to the mock court were Benchers and one had recently become a judge. By this time too the members of the Inns regularly created and performed their own plays at Christmas and on other Grand Days; one in 1526, deemed to represent a satire on Cardinal Wolsey, resulted in its principal author being sent to prison for contempt. Ring-dances around the fire in Hall were survivals of the true medieval 'carol' in its original dance form, stately versions of which were performed by the Inner Temple on Grand Days until well into the eighteenth century. And the solemn revels held in the Inner Temple on 2 February 1734 saw a celebrated actor hired to perform the 'ancient song'. This was the

Setting tables in Hall.

Dining in Hall.

last occasion when the 'old measures', medieval in origin, were performed in any of the Inns; while the song was being sung, the members 'danced, or rather walked, round the coal fire, according to the old ceremony, three times'.

Dining has therefore been a central feature of life in the Inner Temple ever since the knights built their first Hall here over 800 years ago, and kitchens to provide the food were among the first buildings to go up on the site. The dining halls, along with their kitchens, have been rebuilt several times over the centuries; the present Hall dates from the 1950s after war damage necessitated its reconstruction, and a new kitchen was built at the same time. However, the rapid growth in the size of the Inn in the second half of the twentieth century combined with new tastes in food and cooking to require the kitchens again to be upgraded in the 1990s. Under the control of new caterers, and the long-standing and excellent head chef, Martin Cheesman, the standard of food now enjoyed by members of the Inner Temple is the highest it has ever been. And formal dining continues to play its central part in the long tradition of the Inn.

The Chef and the Food

Martin Cheesman joined the Inner Temple as head chef in 1992, having previously been Robert Maxwell's personal chef and also cooked at Downing Street, for royal occasions and as the youngest ever head chef for the Lord Mayor's Banquet. He received two job offers on the same day: one from the Inn and the other from Mohammed Al-Fayed. He chose the Inn and has never regretted it.

Almost immediately on arrival, he started to change the quality and the style both of the food and of the dining environment. The benches were replaced by chairs, and the wooden tables were covered with tablecloths. The spend on ingredients went up and it was not long before the Inner Temple was generally regarded as the best of all the Inns of Court for lunch.

Apart from two weeks at Christmas and the whole of the month of August, the job is a year-round, seven-days-a-week commitment, what with Grand Nights, private guest nights, student dining nights and the massive growth in catering for external functions of all sorts, from banquets to weddings. With his nine staff in the main kitchen and further staff at the Pegasus Bar, Martin is in complete charge of the menus and the ordering, answerable to Charles Vernon, the catering manager for Searcy's, the Inn's contract caterers.

It is a happy environment within which to work; there is low staff turnover, and a strong feeling of community between and within all sections of the Inn. Martin has no plans to move on; he is a happy man where he is and intends to stay until he retires.

Chef Martin Cheesman.

I never practised at the Bar, but was still upbraided over two sartorial solecisms at Inner Temple.

Eating dinners as a student tended to be occasions marking a prelude to social gatherings later in the evening. I was once unwise enough to dine wearing a pink shirt (albeit with a stiff white collar). A handwritten note reached me from the Treasurer: 'Your shirt is not considered to be suitably subfusc' – a reprimand which was the better understood after I had resorted to a dictionary.

The second occasion was during my time as a Member of Parliament. I was about to leave the House of Commons for a dinner at which the Princess Royal was to be installed as an Honorary Bencher, when to my horror I realised at the last minute that the invitation stated 'Gowns to be worn'. A flash of inspiration led to a hasty visit to the Clerk of the House's office and he kindly offered me his gown. My profound sense of relief was quashed when the Treasurer, greeting me on the receiving line, boomed 'Goodson-Wickes, I hadn't realised that you had taken silk'. Needless to say, neither indiscretion was repeated!

CHARLES GOODSON-WICKES

I have very fond memories of my student days when 'eating dinners' became an art form for me and my colleague. Very often we became pleasantly intoxicated towards the end of the meal. In those days two bottles of wine were shared among four students. We made sure to arrive early and seek out students, in particular those from Malaysia, to join us at dinner because these students habitually abstained from drink, so my colleague and I could each enjoy a bottle of wine. That made it easier for us to appreciate what the guest speaker was saying – no matter what he was saying.

IRVING JAMES EBERWEIN

Although I have left the English Bar and now practise in New York, my memories are deep and wonderful. The dining experience was at times sheer delight but could also be rather stressful. I remember one particular night when we were joined by 'real' barristers. I racked my brain for knowledgeable anecdotes that I could impress my neighbour with. I laughed, maybe a little too loudly, at their jokes and tried not to look petrified at their tales of intricate trials. I excused myself and strode to the ladies room – only to be met at the mirror by a row of cranberry-stained teeth. Ah, the port. The rest of the night was spent Japanese style, hand over mouth and drinking water.

HEATHER O'NEILL

AN EXTRACT FROM MAHATMA GANDHI'S AUTOBIOGRAPHY (*MY EXPERIMENTS WITH TRUTH*):

There were two conditions which had to be fulfilled before a student was formally called to the Bar: 'keeping terms', twelve terms equivalent to about three years; and passing examinations. 'Keeping terms' meant eating one's terms, ie attending at least six dinners out of about twenty-four dinners in a term. Eating did not mean actually partaking of the dinner; it meant reporting oneself at the fixed hours and remaining present throughout the dinner. Usually of course everyone ate and drank the good commons and the choice wines provided… I often ate nothing at these dinners, for the things that I might eat were only bread, boiled potato and cabbage. In the beginning I did not eat these as I did not like them; later, when I began to relish them, I also gained the courage to ask for other dishes.

The dinner provided for the Benchers used to be better than that for the students. A Paris student, who was also a vegetarian, and I applied, in the interests of vegetarianism, for the vegetarian courses which were served to the Benchers. The application was granted, and we began to get fruits and vegetables from the Benchers' table.

Two bottles of wine were allowed to each group of four, and as I did not touch them, I was ever in demand to form one of a quartet, so that three might empty two bottles. And there was a Grand Night in each term when extra wines, like champagne, in addition to port and sherry, were served. I was therefore in great demand on Grand Night.

The Library: Its Development and Role

The Inner Temple probably possessed a Library as early as the fifteenth century, although the earliest documentary evidence is from the year 1506. The Library then consisted of a single room on the east side of the Hall, set aside for the reading of books but also used at a later date as an annexe for dining, and for meetings and moots. A legal collection at that time could have been contained in a handful of close presses, so that the use of the room for social and other functions was not as unreasonable as it might seem to us. By 1607, a second room had been added, and there is an early reference to a gift when Sir Edward Coke presented his *Reports* in 1608. The rooms had rushes on the floors, books (at least the more valuable ones) padlocked to iron rods, plaster walls and windows frugally fitted with old glass taken from the Temple Church. During the first half of the seventeenth century steady improvements were made: the flooring was probably tiled, the plaster work renewed and the leaded windows of the upper Library ornamented by two large curtains.

The Bench declined to accept the manuscripts and printed books of John Selden, offered to the Inn in 1654, though it is perhaps fair to observe that acceptance would have incurred the

Sir Robert Smirke's Library and Parliament Chamber (1829); print by Thomas Shepherd.

William Petyt, English school, 1700.

Room C of the modern Library.

expense of building a new library to house the collection. Nonetheless it is still regrettable that the Inn does not possess a single book known to have belonged to one of its most distinguished members.

In 1662, Mrs Anne Sadleir, the eldest daughter of Sir Edward Coke, gave the Inn a number of manuscripts, mainly sermons or texts of a devotional nature, together with a collection of printed books. In the nineteenth century these books were marked with a small red printed label bearing the words 'E Lib Coke', giving rise to the mistaken (and persistent) belief that they were from Sir Edward's own library; in fact, more than half the books date from long after Coke's death.

The Library was wholly destroyed in the Great Fire of 1666. It is not clear, however, how many of the books it housed were saved. Rebuilding followed swiftly and by 1668 it was in use again. By 1670 it was graced by the additional decoration of the Readers' shields, and in 1677 by a handsome Spanish table. The Library, however, still served other purposes, and the upper room was used on occasion for recreation. Another disastrous fire broke out in 1679, destroying a number of residences, and the Library was blown up by gunpowder, after its contents had been removed, in an attempt (unnecessary, as it turned out) to stop the fire spreading.

Once more the Library was rebuilt and by 1680 it was in use again. Of its administration during the seventeenth century little is known. There was, apparently, no catalogue, certainly no official Library Keeper and no rules governing the use of material and the conduct of readers. Then in 1707 William Petyt, Treasurer of the Inn in 1701–2, scholar, antiquary and for many years Keeper of the Records in the Tower of London, left to the Inn a great mass of manuscripts together with a sum of money to construct a building to house them. In so doing he provided the Inn with a manuscript collection of great richness, and also provided the spur for the reorganisation of the Library upon a sound administrative basis. His manuscript collection is still intact after 300 years.

By 1709 the new Library had been built. Samuel Carter, an 'aged and impecunious barrister' was appointed as Library Keeper at a salary of £20 a year. He did the first work on Petyt's books and manuscripts and produced a draft catalogue of the books in the Library, dated 1713, which is still extant, but he died the same year leaving it unfinished. He was succeeded by Joshua Blew, a butler in the Inn, who served as Librarian with distinction for fifty years.

If in the early days the Library's acquisition of books had been haphazard, it was regulated by a Bench Order of 1713 directing the Treasurer to expend £20 a year on books. The responsibility for the selection and purchase of books was delegated to Blew, the Librarian, who also saw to their binding and, on occasion, to the publication of manuscripts. He produced four catalogues, notable for the careful and accurate annotations to entries. On 18 May 1717 a Bench Table Order was issued: 'No copy or transcript is to be taken by any person of any manuscript books in the Library, and no books to be delivered or taken out of the Library without leave of the Table.' Thus was formally established the principle that the Library was essentially for reference only.

Room A as it is today.

In the eighteenth century the great majority of books both purchased and presented were law books; but antiquarian, historical and literary interests were also held by the members of the society, and the purchase or presentation of books reflected those interests, the diversity of which explains the presence today of many valuable works in either original or early editions: Howard's *State of the Prisons* (1777), Strutt's *Sports and Pastimes* (1810), Saxton's *Atlas of England and Wales* (1579) and Seller's *Sea Atlas* (1678). The list of incunabula acquired is shorter but includes the *Nuremberg Chronicle* (1493), volumes of statutes printed by Caxton in 1490 and two out of the three volumes of statutes issued by Machlinia, the first English law printer.

The catalogue of 1773, the work of another librarian, the Reverend William Jeffs, was the last in manuscript and the most scientifically planned to date. In 1784 Randall Norris, a clerk in the Treasurer's department (later Sub-Treasurer) was appointed Librarian, and it was during his tenure that the earliest printed catalogue, dated 1806, was issued. Charles Lamb fondly recalls, in a letter to Crabbe Robinson, 'the erudite look with which, when he [Norris] had been in vain trying to make out a black-letter text of Chaucer in the Temple Library, he laid it down and told me that "in these old books, Charley, there is sometimes a deal of indifferent spelling".'

Randall Norris was succeeded in 1818 by the Reverend William Henry Rowlatt, a member of the Inn (called to the Bar in 1804) who was at that time Reader of the Temple Church. Rowlatt is credited with initiating many overdue improvements during his tenure of office. Scots law, for example, was inadequately represented and it was ordered that books on this subject should be bought at a cost of £200. In 1825 attention was drawn to the fact that the Library was poorly heated. It was suggested that the apertures in the walls should be closed by sliding panels, and that the room to the north of the Library should be fitted with a stove and with shelves for books; it could then be partitioned so that the Librarian might use it to superintend the room to more advantage, since 'in the winter season the severity of the cold weather renders it almost impossible for him to be constantly in the Library'.

A committee of Benchers that same year issued a new and detailed statement on the duties of the Librarian and directed him to make an 'accurate catalogue of the books and manuscripts arranged alphabetically, according to their respective subjects and continue the same as additional books or manuscripts are received into the Library'. Five hundred copies of this classified catalogue were issued in 1833. A new alphabetical catalogue was ordered in 1842 and published in 1843. It shows the Library's holdings as being approximately 5500 printed titles representing over 12,000 volumes, and 492 volumes of manuscripts.

In 1851 the rebinding of the Petyt Manuscripts was initiated, a task that was to extend over twenty years, while in 1856 J E Martin, librarian to the Duke of Northumberland and already Sub-Librarian to the Inn, was appointed to succeed Rowlatt. In 1860 he proposed expanding the Library and this resulted in the accommodation being extended in 1867, 1872 and 1882, by which time it consisted of eight large rooms with a gallery all round. This was sufficient to hold 85% of the entire stock on open access.

Interior of the pre-war Library.

Demolition of the bomb-damaged Library tower.

Admission was strictly confined to members of the society. Others could be admitted only upon special application.

Martin was succeeded in 1883 by J E L Pickering, who had been Sub-Librarian since 1869, and it was under his direction that in 1892 a new catalogue was prepared 'written by type-writer' – then a recent invention. It was to extend to twenty-one volumes, and it was in use for fifty years. It is a tribute to the skill of both Martin and Pickering as Library organisers that the printed plan showing the locations of the various collections was still effective, without alteration, in 1939.

In the early years of the twentieth century the Library acquired by gift one of its most important manuscripts: a set of four fifteenth-century miniatures showing the four courts in Westminster Hall. These were presented by Lord Darling (Treasurer 1914–15), who had purchased them at Christie's in 1894.

Between 1941 and 1942 the Library was destroyed by a succession of air raids. The Benchers had, in 1939, opposed the removal of any printed books, though the manuscripts were taken out of London to safety. It was not until after severe damage was done to the building and several thousand volumes destroyed that the order was given to evacuate the Library, leaving sufficient 'day to day' books to carry on with. The evacuation and the eventual return were overseen by Eric Hart, Librarian from 1939 to 1964. From September 1941 until the final destruction in 1942, books were blown off the shelves while windows, originally of glass and now of linoleum substitute, were blown in daily. The roof was burnt off, rain and snow had to be contended with and books that were frozen hard to the shelves had to be levered off with iron bars. The catalogue and shelf lists were saved but the subject index was not. All the records of the Library up to 1940 – correspondence, memoranda and reports together with the Librarian's files – were burnt. The loss of buildings and facilities was costly but these could in time be replaced. The loss of books was tragic, and the task of restoration was not to be accomplished within thirty years.

In 1942 the Library commenced operating again in four rooms in 2 King's Bench Walk with a stock consisting of borrowed and hastily purchased books. This accommodation was extended in 1949. A new Library on the site of the pre-war building was opened by the Treasurer, Sir Patrick Spens, in April 1958, by which time much of the essential legal material lost in the war had been replaced through the generosity of members and friends. In 1956 Wallace Breem, a distinguished legal bibliographer and (in private life) a successful historical novelist, was appointed Librarian in succession to Hart. Breem had joined the staff in 1950, having previously held a commission in the Corps of Guides, an elite detachment of the Indian Army.

The present Library, designed by T W Sutcliffe, occupies the two top floors of the Treasury building and is in the shape of an L, thus conforming roughly to the plan of the pre-war Library. The style looks back to the late seventeenth and early eighteenth centuries, panelled throughout in English oak, with tables, bookcases, doorways and balustrades to match. The bookshelves, in numbered presses, run around the walls, leaving the centre of each reading room clear for the siting of the readers' desks. The bay windows on the south side contain single desks so that readers may sit in solitude or in company as the preference takes them. Heating is supplied by pipes concealed in the ceilings, while additional warmth is provided by radiators set in the recesses beneath the windows. Comfort cooling was installed in 2001.

The recataloguing of the Library was not completed until 1960. The catalogue (in typescript, supplemented by index cards) was kept meticulously up to date by Daphne Parnham, Wallace Breem's deputy (and wife), who served on the Library staff from 1961 to 1991, when computerised cataloguing commenced. Cataloguing of the manuscript collection was carried out by Dr James Conway Davies during the 1960s. The resulting *Catalogue of Manuscripts in the Library of the Honourable Society of the Inner Temple* was published by Oxford University Press in three volumes in 1972, Dr Davies having died in the previous year. The whole manuscript collection was microfilmed and published, on 256 reels, in 1978.

The new Library also possessed a basement store accommodating older and less frequently used material. In 1991 the Inn decided that the basement should be converted for use as a student common room and bar. The Library would in due course have additional space in the basement of a new building but in the meantime the older legal material, together with the non-law collections then housed in the gallery, was sent into storage. The return of the stored books, to their new home in what had by now been officially named the Littleton Building, was completed in 1997.

Information technology has taken on an ever more important role in recent years. This consideration was to the forefront in 1991 when the Bench appointed Margaret Clay, the Inn's first female Librarian, and set her the task of automating the Library. Users can now access the online catalogues of all four Inns of Court, as well as a variety of legal databases, via the internet. The Library has had its own website since 1997 and Library staff also collaborate with website specialists, ActiveLawyer, on AccessToLaw, a legal gateway providing annotated links to legal and Parliamentary websites.

More than 500 years since its inception, the Library (with a staff of nine) still provides a service to meet the needs of its two main categories of user: members of the Bar and the judiciary, and student members studying for the Bar examinations. Within this deceptively tranquil setting of book-lined shelves and oak-panelled walls it aims to offer a service which combines traditional sources with new technology for the benefit of its readers.

This is an edited version of an article, 'A sketch of the Inner Temple Library', by Wallace Breem, Librarian from 1965 to 1990. Originally published in the Law Library Journal, *vol 64 (1971), it has been revised and updated by current Library staff members.*

The Restoration of the Inns' Teaching Role

Master Southwell

In the 1980s through the then Council of Legal Education (CLE), a team led by Hoffmann J (now Lord Hoffmann) devised a new curriculum for the Bar Vocational Course (the BVC), which placed greater emphasis on practical vocational skills, though with too little emphasis on advocacy skills. More emphasis on advocacy skills, and also the ethics of practice at the Bar, is needed. In 1987 I became Chairman of the Professional Standards Committee of the Bar Council (which dealt with, *inter alia*, education and training of barristers and new entrants to the profession). The Bar was then failing to provide adequate advocacy and ethics training for its new entrants, and I decided that something must be done. In 1987/88 with Hoffmann J and David Latham QC (now Latham LJ) we devised a scheme for continuing professional development (with a strong emphasis on advocacy skills and ethics) for pupillage and after. This was roundly rejected by the Bar Council and the Inns. This meant that apart from the minimal training on the BVC there was still no formal training in advocacy or ethics for anyone entering the Bar whether in pupillage or in the early years in practice.

Once the Bar Council had dealt with the 1989 Green Papers from the government and had begun responding to the Courts and Legal Services Bill as it went through Parliament, a committee was formed, chaired by Potter J (now Potter P) and me with strong support from David Latham, Marion Simmons QC and in particular Lord Benson, who had chaired the Royal Commission on Legal Services in England and Wales, and who had become an energetic Honorary Bencher of the Inn after retirement from a remarkable career in accountancy. We were able by our two reports of 1990 and 1991 to persuade the Bar Council and the Inns to introduce a system of compulsory advocacy and other practical training: first, for pupils during the pupillage year, and secondly, for all barristers during their first three years of practice on their own account.

Acceptance of these proposals meant that some body or bodies would have to provide the advocacy training. The Inns had not themselves engaged directly in any training of barristers for centuries, though they had in the 1870s set up the CLE to carry on the process of training young barristers for entry to the profession. One of the aims of the committee in its recommendations was to persuade the Inns to take on the role of trainers in advocacy skills, because we recognised that only the Inns could bring together a sufficient number of suitable trainers to do this work. Splendidly, the Inns, and in particular the Inner Temple, accepted the new role in providing advocacy training without objection and with considerable care and skill. Advocacy training blossomed with a large number of volunteers from the Bar and from the Bench at the Inn. Several Circuit judges took part, became Benchers and still play a major role in providing this training.

Master Nugee with Lynsey Anne Irving on the night of her call.

Call ceremony in the Temple Church, Michaelmas 2006.

After the training had run for a few years, it became clear at the Bar that those who emerged from pupillage as qualified barristers and those who had done the training for their first three years in practice were proving to be much better grounded in advocacy skills than those who had gone before.

Once the two stages of training in pupillage and in the first three years in practice were firmly embedded, the Inner Temple, ahead of the other Inns, began offering training for those in their third to sixth years in practice, and also training in ethics. Many younger barristers were finding themselves inexperienced in appellate work and in how to work with a QC. They welcomed this training and found it especially helpful. The Inner Temple then moved on to provide training for those in their sixth to tenth years in practice. The work of training those beyond the compulsory training in the third year of practice was coordinated with the training in advocacy and ethics which began to be provided by the Circuits and the Specialist Bar Associations. Overall this has resulted in a strong programme of training in the prime skills which the Bar can offer to its clients; and the Inner Temple has throughout led in the provision of this training.

I was later asked by the Bar Council to chair a committee to consider what further training should be provided compulsorily or otherwise to those beyond the compulsory third year in practice. Quite quickly we found ourselves in entire agreement that the profession must engage in compulsory continuing training and professional development (CPD), like other professions. The idea that even the Bar (whose work is monitored by the judges they address day in and day out) needed to engage in continuing training, particularly to take on board new legislation and case law, seemed to us to be obvious. Our report went to the Bar Council and was met once again with a strong 'no', though this time the Inns were supportive. Fortunately by then the Lord Chancellor's Advisory Committee was in existence, and they asked the Bar Council to reconsider, having consulted me about the background and the need for CPD. Faced with this independent pressure the Bar Council relented and adopted our proposals. The result is that all practising barristers whether in independent practice or in employment are required to undertake training throughout their careers.

One major reason for our recommendation that the more senior barristers should be required to engage in CPD was to encourage them to train themselves by training others, because we knew that, for example, to deliver a one hour lecture may take many hours to prepare; so there is no better way of training than by engaging in the training of others.

The Inns and particularly the Inner Temple have taken as large a part in this as they can, providing the advocacy training which I have already mentioned, as well as series of lectures by distinguished barristers and judges, and others from abroad, with the aim of widening the horizons of barristers, who in the past had tended to be over-insular. Indeed, one of the strangest features of legal education in this country was that universities and those providing the BVC failed to address training in the European Convention on Human Rights except to a small extent, even though the United Kingdom had been the prime mover in the Convention and been a signatory from the 1950s. This the Inner Temple addressed by providing lectures by the President and the Vice-President of the European Court of Human Rights, who became Honorary Benchers of the Inn, and by many others.

Looking back on the changes which have been made since the early 1990s, we can see that the Inn has moved from a position in which it was merely supervising, with the Bar Council, the activities of the CLE (almost entirely devoted to the BVC and not to any training of pupils or barristers in practice) to a position in which it is a major provider of training in advocacy and ethics for those in pupillage, for those in practice in their first three years and for all those who beyond that stage wish to have help in the development of their skills. This has given the Inns an important and significant role in the training of the profession, a role which the Inns abandoned in the mid-seventeenth century and only took up again through the CLE at one remove in the late Victorian age. I have no doubt that in the twenty-first century the Inn will find itself providing more and more training for pupils and barristers and will go forward as a strong provider of this training in collaboration with the Circuits and the Specialist Bar Associations. I sometimes wonder whether the Bar would have survived in its present form if the Inns had not agreed to take on the role of advocacy trainers, and made significant improvements in the skills and abilities of young barristers starting in practice.

Richard Southwell QC was Treasurer of the Inner Temple in 2002 and served as a barrister for forty-two years.

PEOPLE

Some Notable Members of the Inner Temple

Little is known of the Inner Temple in the fourteenth century, although it is clear that it was a society distinct from that of the Middle Temple by 1388, when both names appear in a manuscript year book. Similarly, few names of its members are extant: only five are known for sure, of whom one was William Gascoigne, later Chief Justice of the King's Bench, who died in 1419 and is remembered for his judicial courage in committing Prince Henry (later King Henry V) for contempt.

A little more is known of the fifteenth century, when the titles still in use came into being attached to men's names. Sir Thomas Littleton, who is known to have given a reading before 1453, belongs to this period; he is celebrated both as an eminent lawyer and – mainly – for his masterful work on *Tenures*. Issued within a year of its author's death, this was the first law book printed in England and one of the most enduringly successful; it was the most important law publication between 1300 and 1600, and went into over ninety editions, several in translation. Noted for the clarity of its style and the simplicity of its approach, it was for centuries one of the first books on the law put into the hands of students.

The Inn's first Lord Chancellor was Sir Thomas Audley, who died in 1544, and two other holders of the Great Seal – Sir Thomas Bromley and Sir Christopher Hatton – were also members. Hatton, later a close confidante of Elizabeth I, was also an active force in the plays performed at the Inner Temple in the early years of her reign, which she probably saw when the actors presented their masques at court and through which he may first have come to her attention. But perhaps the greatest of the Inner Temple jurists of the late sixteenth and early seventeenth centuries was Sir Edward Coke (1552–1634). The son of a Norfolk lawyer, Coke first enrolled in Clifford's Inn and was called to the Bar at the Inner Temple in 1578. His skills in effective argument quickly brought him prominence, and his published writings were of paramount importance; his commentary on Littleton's *Tenures*, known simply as *Coke on Littleton*, was the first of four volumes of his *Institutes of the Laws of England*, and his Reports were so fundamentally

Sir Edward Coke (1552–1637), circle of Paul van Somer.

John Selden (1584–1654), after Anthony Van Dyck.

Judge Jeffreys (1648–1689) as Recorder of London.

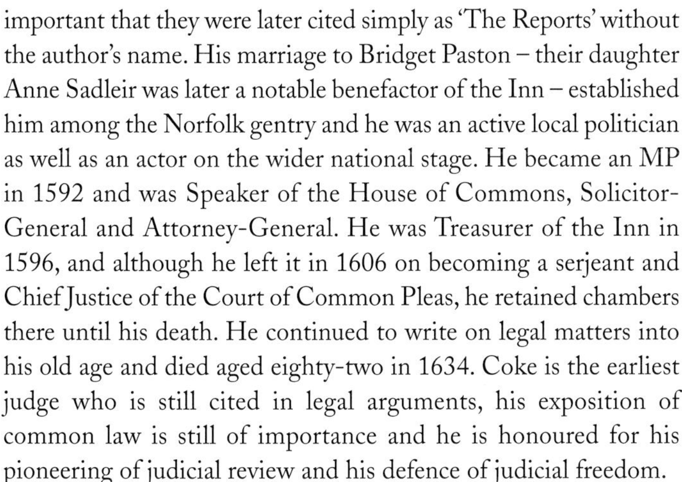

important that they were later cited simply as 'The Reports' without the author's name. His marriage to Bridget Paston – their daughter Anne Sadleir was later a notable benefactor of the Inn – established him among the Norfolk gentry and he was an active local politician as well as an actor on the wider national stage. He became an MP in 1592 and was Speaker of the House of Commons, Solicitor-General and Attorney-General. He was Treasurer of the Inn in 1596, and although he left it in 1606 on becoming a serjeant and Chief Justice of the Court of Common Pleas, he retained chambers there until his death. He continued to write on legal matters into his old age and died aged eighty-two in 1634. Coke is the earliest judge who is still cited in legal arguments, his exposition of common law is still of importance and he is honoured for his pioneering of judicial review and his defence of judicial freedom.

John Hampden, a prominent Parliamentarian who died from wounds received at the Battle of Chalgrove in 1643, is a noted alumnus of the Inn who opposed Charles I's attempt to levy ship money in 1637 and was the defendant in the action brought by the king. His contemporary, John Selden (1584–1654), called to the Bar at the Inner Temple in 1612, was a learned legal historian who was also a poet, a linguist and a friend of such literary luminaries as John Donne and Ben Jonson. Henry Rolle (d 1656), called in 1617, spent his judicial career on the King's (or Upper) Bench, and was appointed Chief Justice in 1648. He refused to be one of the judges in the trial of Charles I. His contemporary on the other side of the political divide, Sir Heneage Finch (1621–82), later the first Earl of Nottingham, spent his early career after being called to the Bar in 1645 in private practice. The Restoration in 1660 immediately transformed his career: he became Solicitor-General that year, in which capacity he prosecuted the regicides. As Treasurer of the Inner Temple in 1661 he gave the first reading after the Restoration, a magnificent occasion with the king himself in attendance at the feast. Appointed Lord Chancellor in 1675, his distinguished position in legal history rests mainly on his work as a great equity judge; indeed, he has become known as the 'father of modern equity'. Another prominent Inner Templar of this time was George Jeffreys (1645–89), the notorious 'hanging judge' who presided over the Bloody Assize following the Monmouth rebellion and the Battle of Sedgemoor in 1685. His earlier legal career had been distinguished: Recorder of London 1678–80, then Chief Justice of Chester and promoted to the King's Bench in 1683, he presided often and ably in civil cases and his judgments were rarely overturned. He prospered under both Charles II and James II, and it was the latter who both elevated him to the peerage and made him Lord Chancellor in 1685. But the flight of the king in 1688 was the downfall of Jeffreys too; he was committed to the Tower in September that year and died there in 1689.

The Inn could boast no fewer than seven Lord Chancellors during the eighteenth and nineteenth centuries, and also spawned a number of distinguished writers on legal and other matters, including Daines Barrington (d 1800), who combined a love of antiquarianism and natural history with the authorship of noted works of legal history. A lifelong resident of King's Bench Walk, he was devoted to the Inn and gave many gifts to the Library as well as tending the garden. John Austin (1790–1859) held the first chair in jurisprudence and the law of nations at the new University of London, but he was an ineffective teacher and his courses rarely attracted enough students, though John Stuart Mill was a devotee. It was only after his death that much of his writing reached publication, through the hard work and dedication of his wife. The historian Henry Hallam was called to the Bar in 1802 and practised as a barrister on the Oxford Circuit for several years before tiring of the law and turning to constitutional history. Sir Edward Hyde East co-edited the *Term Reports in the Court of the King's Bench* from 1785 until 1800, when he took on the whole task himself for the next twelve years. He also wrote *Pleas of the Crown* and served as Chief Justice of Bengal. Later in the century Sir James Stephen (1829–1894) was both an effective lawyer and a prolific journalist and writer. He practised as a barrister and did a great deal of work on legal codification before being made a High Court judge in 1879, and was also in parallel a frequent contributor both on legal matters and increasingly on religious and rational thought to journals like the *Saturday Review* and the *Pall Mall Gazette*. His *History of the Criminal Law*, published in 1883, has endured as a standard work.

Among the distinguished Inner Templars who pursued more conventional legal careers during the eighteenth and nineteenth centuries was Edward Law, later the first Baron Ellenborough (1750–1818). After joining Lincoln's Inn where he was called to the Bar in 1780, he became a member of the Inner Temple in 1782 and initially practised on the Northern Circuit. After taking silk in 1787 he developed a successful career in London where, during the 1790s, he was counsel for the crown in a number of state prosecutions. In 1801 he joined the new government as Attorney-General before becoming Chief Justice of the King's Bench the following year. In 1806 he turned down the Lord Chancellorship but did accept a cabinet post – a decision that was much criticised and which he came to regret. He was the last Chief Justice to join the cabinet. Other prominent Inner Templar lawyers were James Scarlett (1769–1844), first Baron Abinger, who was a highly effective advocate, and George Bramwell (1808–92), who had a distinguished career as barrister and judge, though his judgments were marked by a deep conservatism which seemed outdated even to contemporaries.

More recently, Sir Edward Marshall Hall (1858–1927) became one of the most celebrated barristers of his generation, putting up fine performances for both prosecution and defence in some of the most sensational trials of the early twentieth century. His commanding presence in court, his handsome appearance and his striking oratory all combined to make him a legal celebrity before that word enjoyed its modern wide currency. A member of his chambers who attained equal fame was William Birkett, later the first Baron Birkett (1883–1962), who appeared in many notable cases in the 1930s, including the divorce of Mrs Wallis Simpson for whom he acted. Appointed to the King's Bench in 1941, he was one of the British judges at the Nuremberg trials. Later in the century Michael Oldfield Havers, first Baron Havers (1923–92), became Margaret Thatcher's first Attorney-General in 1979 and served in her war cabinet during the Falklands War where his naval experience during the Second World War was of practical use. He also briefly became Lord Chancellor before ill health enforced his retirement. He defended Mick Jagger on a drugs charge and was the leader for the crown in the case of the Yorkshire Ripper.

Relief carved marble plaque of Sir Edward Marshall Hall by V A La Bouchere.

Among the Inner Temple's many highly distinguished members are several prominent female lawyers, one of whom is Lord Havers' sister, Dame Elizabeth Butler-Sloss. The Inn can also boast the first woman called to the Bar in England. This was Ivy Williams (1877–1966), who took a law degree at Oxford at the beginning of the century and immediately joined the Inn when women were first admitted in 1920. She was called on 10 May 1922, but did not practise as a barrister; her professional life was entirely devoted to tutoring and lecturing in law at Oxford. Another notable woman was Dame Elizabeth Lane (1905–88) who decided to study law when her husband also made that decision and was called to the

Dame Elizabeth Lane, by John Whithall.

Bar in 1940. She practised mainly on the Midland Circuit where she became only the third woman to be appointed QC in 1950. Subsequently she was the first woman Recorder of Derby, the first woman County Court judge and the first to be appointed to the High Court Bench.

Other illustrious members ...

The Bar has always been a stepping stone to a career in politics, and the present and past political landscape is replete with Inner Templars. Two British Prime Ministers have been members of the Inn: George Grenville, Prime Minister 1763–5, and Clement Attlee who served from 1945–51. And there have also been a number of highly distinguished foreign politicians among the membership, among them three of the men who shaped the independence of the Indian subcontinent: Jawaharlal Nehru (1889–1964), Mohamed Jinnah (1876–1948) and Mohandas (Mahatma) Gandhi (1869–1948). Nehru and Jinnah were respectively the first Prime Minister of India and the first Governor-General of Pakistan after the partition in 1947, and Gandhi was the revered 'father of Indian independence' as well as the much respected symbol and inspiration for those who sought to achieve political change through peaceful means. Tunku Abdul Rahman (1903–90), the first Prime Minister of Malaysia after independence in 1957, was an Inner Templar, as was Sir Seretse Khama (1921–80), who became the first President of independent Botswana in 1966.

Jawaharlal Nehru.

John Paston of the letter-writing family was a member in the middle of the fifteenth century and lived in the Inn when he was in London. Cecil Rhodes too was a member, as was John Maynard Keynes though he soon decided to pursue economics rather than the law. A J P Taylor flirted with a legal career after being persuaded by his solicitor uncle that he could fill a gap in the narrow ranks of left-wing barristers; he was however soon claimed by history instead. Roger Fenton, admitted in 1839, pursued an energetic legal career in parallel with his interests as a pioneering photographer: the founder and first secretary of the London Photographic Society, he is noted for his fine landscape and architectural studies but more particularly for his scenes from the Crimean War.

Clement Attlee, Earl Attlee, by Sir Lawrence Gowing RA.

... and some less celebrated

There are some members, unfortunately, who are distinguished for reasons that the Inn would prefer to forget. William Burge was a barrister imprisoned for debt in 1848, and James Townshend Saward suffered a harsher punishment when he was transported for life in 1857 for forging a payment order for £100. Other unworthy members include some whose behaviour was disreputable: one John Clarke was accused of unprofessional conduct in 1901 after demanding fees when acting for a poor man; and Augustus Mirams was particularly vilified because the Inn's Library porter was one of those he defrauded of money that the man could ill afford. It is salutary to note that he was tried and convicted of fraud, and then of course disbarred.

Mahatma Gandhi and the Inner Temple: Disbarment and Reinstatement

Master Sedley

On 7 November 1922 Mohandas Karamchand Gandhi was sentenced at Ahmedabad to six years' imprisonment (he was in fact released after two years) upon his plea of guilty to three counts of seditiously inciting disaffection towards the imperial government. The judge who sentenced him, Mr C N Broomfield, realised that this was no ordinary defendant. He said to Gandhi: 'The law is no respecter of persons. Nevertheless it would be impossible to ignore the fact that you are in a different category from any person I have ever tried or am likely to have to try. It would be impossible to ignore the fact that in the eyes of millions of your countrymen you are a great patriot and a great leader. Even those who differ from you in politics look upon you as a man of high ideals and of noble and of even saintly life.'

Gandhi had been admitted as a student member of the Inn in November 1888 and had been called to the Bar in Trinity term 1891. From here he went to South Africa where he practised for some years before returning to India. Following his conviction, he was ordered at a Parliament of the Inn on 10 November 1922 to be disbarred. He never sought readmission.

Three weeks after Gandhi's disbarment, the periodical *Young India* forecast: 'A time will surely come and that very soon when the Inner Temple will reassert as an honour the fact that the greatest man of our times belonged to her.'

In the event it was sixty-six years later, on 3 November 1988, that the Treasurer, Master Monier-Williams, moved with unanimous support that Mohandas Gandhi be readmitted *post mortem* to the Inner Temple. When his motion was first placed before the Bench Table in July 1988, he recalled that on the centenary of Gandhi's birth in 1969 Lord Mountbatten, the chairman of the United Kingdom committee formed to mark the centenary, had written to the Inn suggesting that readmission might be a fitting gesture, and that the Calcutta Arts Society had offered the Inn a commemorative plaque. The Bench Table had declined readmission, doubting whether it could be done posthumously, but had accepted the plaque with much caution, stipulating that the ceremony must be of the simplest character and that the wording of the plaque be approved in advance. This is the plaque now gracing the Library staircase. It was unveiled in May 1971 by Master Gerald Gardiner in the presence of the Indian High Commissioner, Lord Elwyn-Jones and Lord Denning.

Master Monier-Williams, who had since his student days in 1948 wished to see Gandhi readmitted and had supported the move to readmit him in 1969, now said in support of his motion: 'The readmission of a deceased person to the books of the Inn is, I believe, without precedent, but that does not mean it cannot be done should the Bench wish it. Mahatma Gandhi, although opposed to British rule in India, was a man whose name is revered by millions, both in the East and the West. Many Indians have passed through our Inn and in years to come our own travelling scholars under the Pegasus Scheme will be forging professional links and friendships with the people of India. The action which I propose would, I believe, enhance the name of the Inner Temple both in India and in the countries where Mahatma Gandhi's name is admired.'

Master Platts-Mills, who had been invited to attend the Bench Table because he was the only Bencher who had known Gandhi personally, spoke in support of the motion. The decision was adjourned to November so that the views of the Foreign and Commonwealth Office could be sought. On 3 November 1988, the Treasurer's proposal received the unanimous support of the Bench and Gandhi was readmitted posthumously to the Inn.

Several years later, on a visit to the United States, Master Monier-Williams mentioned Gandhi's readmission to an author friend, Burnett Britton, who was writing a book – *Gandhi Arrives in South Africa* (1999) – on aspects of Gandhi's life and work for publication in the US. The friend suggested that he might add the Inner Temple's proceedings as an appendix to his book. Because Bench Table minutes are confidential, Master Monier-Williams obtained the then Treasurer's permission to disclose them, and the history of Gandhi's readmission became public.

In his valedictory address to Master Monier-Williams at the conclusion of his Treasurership, Master Hugh Griffiths was able to say that to his knowledge the Inn's gesture had been appreciated throughout India. *Young India's* prediction was right, even if it was held up by the law's delays.

The honour of having Gandhi as a member of our Inn now stands alongside the honour enjoyed by the Bar of having Nelson Mandela among its honorary silks. It is pleasant to record that the only prison to have housed both men, the old colonial prison in Johannesburg, has since February 2004 been the seat of South Africa's Constitutional Court, now one of the world's great human and civil rights forums.

The Rt Hon Lord Justice Sedley is Chairman of the Library Committee.

The unveiling of the plaque presented to the Inn by the Calcutta Arts Society to commemorate the centenary in 1969 of Gandhi's birth, by Master Gerald Gardiner in the presence of Lord Elwyn-Jones, the Indian High Commissioner and Lord Denning.

THE INN'S LITERARY CONNECTIONS

There is a possibility that the earliest literary figure associated with the Inner Temple was Geoffrey Chaucer. An Elizabethan antiquary claimed to have seen Chaucer's name in the Inn's medieval archives, but as they are unfortunately no longer extant this cannot be confirmed. However, whether a member or not, it is certain that Chaucer was familiar with the Inns of Court, since he featured the 'gentle manciple' of 'a temple' in the *Prologue to the Canterbury Tales*. This manciple, an administrative official responsible, among other duties, for purchasing provisions for the Inn, was apparently a canny fellow. Although he had more than thirty masters, intelligent and expert in the law, he was able to outwit them all:

A gentil maunciple was ther of a temple,
Of which achatours mighte take exemple
For to be wise in bying of vitaille:
...
Of maistres hadde he mo than thries ten,
That weren of lawe expert and curious
...
And yet this manciple sette hir aller cappe

Several early dramatists have Inner Temple connections, whether through membership of the Inn or through their contributions to the revels. One of these was Arthur Broke (d 1563), the first to translate into English the Italian tale of Romeo and Juliet on which Shakespeare's play was based. He is known to have been involved in the Christmas revels in 1561, overseen by Robert Dudley, though the interludes he wrote for the occasion have not survived. He was granted honorary membership in gratitude for his work, his guarantors being fellow dramatists and contributors to the same revels, Thomas Sackville and Thomas Norton. They were both full members of the Inn, having studied law as part of their education, and their joint contribution on this occasion was a play entitled *Gorboduc*.

The son and grandson of Inner Templars, the dramatist and poet Francis Beaumont (1584/5–1616) became a member in 1600, joining his two brothers there. Though he probably never studied the law seriously, he played a full part in the life of the Inn, contributing a satiric 'Grammar Lecture' to the revels of 1606 and being chosen in 1613 to write the combined Gray's Inn and Inner Temple masque for Princess Elizabeth's wedding. His first dramatic outing, *The Knight of the Burning Pestle*, written when he was only twenty-two, flopped, but he had considerably greater success when

Choosing of the Red and White Roses in the Temple Gardens, *by Henry Arthur Payne; this copy by the artist of his mural in the Palace of Westminster was presented to the Inner Temple in 1911.*

he teamed up with John Fletcher, with whom he wrote nine plays.

The poet William Cowper (1731–1800) came from a family of distinguished Middle Templars, and he too joined that Inn and was called to the Bar there in 1754. However, he transferred his membership to the Inner Temple in 1757, almost certainly because he wished to secure the tenancy of chambers in Inner Temple Lane. He continued to pay the rent on these chambers until his death, although he did not live there. He initially pursued a not very successful legal career and also suffered bouts of depression; but his creativity was aroused when he was asked to co-author a book of evangelical poems which includes some Anglican hymns still in use today. This was followed by other books of poetry in which he described himself as 'William Cowper of the Inner Temple'. His poetry was very popular and influential in his time.

Old Crown Office Row in the nineteenth century; this was the birthplace of Charles and Mary Lamb.

James Boswell (1740–95) started to frequent the Inner Temple because of his great admiration for Samuel Johnson, who lived there and whose *Life* he was later to write. Boswell was a Scottish lawyer, but he spent a great deal of his young adulthood in London, determined to enjoy and immerse himself in the literary life of the capital. Boswell's *London Journal 1762–1763* records him in April 1763 'strolling about the Temple, which is a most agreeable place. You quit all the hurry and bustle of the City in Fleet Street and the Strand, and all at once find yourself in a pleasant academical retreat. You see good, convenient buildings, handsome walks, you view the silver Thames. You are shaded by venerable trees. Crows are cawing above your head. Here and there you see a solitary Bencher sauntering about.'

Boswell met Johnson by chance soon afterwards, and the entry for 24 May records, 'I went and waited upon Mr Samuel Johnson, who received me very courteously. He has chambers in the Inner Temple, where he lives in literary state, very solemn and very slovenly.' Some three weeks later he visited him again: 'He shook me by the hand at parting, and asked why I did not call oftener. I said I was afraid of being troublesome. He said I was not; and he was very glad to see me. Can I help being vain of this?' Boswell had become a member of the Inn in 1761, but was only called in 1786 when he decided to try his luck at the English Bar. He practiced on the Northern Circuit and eventually became Recorder of Carlisle.

Other literary figures connected with the Inn are Charles and Mary Lamb (1775–1834 and 1764–1847), who were born at 2 Crown Office Row. Their father, John Lamb, was employed as a Hall waiter and clerk to Samuel Salt, then Under-Treasurer (a post subsequently known as Sub-Treasurer). Charles was the youngest of seven children, all of whom were christened in the Temple Church but only three of whom survived infancy. Charles looked back with fondness on the first seven years of his life in the Inner Temple in his essay 'The Old Benchers of the Inner Temple'. He described his birthplace as 'Cheerful Crown Office Row… the place of my kindly engendure' and the Temple as 'the most elegant spot in the metropolis'. But both he and his sister were subject to bouts of depression and insanity, which came to a head in Mary's case in September 1796, when she stabbed her mother to death with a knife. By this time they were living elsewhere in London, and Mary was for a time confined in an asylum. Her brother eventually managed to persuade the authorities to release her into his care, and he looked after her for the rest of his life.

They returned to live in the Inner Temple in 1801, initially acquiring residential chambers on the top floor of 16 Mitre Court Buildings (on the present site of 1 Mitre Court Buildings), and later moving elsewhere within the Temple. It was now that they wrote their *Tales from Shakespeare*, as well as other publications for children, and it was in their Inner Temple residences that they entertained their wide circle of literary friends, including Coleridge, the Wordsworths and Southey. Charles, perhaps now best known as an essayist, described his chambers at 4 Inner Temple Lane: 'I have two of these [sitting] rooms on the third floor, and five sleeping, cooking, etc, rooms on the fourth floor. In my best room is a choice collection of the works of Hogarth, an English painter of some humour. In my next best are shelves containing a small but well-chosen library. My best room commands a court [Hare Court], in which there are trees and a pump, the water of which is excellent cold, with brandy, and not very insipid without. Here I hope to set up my rest, and not quit till Mr Powell, the undertaker, gives me notice that I may have possession of my last lodging.' It was not to be; they moved away in 1817.

A P Herbert, by Thomas Cantrell Dugdale.

The author of *Tom Brown's Schooldays*, Thomas Hughes, was an Inner Templar, called to the Bar in 1848 and becoming an MP in 1865, a QC in 1869 and a Bencher in 1870. Another practising lawyer was Sir William Schwenck (W S) Gilbert, called in 1863; but his legal career was not successful – he is said to have both irritated judges and bored juries – and he turned to journalism and drama instead, achieving huge success particularly through his collaboration with Arthur Sullivan on the Savoy operas. His legal roots showed: legal themes and lawyers appear in several of the operas, and *Trial by Jury* includes the jaundiced lines, 'And many a burglar I've restored/to his friends and his relations'. Later in life he became a magistrate in Middlesex, and was also a noted litigant; it is reported that even his milkman, coalman and postman were threatened by him with the law.

Bram Stoker (1847–1912) enjoyed an *annus mirabilis* within an otherwise quiet life in 1890, the year when he was both called to the Bar at the Inner Temple (at the late age of thirty-eight) and began to research the book for which he is famous, *Dracula*. A visit to Whitby that year started him on the trail of the story, which was not published until 1897; it failed to achieve much during his life, either financially or in terms of critical acclaim, but has since become a classic of the Gothic genre. Stoker never practised law, but he did make his hero, Jonathan Harker, a solicitor. A younger contemporary of Stoker's, who wrote under the name Dornford Yates, was Cecil William Mercer (1885–1960). Called in 1909, he combined legal work with writing – he attended the Crippen trial – until after military service in the Great War he abandoned the law for his novels. His legal experience underpinned much of the tale-telling in the Berry series of almost autobiographical works, but he is best remembered for his Chandos thrillers. The Irish patriot Erskine Childers was admitted to the Inn in 1892 but never practised. He is best known in literary terms for *The Riddle of the Sands* (published 1903), but is also a celebrated martyr for the cause of Irish nationalism, being executed in 1922 for the possession of a firearm during the civil unrest of that period.

More recently, Alan Patrick (A P) Herbert (1890–1971) enjoyed early success with his articles for *Punch*, and then with his 1919 book *The Secret Battle*, dealing with the trial and execution of a young shell-shocked soldier. It achieved huge critical acclaim and is credited with changing the courts martial procedures. Having studied law at Oxford, Herbert was called to the Bar in 1918 but never practised, and is perhaps best known among lawyers for his *Misleading Cases*, which are a unique contribution to legal humour if not to the law itself. He combined a long literary career with serving as an independent MP and campaigning on a variety of causes, including those concerned with the rights of authors. And of course still gracing the membership is Sir John Mortimer, whose creation Rumpole of the Bailey is an evergreen evocation of the ethos of advocacy.

Thomas Hughes, by Henry Weigall.

Honorary and Royal Benchers

The prominent part played in the 1561 revels by Lord Robert Dudley is indicative of the place of the Inns of Court within high society at the time and since. A trawl through the membership of the Inner Temple during the sixteenth, seventeenth and eighteenth centuries reveals numbers of members of the peerage and other denizens of London court life who had been appointed as Honorary Benchers; they were not there to study the law but to take part in the courtly entertainments laid on regularly by the Inn and to enjoy the social life afforded by Inn membership. As Master May records elsewhere in this volume, Honorary Benchers continue to be appointed from the ranks of professionals in non-legal disciplines who are willing and able to offer their experience to the Inn in a variety of areas. The membership can boast Academic Benchers too, who are distinguished teachers of law and maintain the links between the Inns of Court and the universities. All are an adornment to the Inn as well as an essential facet of the management of the Inn's affairs.

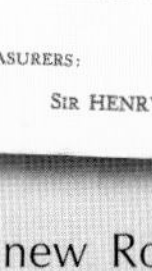

The Honourable Societies of

THE INNER TEMPLE — THE MIDDLE TEMPLE

JOINT BENCH DINNER

On WEDNESDAY, 20th JULY, 1949 in

THE MIDDLE TEMPLE HALL

TREASURERS:

HIS MAJESTY THE KING — HER MAJESTY THE QUEEN

DEPUTY TREASURERS:

THE RT. HON. LORD MERRIMAN — SIR HENRY MACGEAGH

Connections with royalty go back right to the beginning. The Templars enjoyed a close relationship with the monarch during their tenure, and after their dissolution the estate was in royal hands until the time of James I when he granted it to the Inner and Middle Temple. Although monarchs down the centuries are recorded as being entertained by the masques performed at court by members of the Inner Temple, there is no record of them visiting the Inn until Charles II honoured the Reader's feast of 1661 with his presence. In that same year his brother, the Duke of York, later to become King James II, was inaugurated as the first Royal Bencher. He was admitted as a student, called to the Bar and called to the Bench all on the same day, a procedure that has been followed ever since for Royal Benchers. He is known to have taken a personal interest in the fortunes of the Inner Temple; he himself came to the Inn during the Great Fire of 1666 and oversaw the firefighting.

The association with royalty then lapsed for over 200 years until, in the later part of Queen Victoria's reign, her daughter Princess Louise came to open the newly rebuilt Hall and Library, and the opportunity was taken to appoint a new Royal Bencher. This was Prince Christian of Schleswig-Holstein, husband of Princess Louise's sister, Princess Helena. Victoria's husband and son had both become Benchers of other Inns, so the royal connection with the legal profession was now re-established on a firm footing. The next Inner Temple Royal Bencher was Prince Albert, then Duke of York, whose father and brothers had all been admitted to other Inns; the Inner Temple therefore has the distinction of having had two kings among its Royal Benchers, since Prince Albert followed his predecessor as Duke of York in the seventeenth century by succeeding his brother on the throne as King George VI.

The king became Treasurer of the Inn in 1949, and was able to celebrate with his wife, Queen Elizabeth, who was a Royal Bencher of the Middle Temple, at a joint dinner of the two Inns. In the year that their daughter became Queen Elizabeth II she laid the foundation stone of the new Inner Temple Hall which was being rebuilt after the bomb damage of the Second World War, and two years later her husband, Prince Philip, Duke of Edinburgh, became an Inner Temple Royal Bencher in his turn. He served as Treasurer in 1961, and he was joined as a member of the Inn by his daughter, Princess Anne, the Princess Royal, who was admitted in 1990.

Master HRH the Princess Royal, by David Cobley.

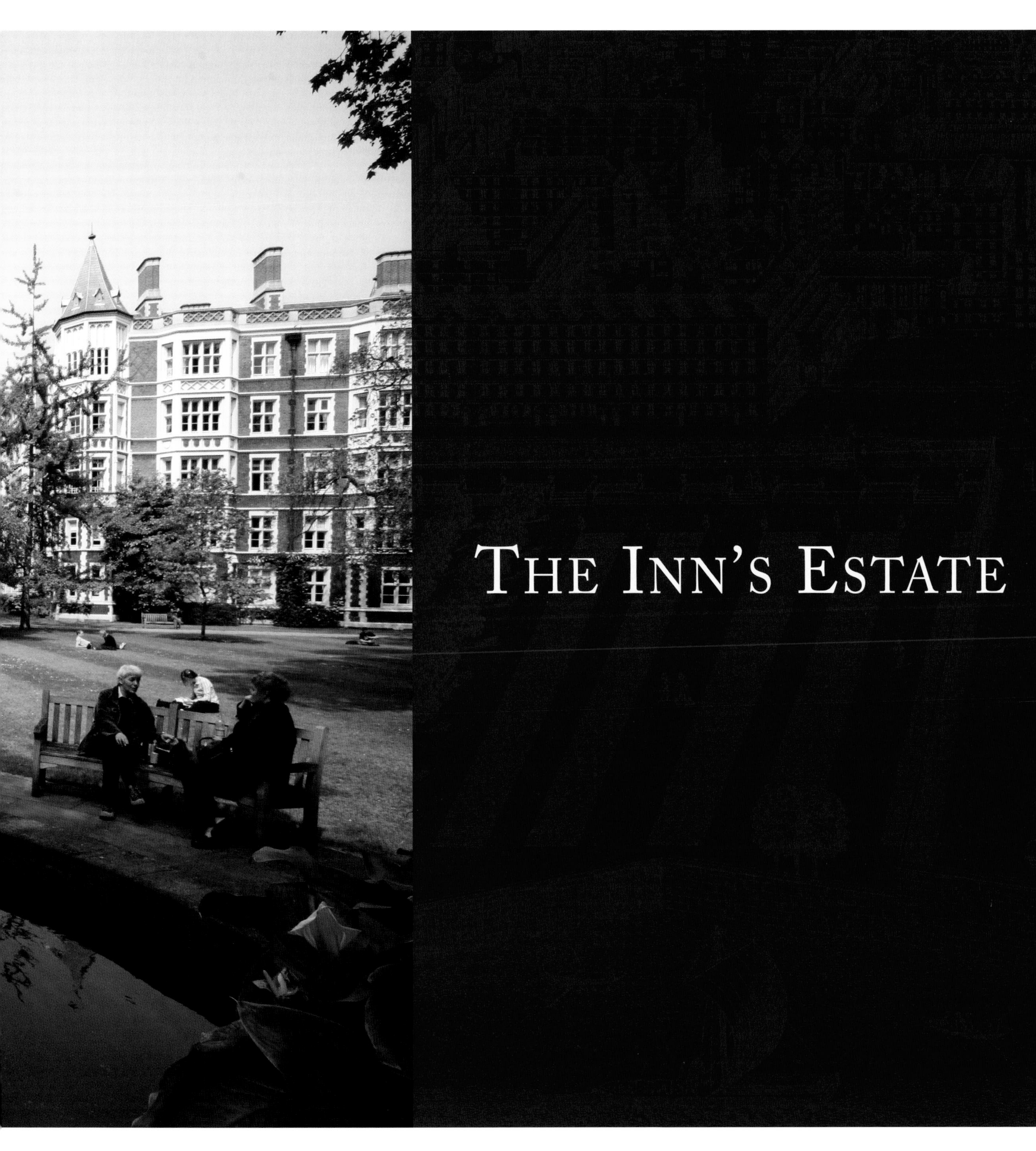

The Inn's Estate

The Buildings of the Inner Temple

Geoffrey Tyack

The architectural history of the Inner Temple begins with the church and preceptory put up by the Knights Templar after they acquired their new site south of Fleet Street in about 1161. The Temple Church, one of the major architectural monuments of medieval London, was consecrated in 1185 and still survives despite the terrible devastation wrought by German bombers in the Second World War. Early thirteenth-century records also mention two halls, one of which almost certainly stood on the site of the present Inner Temple Hall. It was connected to the Church at its western end by a covered way or cloister, and it has usually been assumed that there was another matching cloister at the east, perhaps connected with a dormitory, thus creating a courtyard on the site of the western part of the present Church Court.

The Knights Hospitaller took over the property following the abolition of the Templars in 1312, and in 1347 they leased the 'New Temple' to lawyers, who constituted themselves into two societies: the Inner Temple, which took over the buildings south of the Church, including one of the two Templars' Halls (probably the Priests' Hall), and the Middle Temple, whose property was to the west of the monastic courtyard and included the second hall (probably the Knights' Hall). Both societies shared the Church.

We do not know what the Knights Templars' halls looked like, though the surviving thirteenth-century hall of their preceptory at Bisham, Berkshire (now part of the house called Bisham Abbey) may provide an analogy. And it does not seem likely that much, if any, of the Templars' structure was incorporated into the Hall used by the lawyers of the Inner Temple, which was substantially rebuilt, if not totally reconstructed, in the second half of the fourteenth century. Homely rather than magnificent, it was raised up over a basement and measured 70 by 29ft, with walls of Kentish ragstone and an arch-braced timber roof 23ft high, not unlike the surviving late fifteenth-century roof of the Old Hall of Lincolns Inn (1493). The walls were buttressed and there were Gothic windows lighting the main body of the room, with bay (oriel) windows at the east or high table end and a louvre on the roof to take the smoke from the central hearth which served as the only fireplace. Until its replacement in 1867–70 this was the oldest of the secular buildings of the Inns of Court.

Effigies of knights in the Round.

East of the Hall there was a Library, first mentioned in 1505. It had a chamber underneath it, and nearby were the Parliament Chamber, equivalent perhaps to the solar or Great Chamber of a

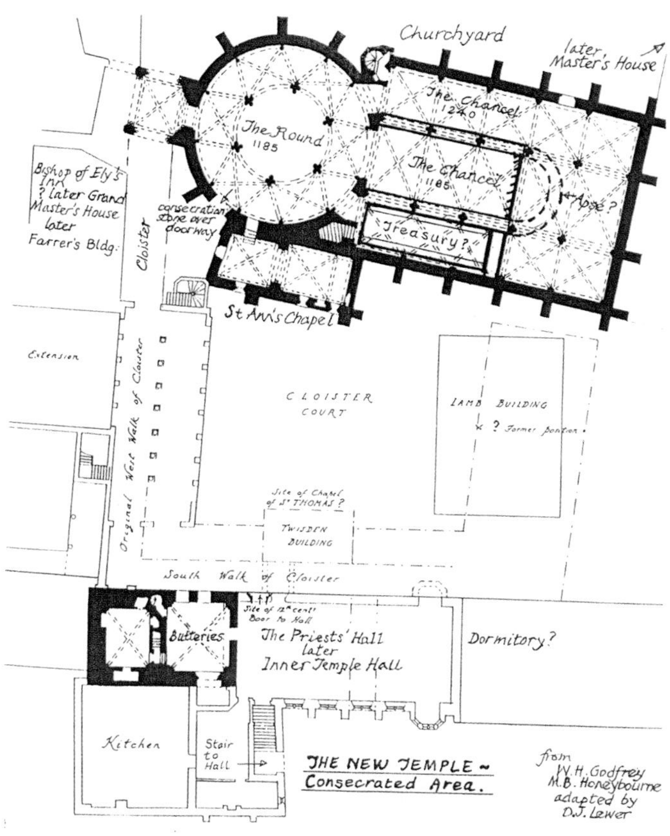

Plan of the consecrated area of the New Temple as it might have been in the time of the knights.

large late-medieval house, and lodgings for the Treasurer. At the lower (service) end there was a two-storeyed block made up of four stone-vaulted rooms – the upper ones later called the outer and inner buttery – probably dating from the fourteenth century. Two of these rooms were demolished in 1868 to enable the Hall to be extended westwards, but the outer pair survive, their much-restored rubble-stone outer wall now visible from Elm Court. With their simple rib-vaulted ceilings and fifteenth-century fireplaces, which bear the arms of Peter Arderne, Chief Baron of the Exchequer (d 1467) and Brian Roclyffe, Baron of the Exchequer, 1452–88 (d 1494), these are the only surviving part of the medieval Hall complex, and the oldest of the Inner Temple's buildings. Their precise purpose is unknown, but the presence of fireplaces, and originally of carved capitals, indicates that they were relatively important rooms which may have formed the lower storeys of a tower mentioned in sixteenth-century documents.

The Inns of Court began teaching law in the fourteenth century, but there was a boom in membership in the sixteenth century, rising to a peak around 1610, when there were about 200 people resident in the Inner Temple at any one time. This led to a big demand for accommodation, which was provided by individual members building speculatively on vacant plots and leasing out chambers. In 1587, for instance, Sir Julius Caesar, son of Queen Mary's Italian physician, spent £300 on building 'divers fair and necessary rooms' at the upper end of the Hall, on the site of an old, ruinous, decayed chamber, 'to the great beautifying this House… and benefit of this House in time to come'. But there was no overall plan; the Inns of Court did not have the landed endowments of the Oxford and Cambridge colleges to which they are often compared, and they were never even legally incorporated. So building took place piecemeal around small courtyards which became the basis of today's courts, some, like Hare Court, preserving the names of their sixteenth-century builders despite the disappearance of the original buildings.

The first visual record of the Inn comes from Wyngaerde's famous panorama of London from the river (*c*1544). It shows a modest grouping of buildings south of the Temple Church – possibly too loose to be dignified with the name of a court or quadrangle – with a garden to the south stretching down to the river wall, built by John Pakington in 1524–5, and a tower at the river end of Middle Temple Lane. Whitefriars monastery lay to the east, Fleet Street to the north and the Middle Temple to the west, beyond which were the grand houses or 'inns' of the Bishop of Bath and Wells and other important ecclesiastics and noblemen, stretching along the banks of the Thames towards Westminster. When Wyngaerde drew his panorama, blocks of chambers called Pakington's Rents (1534) and Babington's Rents (*c*1530) had already been built east of the Library; these were probably on the

Exterior of the old Inner Temple Hall.

Above: Woodcut of the buttery fireplace.
Left: The buttery in modern use.

site of the present Treasury Office and Library building. Then in about 1544 a range called Bradshaw's Rents, named after the then Treasurer, went up on a site running north, roughly on the site of the present east range of Church Court (formerly 1–2 Tanfield Court, named after Sir Lawrence Tanfield, who lived there in the early seventeenth century). Shops had been built against the south wall of the Church by 1593, and chambers had gone up next to the Round by 1612.

There was also expansion to the east and west. Fuller's Rents, named after another Treasurer, went up in 1562 on the site of the present Mitre Court Building, and the building was extended in 1588; the dramatist Francis Beaumont lived here, as did the famous lawyer Sir Edward Coke. In 1577 Queen Elizabeth's favourite, Robert Dudley, Earl of Leicester, was given permission to build a south extension, on the site of 1–2 King's Bench Walk; it housed the Alienation Office – one of several government offices which came to be based in the Inner Temple – and formed, together with Fuller's Rents and Bradshaw's Rents, a three-sided courtyard looking south towards the river. Meanwhile, in or after 1567, Nicholas Hare built a block of chambers west of Inner Temple Lane which gave, and still gives, access to Fleet Street; it formed the south side of the present Hare Court. And in Fig Tree Court, immediately to the west of the Hall, a block of chambers existed by 1573, and possibly earlier, another block following in 1623–4.

In his poem 'Prothelamion', published in 1596, Edmund Spenser referred to the 'bricky towers [of the Inner and Middle Temple] ... where now the studious lawyers have their bowers'. But most of the buildings were probably timber-framed, like virtually all the residential buildings of Elizabethan London. They contained sets of rooms – chambers, rather like flats – reached by a common staircase and furnished by their occupants. Some chambers were shared by two students but others functioned like modern barristers' chambers; Sir Julius Caesar's new building was described in 1596 as having two large sets of chambers on the first floor, with chimneys, each containing a bedroom, study, a room for clients to attend in, a house of office and 'a place thereto adjoining to lay things in'. On the second floor there were two sets: one for a Bencher, with a bedroom, study, gallery or inner chamber with chimney and house of office, and another with a heated bedroom and study. There were two two-room chambers on the third floor, and above them was a gallery with a chimney.

These chamber blocks have all vanished, but the building containing 'Prince Henry's Room' over the Inner Temple Gateway – one of a mere handful of pre-Fire domestic buildings to survive in the City – still gives some idea of what the grander rooms may have looked like. Never part of the Inn, it was built of timber in 1610–11 by John Bennett, its upper floor projecting over the round-arched stone gateway, and contained Bennett's own rooms and a tavern called the Prince's Arms – hence the feathers on the plaster ceiling of the panelled upstairs room which can still be visited. The gateway itself is round-arched, of stone, and is flanked by classical pilasters, like those introduced on a much grander scale into the new Middle Temple Hall in the 1560s.

Opposite: Entrance to the Alienation Office (now 3 North, King's Bench Walk).

3 North
LITTLETON
CHAMBERS

Prince Henry's room interior 1905.

The Inner Temple gateway and Prince Henry's room, Fleet Street, 1905.

Further expansion was influenced by the existence of the garden, newly laid out in 1591 and stretching down to the river. In 1609 Edward Heyward and others built a large new chamber block on its eastern side, 90ft long, 28ft wide and four storeys high, with an 'open gallery' above. Its timber construction earnèd it the later name Paper Buildings, but it was demolished because of its 'weak and unseemllie construction' in 1629, and was replaced by another block of sixteen chambers, one of which was occupied by the famous jurist John Selden; it had a gabled roof-line and lasted until 1685. The ground to the east of Paper Buildings was later laid out as another formal open space, King's Bench Walks. They took their name from the King's Bench Office, rebuilt with the aid of funds provided by the Duke of Buckingham in 1621–2, and subsequently relocated to a single-storey building next to the river. Four-storeyed chamber blocks went up at the upper end of the Walks, on the site of the present numbers 3–6 in 1616 and 1635, and more were built south of the Whitefriars gateway, extending down to the river. But they all fell victim to the Great Fire, and their original appearance can only be surmised from tiny details in Wenceslas Hollar's invaluable views of pre-Fire London.

The most impressive of the Inner Temple's early seventeenth-century buildings went up in 1629–30 in Crown Office Row, looking south over the garden to the river on the site of premises occupied by the Clerk of the Crown since the early sixteenth century; a shorter range projected south along Middle Temple Lane (the site of Harcourt Buildings), and another north to the Hall, where a new entrance was created. The scheme was conceived not by individuals but by the Inn as a whole and was financed 'with the treasure of the house', which recouped part of the cost of £2682 19s 9d by letting the chambers, the rest coming from a tax on members. By now the Inns of Court had come to think of themselves as 'the nurserie for the greater part of the gentry of the realme', comparable to the colleges of Oxford and Cambridge. By planning new buildings on this scale the Benchers clearly wanted to give the Inner Temple an architectural presence commensurate with its prestige as a place of legal scholarship and education. The block – which survived the Great Fire – occupied the site of 1–10 Crown Office Row. It was built of brick, five storeys high and twenty-three bays wide, with a roof-line enlivened with pedimented gables of the type often called Dutch, though probably deriving from Fulke Greville's long-vanished town house in Holborn of 1619; such gables can still be seen at the brick house now called Kew Palace, built for a London merchant in 1631. Had it survived, Crown Office Row would now be recognised as one of the most important London building projects of its time, anticipating the plain, disciplined, classically-based brick architecture which became normal after the Fire. However, part was destroyed in a fire of 1737 and the remainder, remodelled externally in 1838, obliterated in the Blitz.

We do not know who designed these new buildings. A carpenter called John Field was paid for making a new 'bridge' (pier) and river stairs in 1620–1, and was paid £5 in 1624–5 for making 'several plots [plans]... for buildings in the House', but the buildings themselves are not named. From 1638 onwards there were sporadic payments to John Young, later Master of the Masons'

Crown Office Row after the fire of 1737, from a painting by Richard Wilson.

The Master's House in 1927.

Company in the City of London, but again the buildings are not specified; he later went on to design the church at Berwick-on-Tweed – one of the few parish churches built during the Interregnum – and, following the Fire, Apothecaries' Hall, one of the few Livery Company halls to have survived the Blitz largely intact. One project that can be tentatively attached to a known building craftsman was on the east side of Hare Court, flanking Inner Temple Lane. A payment of £20 to 'Carter' for surveying a new building here in 1658 suggests that it may have been built by Edward Carter, son of the Chief Clerk of the King's Works and an associate of Inigo Jones during the 1630s, though the payment may refer to a survey of a building put up by someone else. The block, which was of brick, stood on the site of the present Dr Johnson's Building, and for a period after 1760 was the residence of Johnson himself, whose bulky form is seen emerging from the doorway with its handsome plaster shell-hood in a much-reproduced nineteenth-century drawing. The building was demolished in 1858.

By 1660 the ground plan of the Inn was similar to that of today. Small courtyards clustered around the Church and Hall, with a more spacious layout overlooking the river and gardens to the east and south. But, with the exception of the Church, virtually none of the buildings survived a series of devastating fires in the late seventeenth and eighteenth centuries, a spate of rebuilding in the nineteenth century and finally the Second World War. The first of these catastrophes was the Great Fire of 1666, the westward progress of which was halted in the Inner Temple. By the time it had burnt itself out, as Hollar made clear in his map of the City produced while the ruins were still smouldering, it had destroyed all the buildings in King's Bench Walk, with the exception of Paper Buildings, and the Master's House, east of the Church. The Master's House was rebuilt in 1667 as a neat brick classically-proportioned box of the comfortable type that Inigo Jones had introduced into London before the Civil War (for example in a house for Lord Maltravers, and the row of houses possibly for Lord Arundel *c*1638), and which proliferated throughout England after the Restoration. Three storeys high and seven bays wide, with a central pediment under a hipped roof, it was copied almost to the letter when it was rebuilt in 1955, though alas without its beautiful internal wood carving which perished in the Blitz.

The rebuilding of King's Bench Walk was also planned in 1667, and in 1670 one of the Benchers, Francis Phelips, employed Edward Tasker, 'a skilful surveyor and contriver of buildings', to build a block of chambers which may be the present numbers 1–2 (number 1 was rebuilt after war damage in 1949, preserving only the doorcase). With their plain three-storeyed brick exteriors, pedimented doorways and hipped roofs, they show the influence both of Jones and of the 1667 Rebuilding Act for the City of London, which stipulated the external use of brick construction to minimise fire risk. Numbers 1–2 are clearly shown, together with the adjacent Alienation Office, in a birds-eye view of 1671 which constitutes the first accurate visual record of the Inn, and their external appearance is virtually unchanged. The 1671 view also shows buildings lining the eastern side of the Walks, which are laid out with trees and pathways in the fashionably formal style. Some, on the site of the present numbers 3–6, have somewhat old-fashioned gabled elevations. But the rest (numbers 7–10) are more classical in appearance, as was the rather featureless, four-storeyed block of red-brick buildings (1–3 Tanfield Court) which looked east over the upper end of King's Bench Walk and south over the terrace in front of the Hall and Library.

No sooner were these buildings completed than another fire of 1677 made it necessary to rebuild 3–6 King's Bench Walk again.

Overleaf: A view of the Temple as it appeared in 1671, re-engraved in 1770.

A View of the TEMPLE as it appeared in the Year 1671, when James Duke of York, afterwards James II. *was a member of the Inner Temple, and Sr. Heneage Finch, Ki*

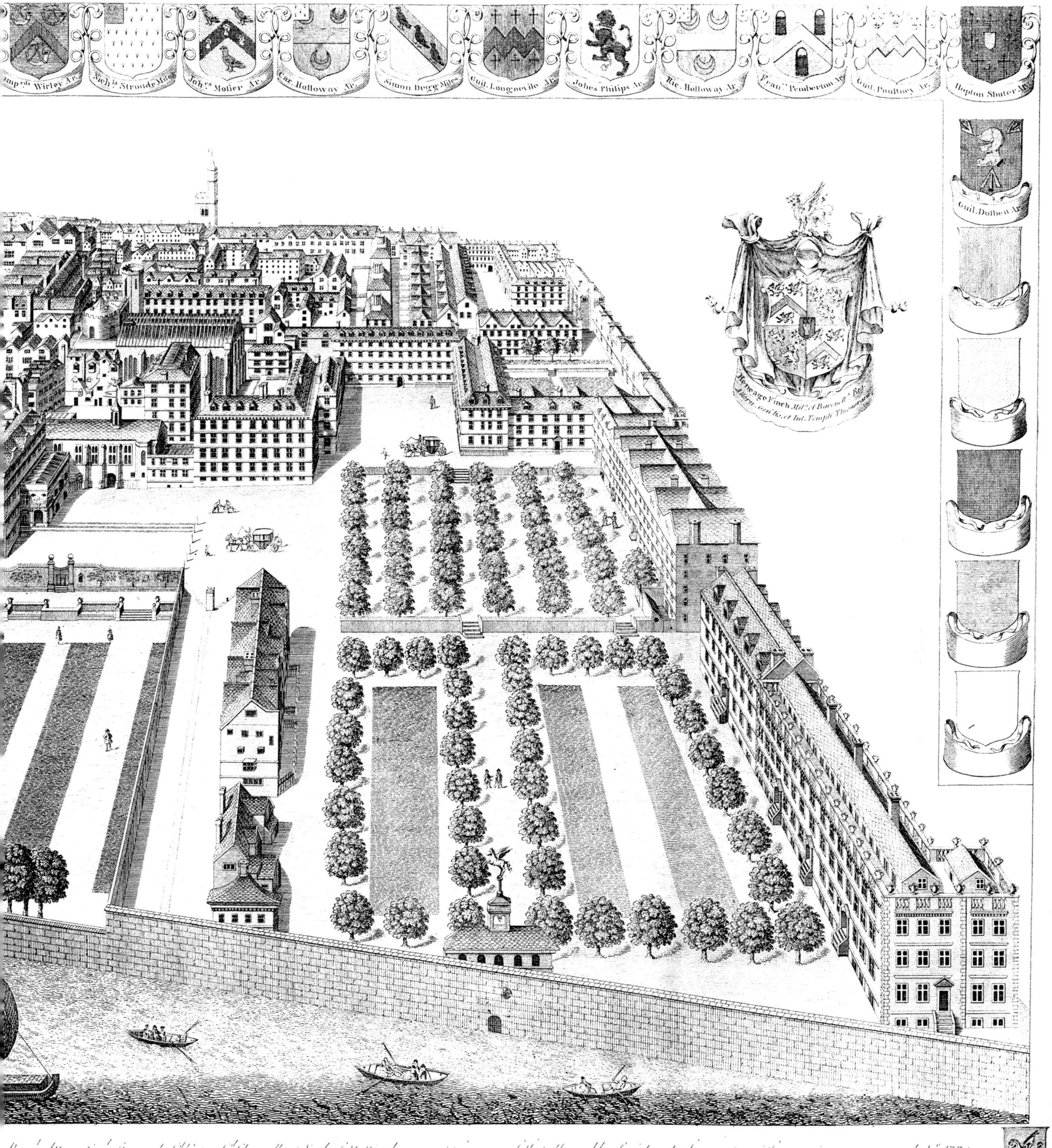

...mp.rus Wirley Ar.
Nich.ls Stroude Miles
Joh.es Mosier Ar.
Car. Holloway Ar.
Simon Degg Miles
Guil. Longnevile Ar.
Johes Philips Ar.
Ric. Holloway Ar.
Fran.s Pemberton Ar.
Guil. Poultney Ar.
Hopton Shuter Ar.
Guil. Dolben Ar.

Heneage Finch Mil.t et Baronett.s Reg. Attorn. Gen.l &c. et Int. Templi Thesaurar.

...Bar.t Attorn. Gen.l afterwards L.d Keeper, L.d Chancellor & Earl of Nottingham, was Treasurer of that Honorable Society; at whose expence the same is now re-engraved An.o 1770.

Occupying the site of the gabled buildings shown in the 1671 view, they survive virtually intact as perhaps the best examples of post-Fire domestic architecture not only in the Inns of Court but in the City as a whole. Each block is of brick, four storeys high, with a basement and an attic hidden behind a parapet, and in each the external decoration is confined largely to the round-arched doorways, in gauged and rubbed brick, framed by classical columns supporting a pediment. At numbers 3, 4 and 6 the unknown architects or craftsmen employed the Doric order, with an inscription on the frieze of number 4 recording the rebuilding in 1678; number 5 has Corinthian columns, with the bases and capitals carved in stone. The doorways are placed at the centre of each building and lead to staircases which give access to the chambers, each of which is made up of sets of up to four rooms – one for the clerk, an office/study, a living room and a bedroom – panelled in wood, and with a heavy outer door for privacy.

A third fire in 1679 devastated the still largely timber-built Middle Temple, leaving only its magnificent Elizabethan hall, and paving the way for its extensive rebuilding by the notorious Nicolas Barbon, the most famous of London's late seventeenth-century property developers. This fire also affected the north-western part of the Inner Temple, leading to the rebuilding of Hare Court with a handsome row of four-storeyed buildings on the west and south sides, their plain brick elevations enlivened by the alternating triangular and rounded pediments over the doorways. The similar Farrars Building, which faced the round nave of the Church, went up at the same time, as did 4–6 Fig Tree Court, next to the medieval 'butteries' adjoining the Hall, with two storeys over a basement and a dentil cornice. The only one of these buildings to survive today is 1 Hare Court.

Entrance to 4 King's Bench Walk.

2 King's Bench Walk interior in the 1950s.

The 1679 fire started in Pump Court, part of the Middle Temple, and destroyed the cloister between it and the present Church Court. This had formed part of the Templars' buildings but it belonged to the Middle Temple whose members wanted to replace it by a block of chambers. The Benchers of the Inner Temple protested, arguing that students had used it from time immemorial for walking in the evenings and 'putting cases'. So, following an appeal to the Lord Chancellor Sir Heneage Finch – a member of the Inner Temple – a classicised 'cloister' was retained, with round arcades and a row of Doric columns inside to support the three-storeyed block of chambers above. The design was provided by no less an architect than Sir Christopher Wren, who had already done surveying work for the Benchers in King's Bench Walk and had designed a similar 'cloister' under the library at Trinity College, Cambridge, and the block went up in 1680–1. Though destroyed in the Second World War, its general appearance was retained when it was rebuilt in 1949–52 by Sir Edward Maufe, who took the opportunity to reinstate the number of arches – seven – originally intended by Wren but unaccountably increased to eight by the builder.

This spate of rebuilding left the Inn with a set of new and handsome, though plain, residential buildings. Writing in 1720 about the Inns, William Strype referred to their 'most beautiful, uniform manner [of building], very lofty, and more substantial and

Plan of the Temple in 1677 from John Ogilby's map of London; the ink line marks the western limit of the Great Fire of London.

Cigarette card of 1 Hare Court.

convenient than before'. By then the Inner Temple, like the other Inns, had ceased to be a place of formal legal education. The last lectures or 'readings' took place in 1678, and when they stopped the Inns reverted to being clubs for lawyers, many of whom continued to reside and have their offices there. The remaining chambers were leased out to tenants such as Johnson and Boswell who appreciated the congenial, quasi-collegiate atmosphere and the convenient situation between the City and the West End; the chamber blocks, with their communal staircases, reminded one writer of apartment houses in Paris and Edinburgh. With fewer resident lawyers and next to no students there was little need to build, except as the result of fire – that scourge of the Inns of Court – or dilapidation. Number 7 King's Bench Walk was rebuilt after a fire in 1684, and 8–11 followed in the late eighteenth and early nineteenth centuries (10–11 are dated 1814). Paper Buildings was rebuilt in brick, and on a larger scale, in 1685, its north wall overlooking the terrace – shown in early eighteenth-century views as a place for fashionable promenading – adorned with paintings of the Virtues; they were repainted by Peter Berchet in 1706. Harcourt Buildings was built on the west side of the garden in 1703, and in 1738, after another fire, the east part of Crown Office Row (numbers 1–3) was replaced by a plain but well-proportioned brick block with fashionable Palladian detailing, designed by the carpenter and master mason Benjamin Timbrell, perhaps the most successful London speculative builder of his time, with much of Mayfair to his credit. It was here that the writer Charles Lamb was born.

The medieval Hall survived all these changes. A screen with elaborately carved wooden doors was introduced in 1574, and the doors themselves were retained when the Hall was finally demolished, only to fall victim to the Second World War. The Library, next to the Hall, was demolished in 1679, supposedly to stop the fire spreading, and was later rebuilt, as was the Parliament Chamber, richly panelled with some Grinling Gibbons-like wood carving of 1705 which was rescued from the devastation of the Blitz and incorporated into the present Parliament Chamber. Within the Hall itself a new screen was built in 1680, and in 1709 Sir James Thornhill, best known for his frescoes inside the dome of St Paul's Cathedral and in the Painted Hall at Greenwich Hospital, was paid £70 for a painting at the east (high table) end showing Pegasus leaping from Mount Helicon, with Mercury, the Arts and Sciences in attendance. Then, following the fire that destroyed the eastern part of Crown Office Row in 1737, the south wall, overlooking the terrace, was remodelled with round-arched windows replacing the earlier Gothic ones. A new south entrance was also created, with an

The modern cloisters.

Smirke had a reputation for 'pleasing men, whom it is proverbially impossible to please', and when John Wigg stepped down as Surveyor in 1819 he took over his position. In this capacity he was responsible in 1819 and 1827–8 for building a new Library and Parliament Chamber on their old site on the south side of Tanfield Court. The proximity of the recently remodelled Hall made the choice of the 'collegiate Gothic' style almost inevitable, but Smirke's meagre south front, with its crenellated roof-line and pointed windows, though arguably more interesting than the late seventeenth-century building it replaced, was no more than a open swan-necked pediment on Doric pilasters containing a relief carving of Pegasus by the great sculptor J M Rysbrack, later removed to the Library and now over the Benchers' staircase.

The Hall had long been regarded as inadequate, especially in comparison with that of the Middle Temple – the finest surviving Elizabethan building in central London – and its replacement was seriously considered in the early seventeenth century, only to be dropped. By 1816 it had become structurally dangerous. Since the 1770s the Benchers had entrusted new building projects in the Inns to their own Surveyors, the first three of whom – John Gorham, James Hall and John Wigg – were successful London builders who did similar work for other City institutions. But when it came to remodelling the Hall they turned to one of London's most fashionable architects, Robert Smirke, the son of a painter who leapt to fame in 1809 as the architect of the new Covent Garden Theatre, the first major monument of the Greek Revival in London. In 1815 Smirke became, along with John Nash and John Soane, one of the three 'attached architects' to the reorganised Office of Works – the body responsible for royal and government buildings – and in 1823 he was entrusted with the new British Museum. At the Inner Temple his task was a more modest one, and in his external and internal remodelling of the ancient Hall he resorted to the romantic medievalism of which he had already shown himself a competent practitioner in his ponderous, though impressive, 'castles' at Eastnor (Herefordshire) and Lowther (Westmorland). With its delicate neo-Tudor woodwork, Readers' coats of arms and three large statues in niches over the screen at the west end, Smirke's interior was, in the words of the Gentleman's Magazine, 'an interesting specimen of the Gothic style of decoration', and his structural repairs made the building serviceable for another generation.

10 King's Bench Walk.

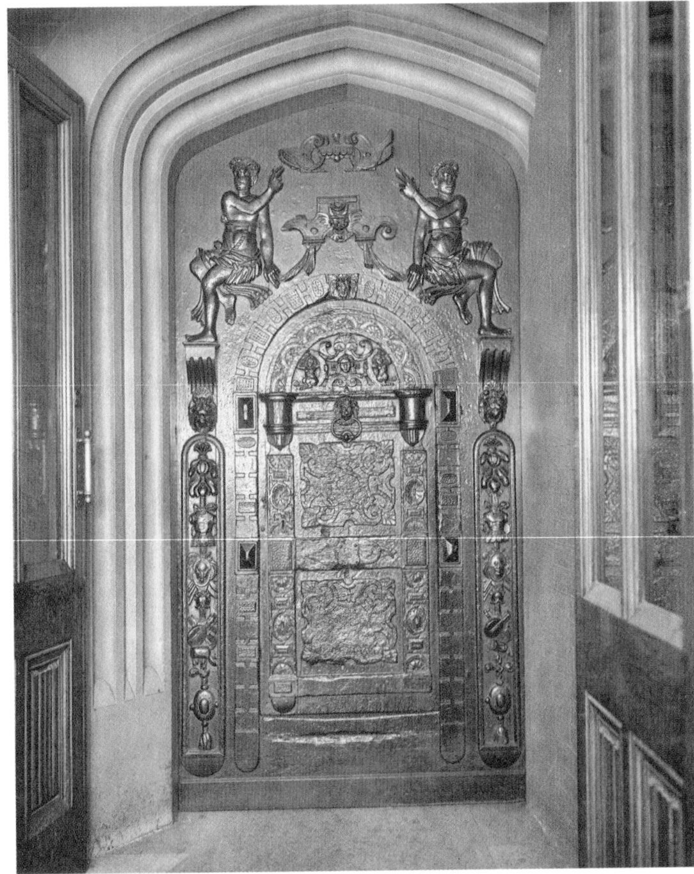

Elizabethan door formerly in the Inner Temple Hall; destroyed in the Second World War.

Eighteenth-century painting showing the north side of Paper Buildings.

covering for a symmetrical, classically proportioned building. The result was bemoaned by Charles Lamb in his *Essays of Elia* (1823): 'They have lately gothicised the entrance to the inner temple-Hall and the Library front, to assimilate them, I suppose, to the body of the Hall, which they do not at all resemble.'

The building of the new Library was the beginning of a programme of modernising the Inn's facilities which continued on and off for the rest of the nineteenth century. £179,620 was spent on buildings between 1824 and 1853, and in designing most of them Smirke did more to change the face of the Inn than any architect before the late twentieth century. In 1825 he finally cleared the shops away from the south side of the Church, a process begun in 1811, exposing the south front to public view for the first time for centuries, and refacing the building in Bath stone. Otherwise the work mainly involved remodelling or replacing seventeenth- and early eighteenth-century buildings in order to provide extra chambers for the growing number of barristers required by a rapidly expanding population. So the western part of Crown Office Row was refaced in 1827, and 4–5 Hare Court altered in 1827 and 1832 (and the Master's House in 1827–31). King's Bench Walk was extended south towards the river with the building of numbers 12–13 in 1829, and number 9 was remodelled by Smirke in 1836–7, as were Mitre Court Buildings, at the upper end of the Walk, in 1830, the east side of Tanfield Court in 1832–3, Harcourt Buildings in 1832–4 and 1–3 Paper Buildings, after a fire, in 1838. The results were solid, workmanlike and restrained almost to the point of dullness: qualities that can still be seen in the Portland stone facade of Mitre Court Buildings, closing the view north from King's Bench Walk, and the plain, unadorned yellow brick fronts of Paper Buildings.

The Rysbrack Pegasus.

Old Inner Temple Hall looking east, indicating the location of the Thornhill painting above the portraits.

Pre-war Mitre Court Buildings.

5 Paper Buildings.

In 1845 Robert Smirke was succeeded as Surveyor by his younger brother Sydney, architect of the Oxford and Cambridge and Carlton Clubs in Pall Mall and later of the round Reading Room at the British Museum and the galleries for the Royal Academy at Burlington House. He completed the restoration of the Temple Church in 1840–3, and in 1847–8 he remodelled the southern end of Paper Buildings (numbers 4–5) in a red-brick and stucco neo-Jacobean style whose variegated elevations, influenced perhaps by the new red-brick Hall of Lincoln's Inn (Philip Hardwick and son 1843–5), earned it the nickname of 'Blotting-Paper Buildings'. In 1858 he went on to rebuild Dr Johnson's Building, whose gloomy grey brick facade, similar to those of many City office and warehouse blocks of the time, still casts a shadow over Inner Temple Lane.

Sydney Smirke redeemed himself with his new Hall, built in 1867–70. Ten years earlier the Royal Commission on Legal Education (1854–5) had recommended amalgamating the Inns of Court and transforming them into a new legal university. This proposal never bore fruit, but it led to a revival of their educational role. Meals had always been an important part of their communal life and, as numbers of trainee barristers increased, a larger hall became desperately needed. The new building – 94ft by 41ft with a 40ft-high roof – was substantially larger than its predecessor, the extra width being obtained by the demolition of a block called Twisden's Building to the north. More space was also obtained by extending the building west over the innermost of the medieval 'butteries'. So, ironically, all but a fragment of the Inner Temple's genuine medieval secular buildings were sacrificed in order to build what turned out to be its finest – though sadly short-lived – example of Gothic Revival architecture. Sydney Smirke was a more convincing Gothicist than his older brother, and his Hall successfully evoked the great halls of the later Middle Ages with its hammer-beam roof, carved wooden screen, mullioned and transomed windows filled with stained glass and its battlemented and pinnacled roof-line. Such features had recently appeared in the new Hall of Lincoln's Inn, as well as at the new Houses of Parliament, and, by employing a similar architectural language in the heart of the Inner Temple, Smirke was making a clear statement about the origins not only of the institution but of the English legal system as a whole: a statement which was underlined by the presence of bronze statues of Knights Templar and Hospitaller, by the sculptor Henry Armstead, on the screen.

Sydney Smirke was the last top-flight architect to hold the position of Surveyor to the Inner Temple. When he resigned in 1870 he was replaced by Arthur Cates, a pupil of Sir James Pennethorne, the architect of the Public Record Office (now the library of King's College) in Chancery Lane. Cates was a competent exponent of the restrained but somewhat humdrum Renaissance style used in many mid-Victorian commercial buildings, as can be seen in his Farrar's Building, next to the round nave of the Church, built in 1875–6 on the site of a late seventeenth-century block of red-brick chambers. He also designed the gateway from King's Bench Walk to Tudor Street in 1886–7. But he also demonstrated his command of the Gothic idiom in his extension to the Library of 1881. The contrast between Sydney Smirke's new Hall and the uninspiring exterior of his older brother's Library block had been painfully obvious, and by adding a pinnacled tower surmounted by a wooden turret, somewhat reminiscent of Big Ben, at the south-eastern corner of the older building, Cates succeeded in balancing the composition while also supplying a visual punctuation mark to the view north from King's Bench Walk: an effect that was unfortunately lost when the decision was made to rebuild the Library in a totally different style after the air raids of 1940–1.

The character of London's legal quarter was permanently changed by the completion of two projects of long gestation in the late nineteenth century: the Thames Embankment and the new Royal Courts of Justice in the Strand. The Embankment was built

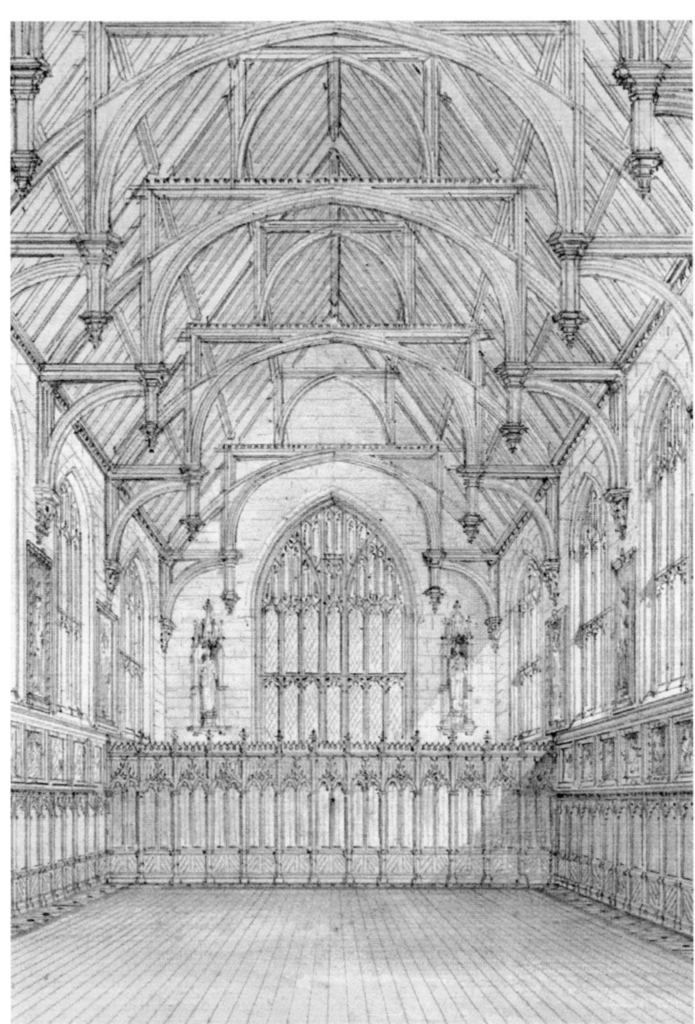

Design for the Hall by Sydney Smirke, 1867.

South side of Sydney Smirke's new Hall.

Two of Henry Armstead's bronze statues.

Farrar's building.

South facade of Temple Gardens c1900.

Early twentieth-century photograph of the Inner Temple Library showing Arthur Cates' tower, added to the east of Sir Robert Smirke's building.

between 1868 and 1874, cutting both the Inner Temple and the Middle Temple off from the river and giving them access by road from the south. Meanwhile the building in 1871–84 of the Law Courts, following years of wrangling, increased the demand for lawyers' chambers. To satisfy that demand, in 1875–9 the Inner Temple and the Middle Temple jointly put up a massive new block, Temple Gardens, at the southern end of Middle Temple Lane. Separated from the new Embankment by lawns, and built of Portland stone, four storeys high with a basement and attic, it adopted the character of a great gateway with a central arch flanked by statues of Learning and Justice (by W Calder Marshall), exemplifying the newly-recovered role of the Inns as guarantors of legal education. The architect was E M Barry, son of the architect of the Houses of Parliament, and he employed the rich and somewhat over-ripe French Renaissance style he had already used in the Charing Cross Station hotel (1863–5): a building which, with its steep-pitched roof and array of elaborately carved gables, it loosely resembled.

The last important Victorian addition to the Inner Temple was very different in character. In 1893 Arthur Cates was asked to rebuild the western side of Hare Court (numbers 2–3), but he withdrew through ill health and the job was given to another architect, Thomas Graham Jackson. He was a pupil of the great Gothic revivalist Sir George Gilbert Scott and had made his reputation in Oxford, where he both surprised and delighted his contemporaries with his bold and eclectic designs for the Examination Schools in the High Street, insouciantly mingling Elizabethan and Italian Renaissance motifs. In Hare Court he employed the red brick and white-painted sash windows which had

The Master's House in ruins, 1941.

The old Lamb Building in Church Court c1910.

given the seventeenth-century buildings he was asked to replace much of their charm, and he even imitated their attractive doorways with their pilasters and rounded pediments in rubbed brick. But he also introduced the bay windows, pedimented dormers and wooden cornices of the so-called 'Queen Anne' style, exploited with great panache by architects such as Norman Shaw, and by Jackson himself, from the 1870s onwards. 'Queen Anne' was conceived as a reaction against the heaviness and solemnity of the architecture of the previous generation, and in his Hare Court building, with its bold elevation to Middle Temple Lane, Jackson brought it into the heart of the Inns of Court.

It is no accident that Jackson's red-brick buildings went up at a time when the remaining seventeenth-century buildings of the Inner Temple, so long despised or neglected, were being carefully recorded in watercolours or photographed. And in 1900–6 the buildings over the Gateway, long covered in stucco, were restored to something believed to approximate to their original half-timbered appearance. This new appreciation of the ordinary domestic architecture of the Inn may help explain why so little new building occurred in the first forty years of the twentieth century.

But in 1940–1 a series of air raids, culminating in a devastating raid on the night of 10–11 May 1941, wrought havoc on a scale unseen since the fires of the 1660s and 1670s. The Temple Church was gutted by incendiary bombs, as were the Master's House, the Hall and Library, the cloister leading into Pump Court, the western part of Mitre Court Buildings, some of the buildings in King's Bench Walk (numbers 1, 6 and 14–15) and the whole of Fig Tree Court, Crown Office Row and Harcourt Buildings. Apart from most of King's Bench Walk, the only buildings to be relatively unaffected were Paper Buildings, Temple Gardens and the complex to the north-west of the Church – Farrar's Building, Hare Court and Dr Johnson's Building. The devastation caused Sir Frank MacKinnon, Treasurer in 1945 and no lover of Victorian architecture, to bemoan, 'Anyone who goes into the Temple and views the devastation in its buildings might suppose that by an irony of fate... things of beauty had suffered, while that which is hideous has escaped. The Master's House and nos 5 and 6 Fig Tree Court are heaps of rubble, while Farrar's Building and Temple Gardens are almost intact.'

The appalling damage wrought by Hitler's bombers presented the Benchers with an opportunity to impose their own architectural taste upon the Inn, and the decisions they and their architects made go a long way to explain its appearance today. Of the buildings destroyed, only the Temple Church, the Master's House and the cloister building – all of them shared with the Middle Temple – were rebuilt in anything like their original form. The Church was entrusted to Walter Godfrey, an architect of great sensitivity and profound knowledge of medieval buildings, and his restoration, completed in 1957, was an unqualified success. For the Master's House the two societies jointly employed their own architects: for the Inner Temple Hubert Worthington, who had enjoyed a great

2 Hare Court detail.

Interior of the Hall after bombing, with the remains of Armstead's bronze statues.

vogue in inter-war Oxford, and for the Middle Temple Sir Edward Maufe, whose finest building is the still under-appreciated Guildford Cathedral, but who was also widely employed by Gray's Inn and some of the Oxford and Cambridge colleges. Their restoration of the Master's House (finished in 1955) reinstated the facade of the 1667 building; and Maufe, making use of a recently discovered drawing by Sir Christopher Wren and acting alone, was also able in 1949–52 to reconstruct the cloister and the chambers above it in the form originally intended.

Until 1940–1 Tanfield Court, between the Church and Hall, was divided into two by the late seventeenth-century Lamb Building, a detached part of the Middle Temple. The Blitz gave the Inner Temple the opportunity to do away with this alien presence in its midst, and few tears were shed when the decision was taken not to rebuild the plain brick building but to create a single court, renamed Church Court, with the Church and Master's House taking up the whole of the north side. The creation of a large new court at the heart of the Inner Temple was a positive benefit to both of the Inns, but the Middle Temple had to be compensated for the loss of Lamb Building by the exchange of land west of the Inner Temple Hall, and the result here was less happy. Fig Tree Court had been one of the most attractive of the smaller enclaves in the Inns, but it was now amalgamated with the adjacent Elm Court – part of the Middle Temple and also destroyed by bombing – to form a rather characterless space, also called Elm Court, surrounded on three sides by unremarkable neo-Georgian blocks of chambers and on the east side by the much-restored and anomalous-looking rubble wall of the medieval butteries adjoining the Hall.

The Inner Temple spent £1,432,082 on its new buildings, most of which came from the War Damage Commission. The most important task was the rebuilding of the Hall and Library. By the middle of the twentieth century appreciation of Victorian architecture had sunk to its nadir, and any suggestion of rebuilding Sydney Smirke's Hall or his older brother's Library in their original form would have been inconceivable. So too, given the aesthetic conservatism of most corporate and educational institutions in the post-war period, would any proposal to employ the architectural style of International Modernism as exemplified by foreign architects such as Le Corbusier and Mies van der Rohe. Such architecture might be appropriate for housing estates or even the buildings of the Festival of Britain of 1951, but not for a society of lawyers which could trace its origins back to the fourteenth century. Admiration of the restrained, gentlemanly, brick architecture of the Inn as it had been rebuilt after the Great Fire continued to increase in the first half of the twentieth century, and in that climate of opinion it is not surprising that the Inner Temple's architect Hubert Worthington should, like his Middle Temple counterpart Maufe, opt for a style of architecture which can broadly be called neo-Georgian: classical in inspiration, brick-built, pitched-roofed and aesthetically undemanding. His design of 1948 for the Inner Temple's new buildings – the east end of Crown Office Row, the Hall, the Library and the Treasurer's office and the east side of the new Church Court – displayed both the virtues and the vices of his architecture: the buildings look dignified and reassuringly traditional in appearance, but the overall effect is bland and the detailing perverse, as can be seen on the exterior of the Hall.

Post-war reconstruction under way.

Exterior of the modern Hall.

Post-war building controls meant that work had to begin on the less-damaged buildings in King's Bench Walk, Mitre Court and elsewhere, and the foundation stone of the new Hall was not laid until 1952. By then Worthington had already fallen foul of the Benchers because of delays on the earlier projects, and in 1953 he was dismissed because of his failure to produce working drawings on time. He was replaced as architect by his assistant T W Sutcliffe, and it was Sutcliffe who brought the building to completion in 1955. From the outside it is distinguished mainly by its large round-arched windows with their rather peculiar, almost Mannerist, stone aprons and carved brackets underneath. The inside is more successful: wide, spacious and notable for the high quality of the craftsmanship, especially the wood panelling and the classical mouldings in plaster on the flat ceiling. It would be difficult to imagine a greater contrast to the solemn medievalism of its predecessor.

The remaining projects were shared between Sutcliffe and Maufe. Sutcliffe took responsibility for the Library and Treasury Office building (1956–8), with its dignified thirteen-bay classical frontage looking south over the terrace. The Parliament Chamber and Benchers' Rooms are placed on the first floor or *piano nobile*, with the L-shaped Library, 'unashamedly modelled', in the words of a *Country Life* article, 'on late seventeenth and eighteenth-century prototypes', on the second floor. Ingeniously divided into bays by beautifully crafted oak bookcases, with galleries above, it is the most successful of the post-war interiors in the Inn. Maufe meanwhile took on the rebuilding of Crown Office Row (1954–5), similar in dimensions to its pre-war predecessor but with a rather dull, repetitive neo-Georgian elevation to the garden and a livelier, pedimented eastern facade to the terrace. It was also Maufe who designed the Francis Taylor Building (1955–7), on the site of 1 Tanfield Court – the eastern side of Church Court – with a plain, well-mannered yellow brick frontage to King's Bench Walk (and a doorway flanked by columns with a distinctive form of Ionic capital deriving from the Temple of Apollo at Bassae in Greece, which Maufe borrowed from the Ashmolean Museum in Oxford and used in his Dolphin Building at St John's College). With the completion of this building, and of the Treasury Office and Library, the post-war reconstruction of the Inn came to an end. Following years of destruction and upheaval, the last fifty years have been, from an architectural point of view, remarkably tranquil: a welcome development for all those who value London's old buildings and who cherish the distinctive charm of the Inns of Court.

Dr Geoffrey Tyack FSA is a Fellow of Kellogg College, Oxford, where he lectures in architectural and urban history.

Queen Elizabeth II laying the foundation stone for the new Hall in 1952.

THE VICTORIAN RESTORATION OF THE CHURCH

J Mordaunt Crook

The restoration of the Temple Church in the early 1840s was a major triumph for ecclesiology and a minor tragedy for several of the individuals involved. Hazards, from the Great Fire to Hitler's bombs, and the fashions of taste, from the age of Wren to the age of Pugin, have combined to make the Temple Church an architectural palimpsest of extraordinary interest. Its construction during the twelfth and thirteenth centuries had been a milestone in the development of the Gothic style. The alterations of the seventeenth and eighteenth centuries represent an interesting commentary on the vagaries of liturgical fashion. Its restoration during the nineteenth century was an early landmark in the history of the Gothic Revival. Its partial destruction in 1941 made possible the most drastic and the most accomplished restoration of all.

Both the Inner and Middle Temple contributed to the remarkable expansion of public building during the post-Napoleonic period. In 1819 both societies appointed a new architect with a mandate for reconstruction. The Inner Temple chose Robert (later Sir Robert) Smirke. The Middle Temple chose Henry Hakewill. Smirke held office until his retirement in 1845, when he was succeeded by his younger brother Sydney. Hakewill died in 1830 and was succeeded by James Savage. Smirke's predecessors had all been surveyors rather than architects, concerned with running repairs rather than rebuilding or restoration. Now there was to be a considerable amount of rebuilding in both Gothic and classical style, led by Smirke as the appointee of the richer of the two institutions. Before long, the various 'Gothicisings and Smirkefyings' were causing Charles Lamb to lament the transformation of the Inner Temple he had known as a child. But the restoration of the Temple Church was the joint responsibility of both societies. From the Blitz-scarred manuscripts of the Inner Temple we have now sufficient evidence to reconstruct the circumstances of this architectural *cause célèbre*.

The Temple Church entered the nineteenth century a dilapidated hybrid. Repairs over the previous two centuries had bestowed upon the ancient exterior what were described as 'odious overlayings', and the outline of the Church was effectively obscured by a clinging jumble of shops and lodgings. Inside were 'Vandalic encroachments and beautifications', with the Round divided from the chancel by a pilastered organ screen and the whole interior encrusted with medieval brasses and classical monuments.

Interior of the Round, 1809; acquatint by Pugin and Rowlandson.

After a feeble attempt at repair in 1810, the Inner Temple employed Smirke in 1825 to complete the clearance, begun in 1811 and 1819, of the south side and reface it with Bath stone. Among other alterations, the southern 'Doric' doorway was walled up, the battlements on half the Round became a corbelled parapet and the

Church interior after the completion of the Victorian restoration in 1843.

old belfry was removed. As work progressed the zeal for restoration increased and expressed itself characteristically in an attempt to improve the symmetry and convenience of the Church through the obliteration of the thirteenth-century Chapel of St Ann and the removal of the organ screen. The chapel's demolition was denounced as 'an unpardonable outrage', but its removal undoubtedly improved the southern aspect of the Round. Smirke carried out several more alterations until lack of funds prevented any further work.

It was not until 1840 that work started again, when both societies agreed upon a programme of restoration, repair and cleaning. But these remedial measures rapidly appeared mere preliminary steps towards a complete transformation of the Church. A great many of the details of the interior were sold or removed and much of the plaster- and stonework was 'indignantly and contemptuously torn away'. But in the process, serious structural weaknesses were exposed. From being merely a matter of running repairs, the restoration of the Temple Church became a work of national interest, involving many of the country's leading architects, artists and craftsmen.

It was now that an investigation of the Temple Church accounts revealed that James Savage, who had been left in sole charge of the work after Smirke's withdrawal through illness, had grossly exceeded his estimates. Smirke, brought back to disentangle the confusion, advised immediate suspension of the restoration, but

The Church in 1828 as drawn by Thomas Shepherd.

that Savage should be in control of individual contracts with tradesmen which would be let after he (Smirke) had examined all the specifications. However, despite his protests that he could not have foreseen much of the work he was called on to do, the Joint Committee decided that Savage should have no further part in the work and dismissed him. Since Smirke's ill health now prevented him from continuing with the project, his brother Sydney was appointed together with Decimus Burton.

The scope and expense of the restoration continued to expand. The Round was given a conical roof and polychromatised vaulting, a new bell turret was added, a reredos, pulpit and Caen stone font were installed, along with new stalls and stained glass, and the floor was fitted with new tiles. However, in the enthusiasm for restoration, ecclesiology engulfed antiquarianism, and thirteenth-century relics were subjected to what can only be described as vandalism. The 'decayed and decaying remains of coffins and human bodies' below the pavement were replaced by 'a stratum of lime rubbish and concrete… to keep down the damp and prevent all noxious exhalations'. The decomposing remains were visited by curious thousands before being 'heterogeneously thrown into a vaulted grave dug in the reconstructed Round'. The effigies were drastically restored and the 'pagan tombs and scoffing epitaphs' of the sixteenth, seventeenth and eighteenth centuries were bundled unceremoniously into the triforium and vestry.

The final bill was in the region of £70,000, a figure which the Joint Committee excused by explaining that 'the increase has arisen almost wholly from difficulties which could not have been anticipated' – a defence that made nonsense of Savage's dismissal. The restored Temple Church never won the full approval of thoroughbred ecclesiologists; but the Inns were satisfied: 'Exceptions to the details might be justly taken; yet on the whole they appear the best of the kind which our age has yet accomplished – right in spirit and well executed, considering the sort of mixed tribunal which superintended them.'

Professor Joseph Mordaunt Crook FBA FSA is an English architectural historian and specialist in the Georgian and Victorian periods.

Wartime Bombing and Fighting the Fires

Cecile Robinson

The first bomb in the Inn shook us up mentally as well as physically; I was astounded the next morning to see the mess and confusion it had created. A bomb is a most untidy affair. There was any amount of debris about – broken glass which scrunched as we walked home, lots of splinters, some beams of wood and oh! the dust. Everything looked like a housemaid's bad dream.

Until then the first nights of the raids in September 1940 had been fearful but rather exciting. When the sirens sounded each night I had joined about seven others in the shelter at 2 Dr Johnson's Building and settled down for an uncomfortable night. My husband did not accompany me. He spent each night at Inner Temple Hall with his fire-fighting team. My shelter companions were a pleasant crowd and we got on very well. Each evening the sirens sounded a little earlier, which meant that our evening meal was cut out so we started to picnic in the cellar. An electric kettle was used for making tea during the night if things got very noisy. When Inner Temple Hall received a direct hit I was extremely pleased to see my husband emerge safe and sound with his companions. It seemed a miraculous escape and I think we made a lot of tea that night.

Soon after this we resumed sleeping in our chambers in King's Bench Walk, which was more comfortable, cleaner and warmer, and one could undress. During Christmas 1940 the raids ceased and we got used to sleeping at home in comfort. But then on 29 December, as I was preparing dinner, we heard the noise of incendiaries. We ran downstairs quickly. Incendiaries were falling like hailstones. We ran for sand and started to extinguish as many as possible. Soon the remains of the Library caught fire and were blazing furiously. The Inn seemed full of firemen and hoses and the glare was terrific – no torches were needed. By this time the Library looked a hopeless case and 1 King's Bench Walk was well on fire at the top. It seemed impossible that it would ever be extinguished and that all the Temple, indeed all London, must burn.

Crown Office Row after a bombing raid.

The next few nights were fairly quiet but at 1am on 3 January I was awakened by a terrific noise followed by a familiar rocking of the house and then something fell on the back of my head. When my husband and I put our feet out of the bed we were surprised and relieved to find the floor still there and the blackout intact. My husband groped his way to the door and turned on a light and found that no damage had been done in the bedroom. What I had thought was the ceiling falling on my head had only been the electric light fitting dislodged by the blast. We went into the street. The air seemed solid with dust. It was impossible to see a foot ahead even with a torch. Saturday 11 January was another memorable night. We had several incendiaries followed by a high explosive bomb which also demolished most of the Master's House. By now our shelter population had diminished. Many people had left the Temple or were sleeping in what they felt were safer areas. Also it was very cold there and one weighed up the chances of being killed by a bomb or pneumonia. So we went on, with a few nights when it seemed as if the Hun had given up his horrid ideas: and then a nasty night. Until the night of 10–11 May I had never realised what an air raid could be like. That night was one of terror.

Trouble started at 11pm and right from the beginning everything was hectic. HEs fell in all directions – one explosion followed by another. I had decided to be a fire watcher that evening and found myself in Middle Temple Lane. As the bombs fell thick and heavy we were not ashamed to duck occasionally under the archway leading to Pump Court. My husband joined us and I thought a cup of tea might bolster up our spirits a little. I went to Temple Gardens to make the tea. Just as the kettle boiled there was a series of loud explosions as a stick of bombs dropped very close.

I postponed making tea and went out into Middle Temple Lane to be met by J W Morris KC with the news that my husband had been injured. He had been standing near the letter box in Brick Court and, unlike the rest of us, considered it undignified to duck. I hurried up the lane and found him sitting on the steps of 2 Hare Court with a handkerchief round his leg. He asked for a cigarette. Nobody had one so I said I would return to our chambers and get some. Mr Morris went with me. As we approached King's Bench Walk we saw a lovely blue green light on my roof. I have seldom moved so quickly. I told Mr Morris where the sandbags and the stirrup pump were and we were on the roof in no time. A sandbag put paid to one incendiary but another had gone through the slates and was burning inside the rafters. Still a little excellent work with the stirrup pump and we had the fire out.

Inner Temple Hall after bombing, viewed from Church Court; the remains of the Lamb Building are on the left.

Incendiaries and HEs dropped incessantly that night. Planes were overhead all the time. The Temple Church caught fire and it was then we discovered that we could not get any water to it. We had to watch the fire spreading and were not able to do a thing to help. The fire brigade stood by helplessly. I asked the man in charge if he couldn't get the apparatus needed for relaying water from the Thames. He assured me that he had tried but the tide was too low. The fire was spreading and rapidly approaching the Round. The fires were also raging throughout the Hall, Crown Office Row and Harcourt Buildings. We went into the old Treasury Office and started a rescue train – passing anything we could find one to another. At last it became too hot to stay any longer in the office and people were shouting outside that the roof was likely to come in.

It was not until 6am that the 'all clear' sounded. We did not notice daybreak – the flames were so bright that there was no transition from night to day. After this many people left their shelters and soon the Inn was crowded with sightseers. At about this time the fire brigade got some water and although the pressure was not that great it was something. The cloisters were now well alight and at about 9am the Lamb Building also caught fire.

At home we had no water, gas or electricity so there was nothing for it but to light the open fire in the sitting room and then go out and get a little water from a fireman. Soon I was able to make a cup of tea which helped pull us together. All Sunday the fires raged and it seemed with the approach of evening the raiders would return and find us quite unprepared. The extinguishers needed filling, the buckets and stirrup pumps were missing and the fires made a wonderful target for the enemy. The fires burnt for several days – even a fortnight afterwards we had to call in the fire brigade to a fire which had started again in the cellar.

Since the Treasurer's Office had been destroyed everybody called at our chambers. As I had to cook on the coal fire the one room became a combined office, reception room and kitchen but there was no alternative to this gypsy life. As evening approached we lit candles – sparingly because they were difficult to get. We kept wonderfully good tempered which was astounding in view of our numerous difficulties. That was certainly our worst night.

Cecile Robinson, who died last year, was the wife of Roy Robinson, Sub-Treasurer 1927–58.

Mrs Robinson's living room in 3 King's Bench Walk.

Serjeants' Inn

Master Baker

The purchase in 2001 of the site of Serjeants' Inn, Fleet Street, was the most significant acquisition of real property in the Inns of Court for five centuries. It is a site full of legal interest, having been used by judges and serjeants for about 300 years, and more recently by solicitors and barristers.

The site consisted in medieval times of a messuage or townhouse in the parish of St Dunstan in the West, bounded on the west by the Ram Inn, on the south by what became the Alienation Office garden (now the Littleton Building) and on the east by the Carmelite Friars (or Whitefriars), with five shops and an entrance gateway on the Fleet Street frontage. In 1409 the freehold was purchased by the Dean and Chapter of York out of moneys left by Master Thomas Dalby to found a chantry in York Minster. The rents supported Dalby's chantry until the legislation of Edward VI provided for chantries to be confiscated by the crown. The effect of the statute upon the title of the Dean and Chapter became the subject of litigation in the seventeenth century, which the corporation eventually won on the grounds that the Inn was not chantry land within the meaning of the statute.

Amicable Life Insurance Society office, 1801.

When the serjeants first went into occupation is not recorded. In 1442 the Dean and Chapter granted a lease for twenty-four years to a London tailor, describing it as a messuage and garden 'in which John Ellerker and other serjeants at law lately dwelt'. Ellerker died in 1438, and the past tense seems to import that the serjeants no longer lived there. That, however, is not necessarily so. The stained glass windows as noted in the Hall of the Inn in 1599 included the arms of a judge who died in 1439 and of serjeants called in 1453 and 1463. Of course, it cannot be assumed that the arms were contemporary, but there is supporting circumstantial evidence in that a number of judges in the second half of the century were buried in the Whitefriars. Indeed, Mr Justice Sulyard, whose arms were noted in the windows, referred in his will (1487) to 'my chamber in my Inn next to the Whitefriars' (camera mea apud hospicium meum juxta fratres Carmelitas), which suggests that a Serjeants' Inn was then in being. If so, it was also the residence of Chief Justice Hussey, who the previous year was reported as asking a question of Sulyard 'at his Inn after dinner' (a son hostel puis manger). Hussey's arms were also in the Hall windows. It seems likely, therefore, that the judges and serjeants were in residence as under-lessees in the second half of the fifteenth century; and at least possible that they had continued there since the days of Ellerker. The other Serjeants' Inn, in Chancery Lane, was established during the same period. But it was still common for judges and serjeants to live in their own separate houses, and we do not know whether at that period the two Inns had social constitutions or a wider membership in commons than the residents alone.

The Inn was certainly established as an ordered society well before 1521, for when new serjeants were called in that year it was recorded that 'the old order of the serjeants' chambers in Serjeants' Inn in Fleet Street is to cast lots for their chambers'. Seven years earlier, in 1514, Serjeant Caryll reported an opinion entertained by 'Pollard [J] and all the members of our house', evidently meaning the Fleet Street house. It seems unlikely that 'all the members' could take part in legal discussions of this kind unless they kept commons together. And in 1516 Serjeant Palmes made his will in an upper chamber of the house or inn 'commonly called Serjeants' Inn situated in the street called Fleet Street' – the first known reference to the Inn by that name. For the next 200 years the record is clear, if thin. On 20 June 1523 the Dean and Chapter granted a head lease for twenty-one years to Mr Justice Pollard, seven serjeants at law and an auditor, who were said to be already in occupation. All these lessees had their arms set in the Hall. The Inn was described in the lease as a tenement and garden near the Whitefriars, and the rent was 53s 4d per annum. By 1596 the Inn had a Treasurer, the earliest known holder (in that year) being Sir Christopher Yelverton. Sir Edward Coke was a member, and had a passage made through to the Inn from the chambers which he was allowed to retain in the Inner Temple.

The Inn was employed for public as well as private purposes. By the end of Henry VIII's reign the judges' chambers were being used for judicial business out of court, and the Hall for deliberative assemblies of the judges. Here was argued *Shelley's Case* in 1581, and many other leading cases. The Hall was sometimes used for regular courts as well: for instance, in the time of Queen Anne, it was appropriated for vacation sittings on the equity side of the Court of Exchequer. It was also used for serjeants' feasts at 'private' calls, the first being in

1616, when there was a controversy as to whether the members of the other Inn should attend or have exceedings in Chancery Lane instead.

Nothing is known of the appearance of the original Inn, which was completely destroyed by the Great Fire of 1666, save that the Hall was rebuilt in Jacobean times in brick and freestone. A chapel was built around 1620, using a legacy left by Serjeant Bendlowes in 1584, and consecrated in 1621. The layout of the Inn as rebuilt around 1669–76 is shown in Ogilby and Morgan's map of London (1677), and also in the aerial views of the Temple engraved in 1755 and 1770. There was one main court, with a west range of chambers adjoining Ram Alley, an east range and a more substantial south range with gables overlooking a back garden which adjoined the Alienation Office garden. The new Hall was set back in the east range, extending into the old Whitefriars on land purchased in 1615. It was first used for Serjeant Turnour's feast in 1671, but when only thirty years' old was consumed by the fire of 1702 which also destroyed the new chapel of 1676 and some of the chambers. A fourth hall was completed in 1703 on the same site, and was a 'good large room, ascended up by several freestone steps', the walls fortified with buttresses. By the time the serjeants quit, the Inn was 'far more glorious and stately than formerly it appeared, having now a very fine chapel, an hall, and stately court of tall brick buildings'.

The judges and serjeants were not the best of tenants. They were in dispute with the Dean and Chapter at least as early as 1661, when the latter obtained counsel's opinion that the latest lease was voidable for misrepresentations made by the judges. That dispute was settled by Act of Parliament in 1670, but the sixty-year lease which was then granted proved to be the last. As the lease drew near to expiry, the judges and serjeants increasingly set their heart on the purchase of the freehold and prevaricated in discussions over renewal. The Dean and Chapter were also increasingly difficult, refused an offer of £2000 for a renewal fine and proposed letting each chamber separately for the market price. Throughout the reign of George I, the society discussed with Gray's Inn the possibility of moving into the gardens there; but these plans came to nothing. The day before the lease expired in 1730, no progress having been made in the negotiations, the judges and serjeants filed a bill in Chancery on the footing that the boundary between the leased property and the land purchased in 1615 had become obscured as a result of the Fire. The suit was decided in favour of the Dean and Chapter in 1731, by Lord King LC – a member of the Chancery Lane Inn. The Dean and Chapter then brought an ejectment action to evict the judges and serjeants, who took every technical point at their disposal to delay the outcome. While the suit was pending, agreement was almost reached for a sale of the freehold for £7000 plus arrears of rent. Mr Justice Page was deputed to clinch the deal, but was so rude to the Dean that discussion was postponed. Mr Baron Comyn then 'with great civility' offered the Dean £8000, to include the arrears of rent and costs of the suit, but the Dean declined to accept less than £9000.

Serjeants' Inn today.

By 1733 these discussions had reached a final impasse. The judges and serjeants – having delayed eviction for three years – received individual notices to quit, and by the end of May they had all joined the Chancery Lane Inn. The Fleet Street society, which was unincorporated, thereupon ceased to exist and merged with the Chancery Lane society. The modest collection of plate, comprising a communion flagon, cup and plate, three silver salts and twenty-three spoons, was added to that of the other Inn, and presumably dispersed by sale in 1877. The arms of both Inns were painted in 1738 for the Hall windows of the Chancery Lane Inn and are now on the grand staircase in the Law Society Hall. The Fleet Street society had used the arms *Gules two garbs in saltire* or; and a panel with these arms, dated 1669, survived until the Blitz. They alluded to the arms of the Dean and Chapter of York (*Gules two keys in saltire* or), and a possible explanation of the garbs, or sheaves, is that they were a misunderstanding of fasces, a symbol of magistracy.

Most of the buildings erected by the serjeants, though relatively new, were demolished in 1735 under a building lease. The Hall and chapel were given a temporary reprieve and let to the Amicable Life Insurance Society, which pulled them down and rebuilt them as the society's office in 1792; the building was later occupied by the Church of England Sunday School Institute. It is this Georgian building which is seen in the engravings of 1801 and 1804. When the Dean and Chapter sold the site, under a private Act of Parliament of 1837, the property was divided into a number of separate freeholds – all houses being purchased by barristers or solicitors. The later vicissitudes of the site included another near-total destruction of the buildings in the 1941 Blitz.

The Development of the Estate

Master Davidson

To the casual eye the Inn may look much as it must have done in 1960: Church Court has been enhanced by the magnificent Millennium Column, but the only new building in that time has been the Littleton Building, successfully creating modern chambers on the site of the old Niblett Hall.

To the more appreciative eye the exterior has been greatly improved: look at the Church, from any standpoint, on a cloudless day, or look at the spires and chimneys on 5 Paper Buildings; and look everywhere at the care given to detailing (especially to Pegasus wherever it appears). So many buildings are superb.

But because so many of the Inn's buildings are listed, an appreciable number Grade I or II*, and the Temples are a conservation area, the key challenges for the Inn are two: the redevelopment of Serjeants' Inn (now with ambitious plans to demolish the 1950s building and create a courtyard in sympathy with tradition); and the continued preservation and adaptation of buildings, mainly centuries old, to give us and our successors both the benefit of their beauty and the place in which to conduct the work of our age, preferably with comfort cooling.

Francis Taylor Building.

It is a pity that so few get to see how the interior of such buildings is being transformed. Even as one closely concerned with what is going on, I am still often amazed when I see the results. Just before writing this I visited the transformed Francis Taylor Building; gloomy before, it now makes brilliant use of light, space and the views which its windows afford over Church Court, the eastern wall of the Church and the Master's garden, and every client will get a good sight of the unique quality of the Temple. It also has excellent access for the wheelchair-bound. Like so many of the Inn's buildings it has the impediment of significant steps up to the entrance. It has been equipped with one of the elegant and unobtrusive external lifts which we use to address this problem where we can, and then has a good internal lift to access the other floors. Our external lifts are instanced by the Corporation of London as fine examples of provision for the disabled.

Francis Taylor Building has been a brilliant job, following very successful work in Hare Court (by the same architects, GHK). There is a moral here. Until recently the Inn has virtually never been able to have possession of an entire building at a single time. When that can be achieved, the building can be renovated to immensely better effect than is usually possible if we have possession of part only. My biggest disappointment as Chairman of the Estates Committee has been the reluctance of a professional tenant to vacate a modest number of rooms, vacation of which would have enabled us to address a certain other building in at least the same way.

I hope that we will have the opportunity to do similar work regularly throughout the Inn. It will take time for Serjeants' Inn to be digested, but I expect to see a fine result there. Then I hope we may see three types of project which may impact little on the casual viewer but make a substantial difference to tenants. The first is that there is scope for building out, to some extent, at the back of the

Francis Taylor Building waiting room.

The clerks' room in Francis Taylor Building.

southern section of King's Bench Walk. The second is a project I would very much like to see – the provision of a glazed external lift at 1 Mitre Court, between our building and Hoare's Bank. The design for this shows that it would transform the look of that area: those who have been inside Mitre Court know that it has many fine rooms and qualities (including on each floor some windows looking on to the Master's garden); this project would bring the building to life on the side of its presently poor entrances. Thirdly, we would like to introduce cooling wherever we can.

Many of us take it for granted that we see daily, and some of us work in, buildings of rare character and quality (for the devotion to which we thank the Inn's Surveyor, Roderick Cunliffe ARICS). In fifty years' time I expect that the Inn will look, from its centre, much as it does today (unless we find we can fulfil another dream, creating an underground car park!). The careful preservation of its appearance will conceal an enlargement of space, and improvement of facilities, which will testify to generations' love of the buildings, and thoughtfulness to keep them alive rather than as museum pieces.

Nicholas Davidson QC is a practising barrister and Chairman of the Estates Committee.

View northwards from Mitre Court Buildings.

Gardens and Waterfront

Master Simon Brown and Master Sells

The measure of a city's greatness is to be found in the quality of its public spaces, its parks and squares.

John Ruskin

Early eighteenth-century print of the Inner Temple garden from the Thames.

The Inner Temple has one of the largest remaining private gardens in London. It has great historic importance with a prime location besides the River Thames. It is on land reclaimed from the river: in Roman times, the north river bank was along what is now the Strand, and in medieval times it was along what are now Crown Office Row and Tudor Street. In Tudor times, the garden was successively under church and then crown freehold, and after the granting of the Charter by James I to the Inner Temple in 1608, it extended down to a line between what is now the end of 4 Paper Buildings and Temple Gardens.

In 1621, the fashionable lower walks of Gray's Inn embowered by long shady avenues of elm were regarded as 'the pleasantest place about London'. The gardens of the Temple were also highly rated and set an example for a Royal Commission to ensure that Lincoln's Inn Fields were set out into 'faire and goodlye walks, [which] would be a matter of greate ornament to the Citie, pleasure and freshnes for the health and recreation of the Inhabitantes thereabout, and for the sight and delight of Embassodors and Strangers coming to our court and Cittie, and a memorable worke of our tyme to all posteritie'. During the seventeenth century, the Inner Temple garden evolved as one of London's 'handsome Open spaces, with very good Buildings well inhabited'. 'A View of the Temple' as it appeared in 1671 when James, Duke of York, afterwards James II, was a member of the Inner Temple, depicts a formal top terrace, an orchard and formal walks. Middle Temple Lane beside the orchard led down to the Temple Landing on the Thames.

By 1720, the garden had been re-landscaped in the Dutch William & Mary garden style still prevailing as depicted in John Kip's and Leonard Knyff's engravings and drawings. The orchard had vanished and the whole garden became an enclosed area with three rectangular grass plots interspersed with small trees dissected by gravel paths.

In 1722, Thomas Fairchild published his famous seminal work, *The City Gardener*. In it he remarked upon this 'plain way of laying out Squares in Grass Plots and Gravel Paths'. He opined that it did not 'sufficiently give our Thoughts an Opportunity of Country Amusements'. He continued: 'I think some sort of Wilderness-Work will do much better, and divert the Gentry better than looking out of the Windows upon an open figure.' He detailed five steps to improve the quality of these areas: first, a wilderness would be a harbour for birds; secondly, a variety of trees would be 'goodly to the Eye'; thirdly, 'Groves and Wildernesses would be new and pleasant in a London prospect'; fourthly, 'The Walks, tho regular as the Walks in the common Squares, would be more shady and more private, and the Hedges and the Groves of Trees in every

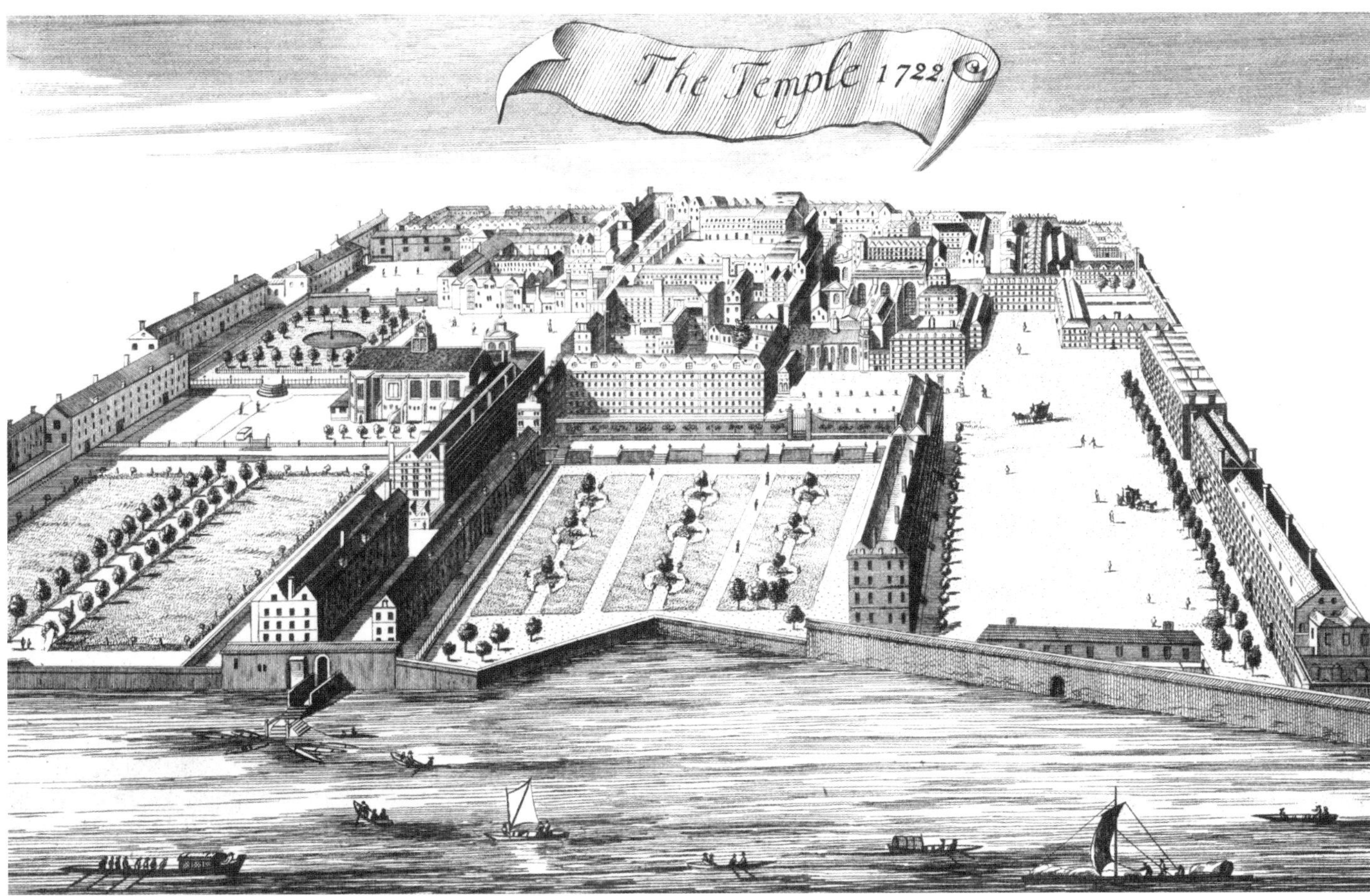

Bird's-eye view of the Temple in 1722.

Quarter would hide the prospect of the Houses from us; every House would command a prospect of the whole, as well as it was lay'd out in plain Grass Platts and Walks'; fifthly, every fountain in such places would have double the beauty that it would in plain squares.

He also detailed the trees and plants suitable for London gardens for Persons of Distinction whilst they were in London. He was convinced that the trees and plants in the Temple gardens thrived better than elsewhere in the City because the atmosphere was cleaner and benefited from the moisture of the river.

In 1771 John Stewart published his *Critical Observations on the Buildings and Improvements of London*. He observed that the best enclosed gardens 'conspired to create an illusion, and we feel ourselves as it were beguiled into the country, in the very centre of business and care'. This was the essence of the garden developed out of Fairchild's earlier strictures in which Dr Johnson took his 'walking exercise' everyday at 4pm with James Boswell while living in Inner Temple Lane when he was writing his famous critical essays on the works of Shakespeare. During the mid-eighteenth century, citizens took delight in 'the walking exercise'. According to the Foreigners Guide of 1744, the large and pleasant walks of the Charterhouse Draper's Hall, Moorfields, Somerset House and the Inns of Court were generally open 'to every person above inferior rank', and the fine walks and shady groves of the Royal Gardens of Kensington were open 'only for persons of Distinction'. Garden squares were open to key-holding residents.

From the late eighteenth century onwards, the fashion for formal French and Dutch style gardens gave way to a landscaped naturalistic style with trees, shrubs and flowers imported from the Orient and distributed by London nurserymen. Landscape gardeners such as Humphry Repton regarded this 'a matter of Public Concern' and 'took a sort of Pride to the Embellishement of the Capital'. Botanists such as Sir Joseph Banks were eager that trees and plants such as Magnolia and the Banksian Rose from China should be displayed in London gardens, as they are in the Inner Temple to this day. In 1814, Hermann Von-Puckler-Muskau remarked, 'Country and town in the same spot is a charming idea. Fancy yourself in an extensive quadrangular area surrounded by the finest houses, and in the midst of its delightful plantations, with walks, shrubberies and parterres of fragrant flowers, inclosed in an elegant iron railing, where persons of fashion are taking the air.'

In 1822 however, John Loudon enthused in his *Encyclopedia of Gardening* about how gardens in the City might be 'laid out in terraces like Isola Bella, or the gardens of Babylon'. And in 1840 there was a proposal for a viewing platform across the whole of the bottom of the garden beside the Embankment. Yet while

Print of the Inner Temple garden, 1820.

Chrysanthemum show, 1854.

landscaping and the plethora of plants made such Italianate designs possible, the prevailing view was that this was in bad taste: 'The inhabitants should be presented with the refreshing verdure of an open lawn in each direction, terminated by foliage not in one unbroken mass, but admitting through two or three apertures perspective display of the ultimate verdure. Trees should be sparingly admitted, the foliage being principally composed of shrubs, supplying shade and shelter to an included curved walk, furnished with appropriate seats,' asserted Jonas Denis in *The Landscape Gardener* (1835).

By 1850, the garden, transformed in this naturalistic style, was idyllically positioned beside the Thames on the bend in the river between Westminster Abbey and St Paul's with the finest river bank promenade in London. Since it was a large garden with river frontage, it was felt that growing trees large enough to survive the infamous London smogs that prevailed until the Clean Air Act 1950 would help to provide fresh air even in the City to its inhabitants.

In 1854, the upper terrace was used for the prestigious Chrysanthemum Show. Then the Victoria Embankment was built in 1864–70, which provided a pleasant public walk and carriageway alongside the River Thames, but considerably diminished the width of the river and denied the Temple its direct frontage. In 1888, the

Royal Horticultural Society's Great Spring Show (now the Chelsea Flower Show) moved from its site in the RHS garden in Kensington to the Temple where it was held under canvas until 1911. The last Temple Flower Show in May 1911 was attended by George V.

By around 1900, at the start of the Edwardian age, the garden had become much as it still is today with three grass tennis lawns marked out. Yet, with no grand borders, it was rather austere, though far more handsome than the industrial view over the commercial river. A great battle again raged at this time between the 'formal' and 'natural' schools of gardening, with the architect Sir Reginald Blomfield, who lived in the Temple at this time, advocating a return to 'the refinement and reserve' of the seventeenth century in order to give grand buildings their stately settings. In his important book, *The Formal Garden in England* (1892), 'he dogmatically opposed the freer and informal style of gardening energetically supported by William Robinson. He strongly advocated a return to formal gardening, using architectural shape, structure and materials with plants as decorative adjuncts. To him gardens were primarily works of art,' according to the *Oxford Companion*. In 1895 he produced a watercolour design of the garden showing a formal top terrace walk buttressed by a brick walk with six rectangular formal flower beds beneath it. The 'natural' school, led by William Robinson, countered that nature and plants should prevail everywhere and wherever. The only thing Blomfield and Robinson agreed upon was their distaste for the gaudy high Victorian parterre. Eventually, the Jekyll/Lutyens compromise of grand herbaceous borders and formal shrubberies was achieved and the garden has remained much as it was since those Edwardian salad days.

It is a tragic irony that a wonderful garden in the middle of a great city that was created by forcing Old Father Thames to retreat should be so severely damaged by the unforeseen twentieth-century consequences of one of those retreats in the nineteenth century. Today the motor vehicle engulfs the garden. The cars of members of the Inn itself are to be found literally right at the gates of the garden and its railings, and those of the public remorselessly drone up and down the Embankment emitting their noxious fumes. The wonderful King's Bench Walk alongside paths and a building by Wren were once beautiful but are now littered with motor cars.

However, the garden is still a barrier to the ravages of the twenty-first century and an oasis within it. Within its curtilage there are very many joys that keep the barbarians at bay: a cathedral of London plane trees, exquisite Banksian roses, wondrous tree peonies revered above all other flowers by the Chinese, a magnificent *Magnolia Salicifolia* dressed in white as a bride in spring, an old Indian Bean tree that has seen generations of visitors come and go, a soaring Gingko tree that would adorn any Temple, an imperious Tulip tree and many other delights both large and small.

King George V and Queen Mary visiting the Inner Temple garden for the Royal Horticultural Society Flower Show in 1911.

The gardens today.

It is a rare and true privilege to be the current Masters of the Garden – reporting to nobody except, ultimately, to the garden itself: a very exacting master! Perhaps the title is an oxymoron and should henceforth be Servant of the Garden. In future, whatever form it takes in terms of changing fashions in gardening, the garden needs to remain a haven for wildlife, a home for its trees and plants and a place where all human beings are just visitors who can enjoy it in whatever way gives them true pleasure without destroying the source of that enjoyment itself. In writing these words, and in glancing from the same vantage point that Charles Lamb may have had, one can see two 'old Benchers' as he would have called them, sitting down on one of the mid-Victorian benches studying the flowers, while a group of young choir boys energetically and gleefully play football; one is reminded of the words of Charles Lamb on the fountain within the garden: 'Lawyers, I suppose, were children once.'

Our plans for the garden in the year leading up to the 2008 celebrations of the granting of the Charter to the Inn 400 years ago are to continue the traditions of the past as described above and to make the garden ready for its celebrations and those of the Inn on their 400th official birthday. We intend to enhance it as a leading botanical garden and as an exemplary, environmentally friendly, vital green space in the middle of the City, to refurbish its pleasurable walks and lawns and to make it a place for everyone to enjoy as a resource open and available to all. It is, not surprisingly, one of the most desired large open areas in London for corporate hospitality, private parties and weddings; but in 2008, God willing, it will be resplendent in all its majesty for its own wonderful celebration.

His Honour Judge Simon Brown QC is a Specialist Mercantile Judge and Joint Master of the Garden.

Oliver Sells QC is a practising barrister at 5 Paper Buildings, member of the Church Committee and Joint Master of the Garden.

The Inn's Treasures

MANUSCRIPTS

Michael Frost

The Inner Temple Library has never been a law library to the exclusion of all else. Few, even among the Library's regular users, will be aware of the extent (or even the existence) of its holdings in such areas as history, topography, biography and heraldry. The manuscript collection likewise covers many areas besides law, which is hardly surprising when one considers that all but a very few of the manuscripts were presented to the Library, and therefore reflect the interests of the donors; there has been little in the way of deliberate collection building.

The manuscripts fall into five groups: The Petyt Manuscripts (386 volumes), the Barrington Manuscripts (57 volumes), the Mitford Manuscripts (79 volumes), Miscellaneous Manuscripts (211 volumes) and Records of the Inner Temple (39 volumes).

The Petyt Manuscripts include those left to the Inn by William Petyt (1636–1707), Treasurer in 1701–2. Petyt also bequeathed his collection of printed books, and a sum of money for the construction of a new building to house both collections. In addition, upwards of 100 volumes that are classed as Petyt manuscripts have in fact no connection with him. The donors of these, in so far as they are known, include Anne Sadleir, daughter of Sir Edward Coke, Sir Martin Wright and King George III.

The Barrington Manuscripts (57 volumes) were presented by the Hon Daines Barrington, Treasurer in 1784–5, or after his death by his brother and executor, Shute Barrington. They comprise for the most part law reports, precedents and commonplace books; other items include (most importantly) a manuscript of Littleton's *Tenures* dating from the late fifteenth century.

The Mitford Manuscripts are associated with John Mitford, first Lord Redesdale, Treasurer in 1795–6, either as creator or collector, and include the notes he took in court as Lord Chancellor of Ireland. The collection, which alone of the five under consideration is exclusively legal in nature, was presented in 1957 by Lord Dulverton.

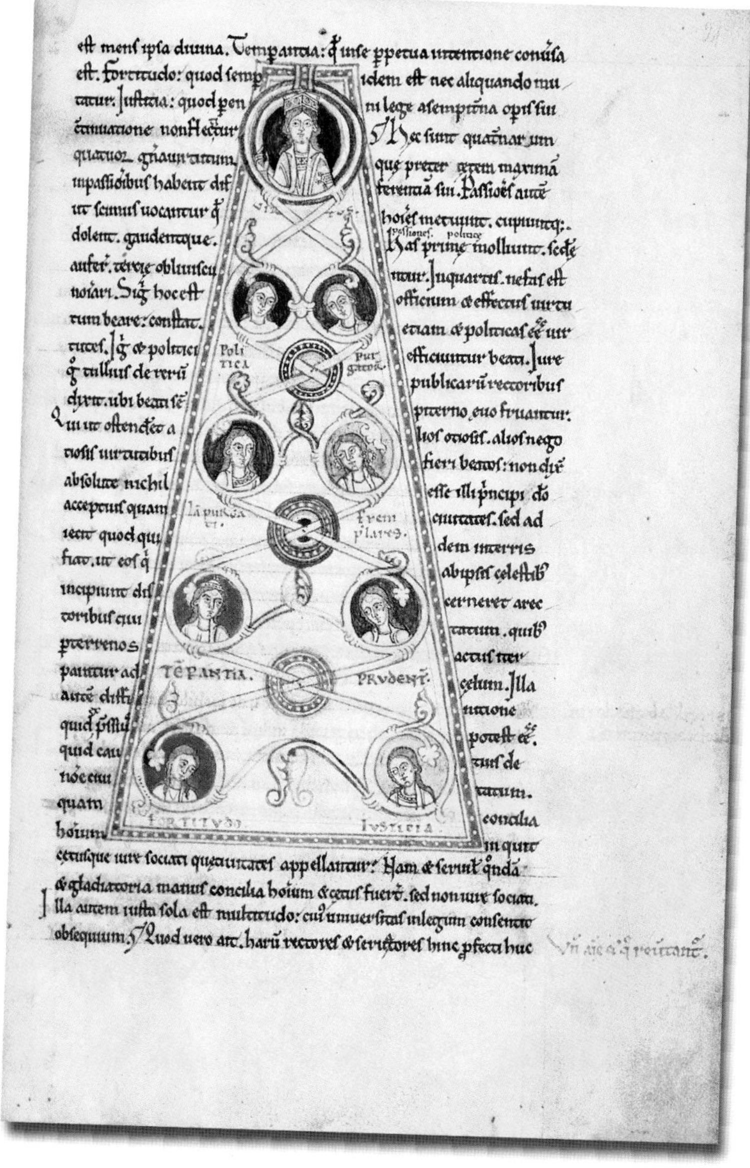

Petyt MS 511.10: Macrobius, Commentary on Somnium Scipionis, early twelfth century.

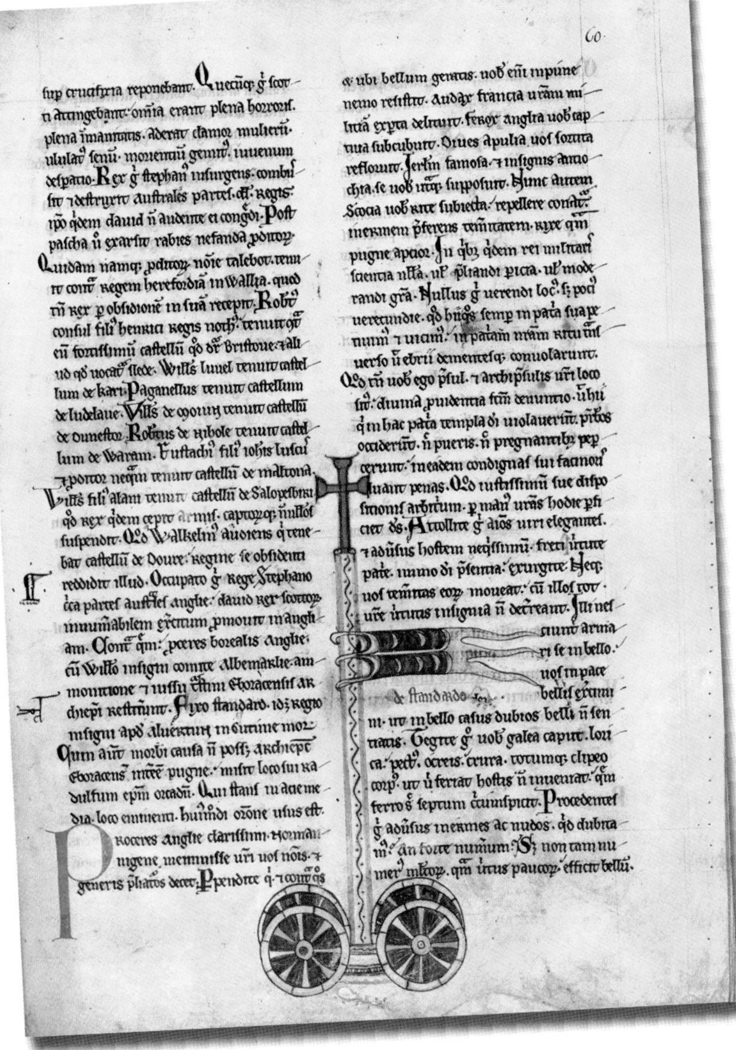

Petyt MS 511.2: Roger de Hoveden, Chronica, *early thirteenth century.*

The Miscellaneous Manuscripts are not a collection in the strict sense, being associated with no one person (or institution) as originator or donor. They are largely legal as regards subject, but also included are, for example, a 1505 Grace Book and a number of mathematical manuscripts presented by Francis Maseres.

Records of the Inner Temple, some volumes of which are rather confusingly labelled 'Miscellanea' (see previous paragraph), are documents generated in the course of the Inn's business, chiefly letters, accounts and memoranda, ranging in date from the late sixteenth to the mid-nineteenth century.

Considering that the collection comprises getting on for 800 volumes, and that some volumes contain several dozen individual items, it is only possible to comment in any detail on a few manuscripts of particular historical significance or artistic merit.

Our earliest manuscript is an illuminated copy of a commentary by Macrobius (AD 395–423) on the 'Dream of Scipio', the last section of Cicero's *De Republica*. It is written in hands of Christ Church, Canterbury type and is identifiable as the first of eleven copies of Macrobius known to have belonged to the Christ Church library. Dating from the early twelfth century, the illustrations are typical of Romanesque manuscript illumination. One folio in particular, featuring a complex geometric design, inspired the garden designer Kathy Brown in her recent scheme for the Hare Court garden in the Temple.

The Inn possesses one of the earliest surviving manuscripts of the *Chronica* of Roger de Hoveden (Howden, Yorkshire). Copied out in the early thirteenth century (the author having only died in around 1201), it has illuminated capitals in red and green and captions in red. Marginal notes suggest that the manuscript, from soon after its creation, belonged to the Abbey of Rievaulx ('Ryevalle').

Walter Hilton's *Scala Perfectionis*, or Ladder of Perfection, is one of the key texts of medieval mysticism and the Library's fifteenth-century copy has particularly fine marginal illuminations, with some gilding. N R Ker, not by any means given to effusive value judgements, allows it to be 'a very handsome copy'. Despite its Petyt class number it is not among those items presented by Petyt; in fact its immediate provenance is unknown, but it does appear once to have belonged to Stephen Gardiner, Bishop of

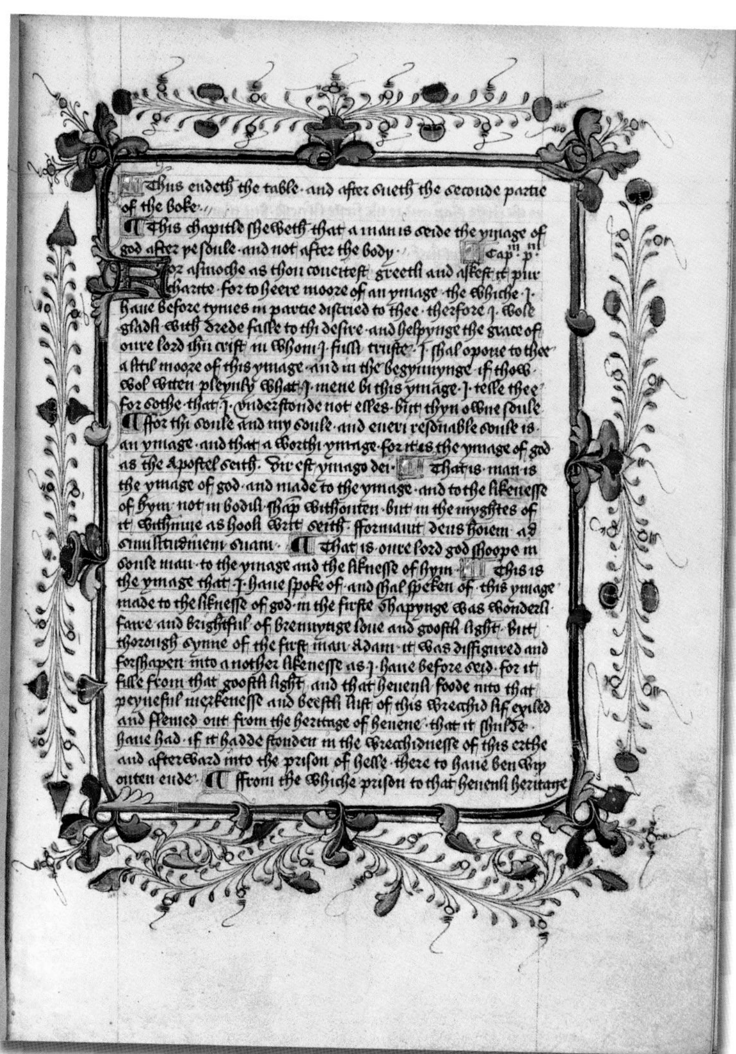

Petyt MS 524: Walter Hilton, Scala Perfectionis, *fifteenth century.*

Misc MS 188: Court of Exchequer c1460.

Winchester (*c*1495–1555) whose signature 'Stephani Winton.' appears on folio 148.

If we speak of the Inn's manuscript 'treasures', then the crown jewels are without a doubt the four miniatures depicting the Courts at Westminster (the Courts of King's Bench, Common Pleas, Chancery and Exchequer) in the reign of Henry VI. These constitute a very early source for English court dress: they are perhaps the earliest coloured illustrations of judges wearing scarlet gowns, hoods and mantles furred with white miniver, direct precursors of the full dress worn today. These folios may in fact very well be the earliest depictions of these courts in session, and have for that reason attracted a great deal of attention from legal historians and other scholars. They are by far the most often reproduced manuscripts in the collection: this is no doubt due in part to their immediate visual appeal, the colours still rich and vivid after five and a half centuries. They may have served as illustrations for an early abridgement of the law, since the folio depicting the Court of Common Pleas bears part of an alphabetical table of contents. The fact that it is somewhat less well preserved than the other three suggests that it may have functioned as the title page. Despite their early date (around 1460) they were added to the collection relatively recently; they were presented by Lord Darling (Treasurer 1914–15), who had purchased them at Christie's in 1894.

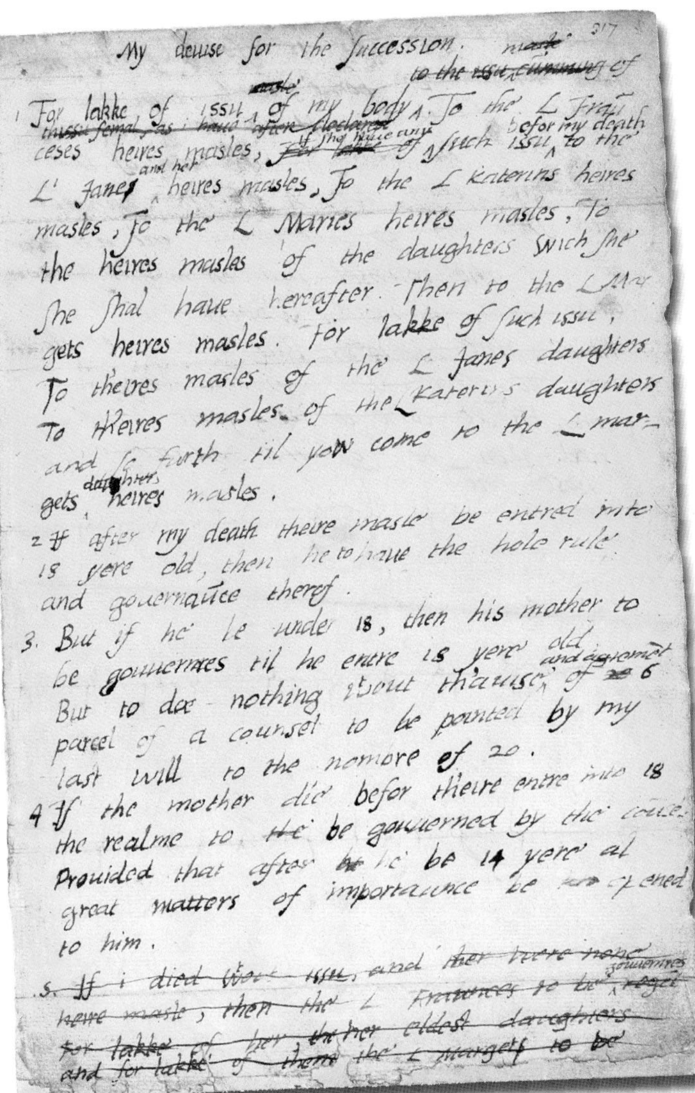

317

My deuise for the Succession.

1 For lakke of issu of my body, To the L Fraunceses heires masles, if she haue any such issu befor my death to the L' Janes and her heires masles, To the L Katerins heires masles, To the L Maries heires masles, To the heires masles of the daughters wich she shal haue hereafter. Then to the L Margets heires masles. For lakke of such issu, To theires masles of the L Janes daughters To theires masles of the L Katerins daughters and so forth til yow come to the L Margets daughters heires masles.

2 If after my death theire masle be entred into 18 yere old, then he to haue the hole rule and gouernaunce therof.

3. But if he be under 18, then his mother to be gouuernres til he entre 18 yere old and agreement But to doe nothing w'out thavise of 6 parcel of a counsel to be pointed by my last will to the nombre of 20.

4 If the mother die befor theire entre into 18 the realme to be gouuerned by the counsel. Prouided that after he be 14 yere al great matters of importaunce be opened to him.

~~5. If i died wout issu, and ther were none heire masle, then the L Fraunces to be gouuernres ... for lakke of her, her eldest daughters and for lakke of them the L Marget to be~~

Petyt MS 538.47 fol 317: Edward VI's Devise for the Succession, *June 1553.*

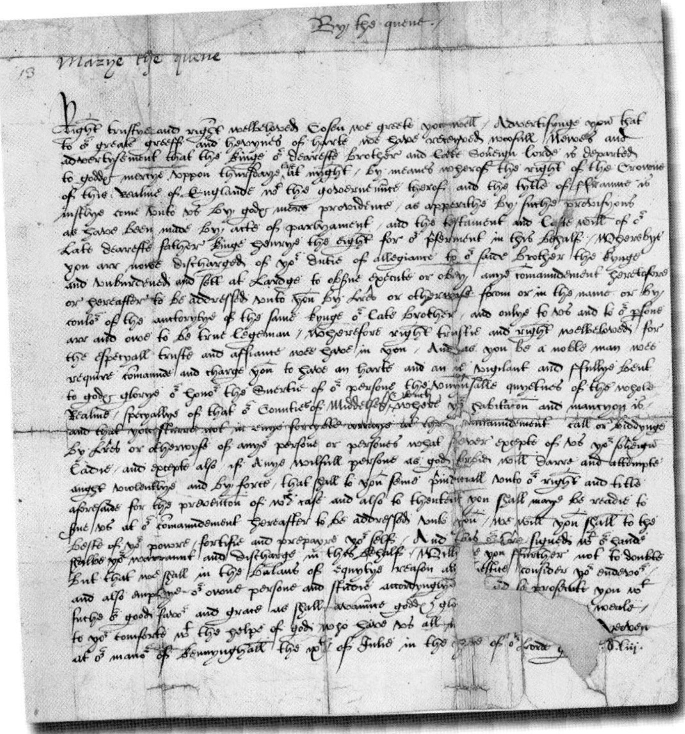

By the quene

Marye the quene

Petyt MS 538.47 fol 13: Mary I's letter to Sir Edward Hastings, 9 July 1553.

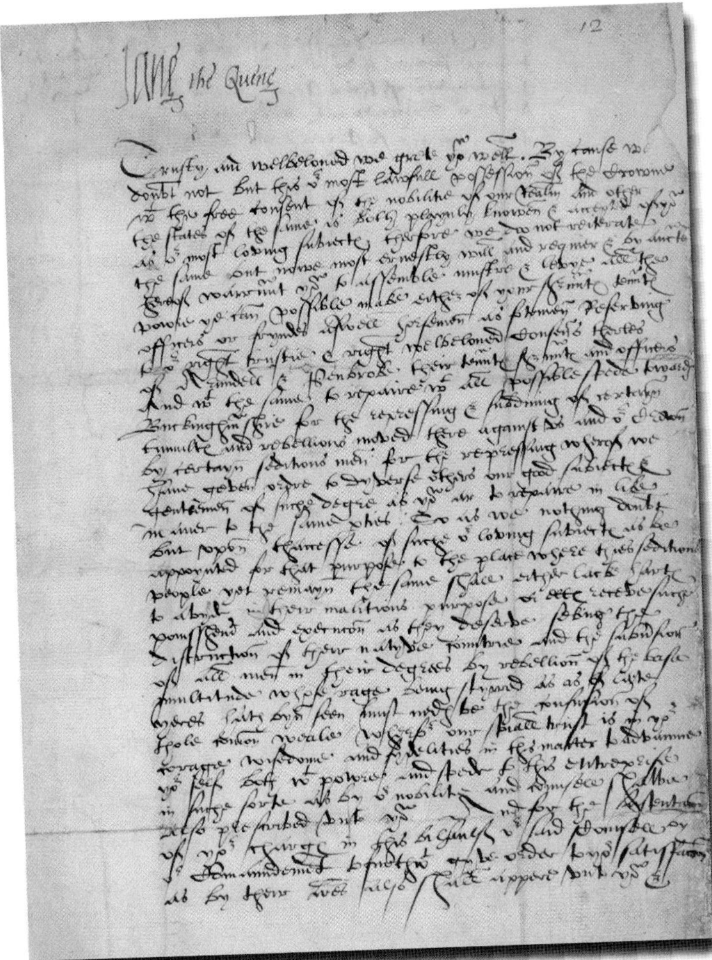

Jane the Quene

Petyt MS 538.47 fol 12: Lady Jane Grey's letter to Sir John St Lowe and Sir Anthony Kingston, 18 July 1553.

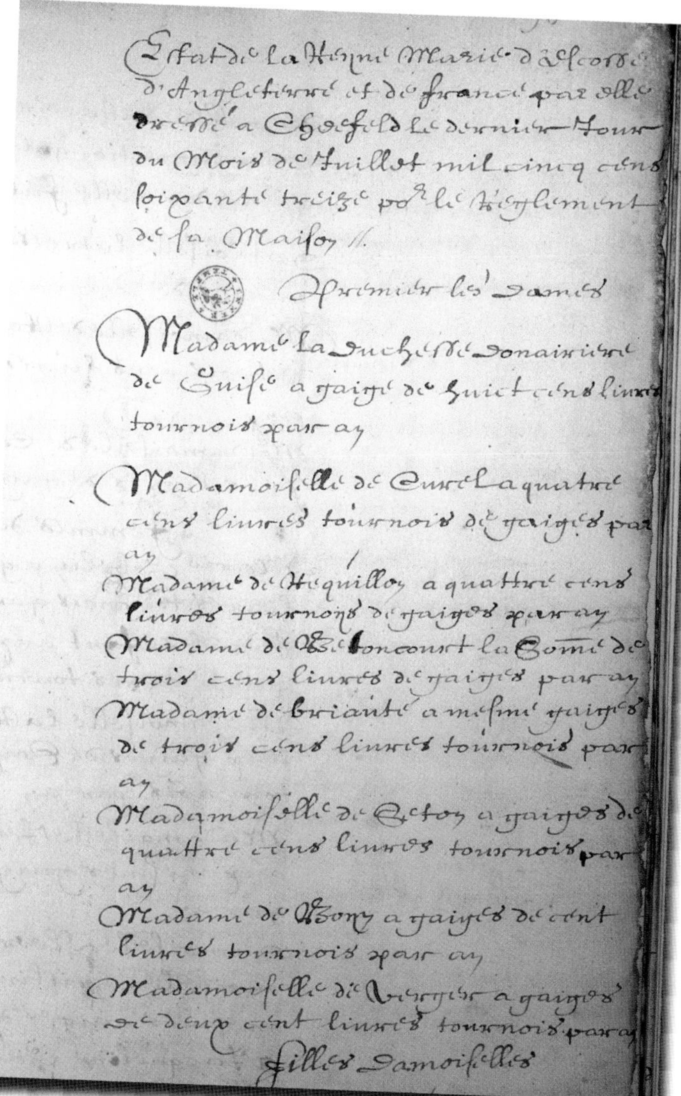

Estat de la Royne Marie d'Escosse d'Angleterre et de france par elle dressé a Cheffeld le dernier Jour du Mois de Juillet mil cinq cens soixante treize pour le reglement de sa Maison //

Premier les dames

Madame la duchesse douairiere de Guise a gaige de huict cens livres tournois par an

Madamoiselle de Curel a quatre cens livres tournois de gaiges par an

Madame de Hequillon a quattre cens livres tournoys de gaiges par an

Madame de Bresoncourt la Conte de trois cens livres de gaiges par an

Madame de briante a mesme gaiges de trois cens livres tournois par an

Madamoiselle de Seton a gaiges de quattre cens livres tournois par an

Madame de Rony a gaiges de cent livres tournois par an

Madamoiselle de Vergier a gaiges de deux cent livres tournois par an

Filles damoiselles

Misc MS 41, no 90: Inventory of Mary Queen of Scots' household in Sheffield, 31 July 1573.

A group of documents with royal associations, which can be conveniently considered as a sequence here, illustrates the succession 'crisis' following the death of Edward VI. The first is Edward's own 'Devise for the Succession', drafted in the king's own hand in June 1553. Knowing that he would shortly, barring a miracle, die without 'heires masles', he sought, by this innocent-looking document, to exclude his half-sisters Mary and Elizabeth from the succession in favour of his cousin, Lady Jane Grey. To what extent Edward was expressing his own will in doing this, and to what extent that of his protector, the Duke of Northumberland (Lady Jane's father-in-law), is a matter for conjecture. Edward died on 6 July 1553. Three days later Mary wrote a letter, signing herself (prematurely, as it turned out) 'Marye the Queen', in which she announced the death of her brother, claimed the crown as hers by Act of Parliament and by the will of Henry VIII and ordered her supporter and confidant Sir Edward Hastings to secure 'the surety

Elizabeth R

By the Quene.

Most Reverend father in God. Right trusty and right welbiloued we grete you well. Where we required you as the Metropolitan of our Realm, and as the principall person in our commission for causes ecclesiasticall, to have good regard, that such uniform order in the devine service and rules of the church might be duely kept as by the Lawes in that behalf is provided and by our Iniunctions also declared and explaned, and that you shuld call unto you for your assistance certeyn of the Bisshops to reforme the abuses and disorders of sundry persons seking to make alteration therin: We understanding that with the help of the Reverend fathers in God the bisshops of Wynchester and Ely and som other ye have well entred in to som convenient reformation of things disordred, and that now the said Bisshop of Ely is by our commandement repayred in to his Diocese whereby you shall want his assistance: We minding earnestly to have a perfect reformation of all abuses attempted to deforme the uniformitie prescribed by our Lawes and Iniunctions, and that none shuld be suffred to declyne either on the left or on the right hand from the direct lyne limitted by authoritie of our said Lawes and Iniunctions, do earnestly by our authoritie Royall, will and charge you, by all meanes lefull to procede therin as you have begon, And for your assistance we will that you shall by authority herof and in our Name send for the Bisshops of London and Sarum and communicate these our lres with them, and straightly charge them to assist you from tyme to tyme betwixt this and the moneth of October, to do all manner of things requisite to reform such abuses as afore are mentioned in whom soever ye shall find the same. And if you shall find in any of the said Bisshops (which we trust ye shall not) or in any other whose ayde you shall require, remissnes to ayde and assist you, if uppon your admonition the same shall not be amended, we charge you to advertise us, for we mean not that any persons having credit by their vocation, to ayde you, shuld for any respect forbear or be remiss in this service tending to thobservation of our Lawes, Iniunctions and commandements. Geven at our Manor of Hatfeild the tenth day of August in the thirtenth yere of our reign.

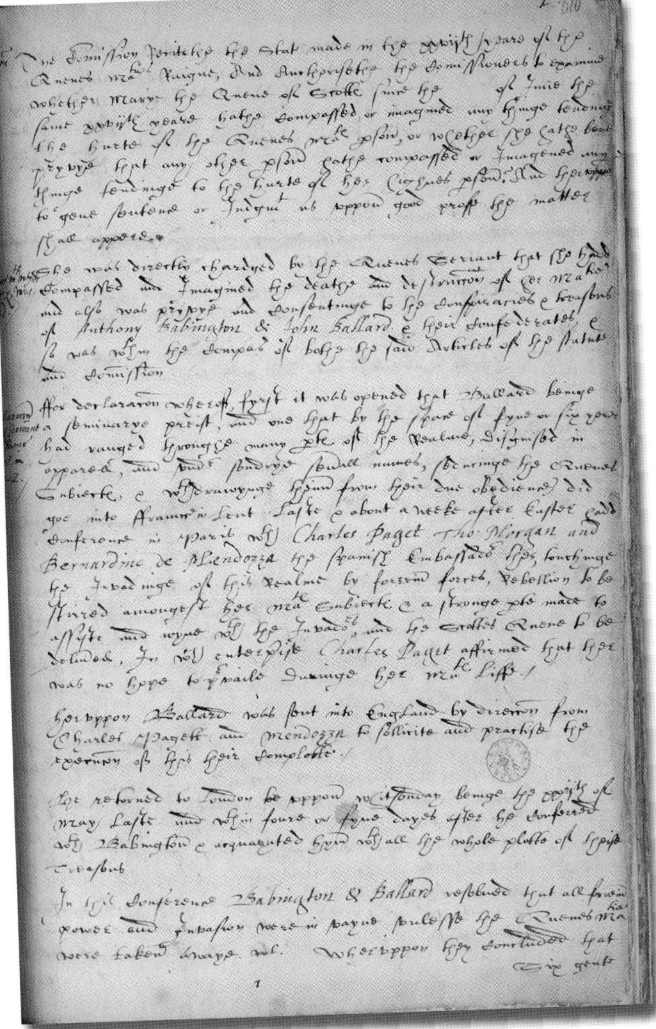

Barrington MS 29: Brief in proceedings against Mary Queen of Scots, 1586.

of our person [and] the universal quietness of the realm', especially in the counties of Middlesex and Buckinghamshire. Lady Jane Grey was proclaimed queen by Northumberland the following day. Given that her reign lasted only nine days, letters dictated by her as queen must be rare indeed. The one in our possession, dated 18 July 1553 and addressed to Sir John St Lowe and Sir Anthony Kingston, states confidently that 'Our most lawful possession of the crown, with the free consent of the nobility or our realm… is both plainly known and accepted.' In fact, Jane had limited support, and Mary was proclaimed queen the next day.

The collection is rich in documents relating to the religious controversies of the sixteenth century, among them two letters under signet and sign manual of Elizabeth I to Matthew Parker, Archbishop of Canterbury, the first concerning observance of Uniformity, the other prescribing certain rules of conduct within cathedral churches and colleges.

There are two items of particular interest to be noted in connection with Mary, Queen of Scots. The first is an account of Mary's household as it was in late July 1573, when she was in the custody of the Earl of Shrewsbury at Sheffield. It gives the names and wages of her attendants, who at that time numbered around 150. The second is the original brief of Sir Thomas Egerton, Solicitor-General, in the proceedings against the queen in the Star Chamber. Dated 20 October 1586 and endorsed 'Mr Solicitor his breviate on the Queen of Scots', it constitutes a summary of the evidence against Mary.

In 2008 we commemorate the generosity of our first Stuart monarch, James I, towards the Temples. His successor, Charles I, did not always accord our Inn his wholehearted approval, for in March 1633 he wrote to the Benchers of the Inner Temple laying down rules for the due observance of Lent, and noting that 'One of the Readings in your House usually falls in this time of Lent and… they are of late grown to an excess of entertainment and charge, much beyond that of former times, which we wish reformed…'. We trust that Her present Majesty will look more indulgently on our celebrations.

Michael Frost is Assistant Librarian of the Inner Temple.

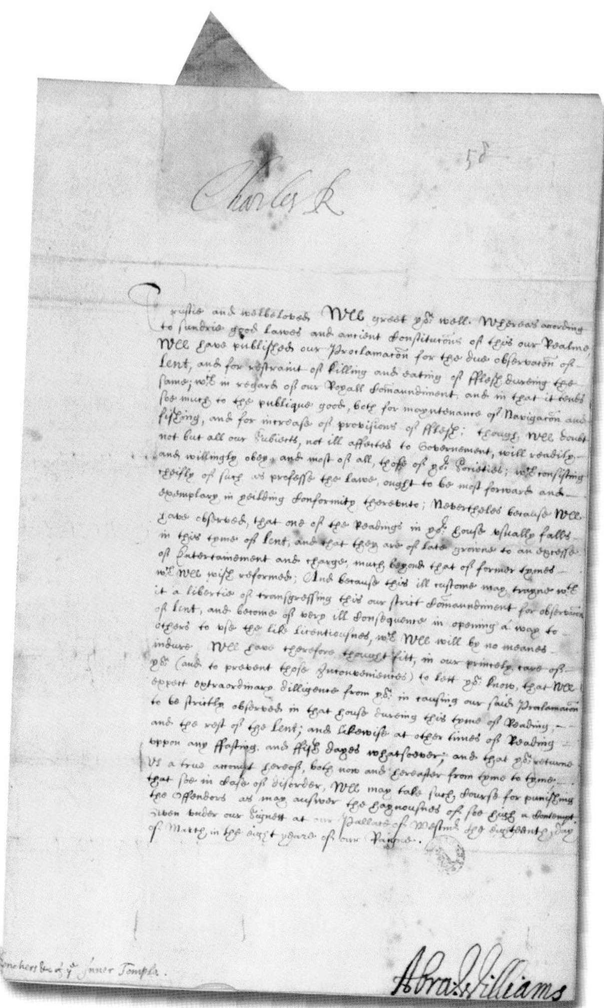

Misc MS 30, fol 58: Charles I's letter to the Benchers of the Inner Temple, 18 March 1633.

Opposite: Petyt MS 538.47, fol 50: Elizabeth I's letter to Matthew Parker, 20 August 1571.

Archives

Clare Rider

The Inner Temple, like other medieval associations, would have kept administrative records from its earliest days. These may have been among the lawyers' papers burnt by Wat Tyler's rebels when they sacked the Temple in 1381. Yet apparently some of the Inn's records escaped destruction since a sixteenth-century antiquary claimed to have seen Geoffrey Chaucer's name in the ancient rolls of the Inn. Unfortunately, the fourteenth- and fifteenth-century archives have since been lost, despite being kept in a 'convenient chest... with divers locks' specifically designed for record keeping. The extant records of the Inn commence in 1505, with a volume of 'Acts of Parliament', the name given to the minutes and orders of the Inn's chief governing body. Despite the charring of the earliest volumes in the Second World War, this series survives in an unbroken sequence to the present. Now reserved for formal decisions, the Acts of Parliament are incorporated in the minutes and orders of the Bench Table, the executive body which took over the everyday governance of the Inn from the mid-seventeenth century. Membership records were maintained from at least the fifteenth century: a pension roll, listing those in residence, was mentioned in 1492 and the first surviving admissions register, which commences in 1547, was apparently copied from an earlier admissions roll. On the financial side, the Treasurer's accounts can be found with the records of Parliament until separately recorded in the seventeenth century, and Sub-Treasurer's account books survive from 1682. Similarly, records of admissions to chambers were originally recorded only patchily in the minutes until separate chambers rentals were compiled in the mid-sixteenth century.

Despite the ravages of war and damp, the Inn's archives are now safe for posterity, thanks to the efforts of Master Monier-Willams, who initiated a programme of repair in 1985, Master Hames, the first Master of the Archives, and his successors Masters Parker, Sumption and Baker. The Inn's first archivist, Ian Murray, was appointed in 1989, and was succeeded in 1997 by Clare Rider. Treasures of the collection include a stunning painting of the Pegasus in an evidence book of 1607, the sixteenth-century Acts of Parliament and admissions registers, beautifully written in manuscript, a Christmas account book for 1614–82 in its original binding, containing accounts kept by the seventeenth-century Christmas stewards for seasonal provisions and entertainments, and a series of plans and photographs, including images of war damage and reconstruction. The disciplinary papers make amusing reading, particularly those relating to a member called Sutherst, who married his daughter to the ageing Lord Townsend under false pretences, while the papers generated by new building works and the restoration of the Temple Church in the nineteenth century offer a fascinating insight into the work of Sir Robert Smirke, his brother Sydney, James Savage and Decimus Burton. The main series of records have been made accessible by the printed calendars of minutes and accounts from 1505 – painstakingly transcribed and edited by F A Inderwick, R A Roberts, Barbara Given and, currently, Celia Charlton – as well as the admission register indexes, compiled with dedication by R L Lloyd in the 1950s, and the online Inner Temple admissions database completed in 2006 with a grant from the Heritage Lottery Fund. By these means, the Inn will ensure that its rich recorded history will be available for generations to come.

Illuminated letter from Book of Evidences 1607.

Opposite: Plan of the Inn in 1820.

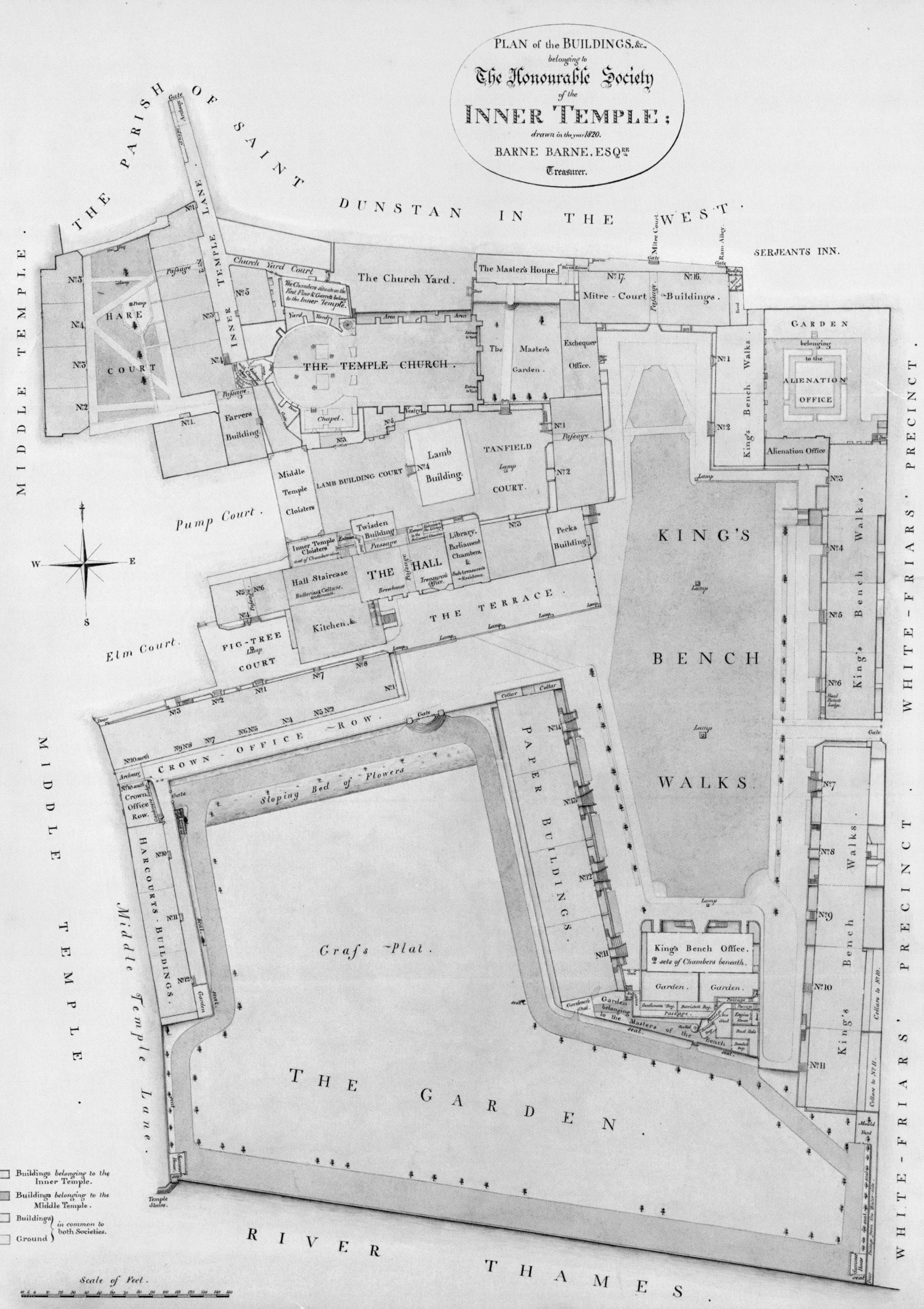

PLAN of the BUILDINGS, &c.
belonging to
The Honourable Society
of the
INNER TEMPLE;
drawn in the year 1820.
BARNE BARNE, ESQre.
Treasurer.
THE PARISH OF SAINT DUNSTAN IN THE WEST.
SERJEANTS INN.
MIDDLE TEMPLE.
INNER TEMPLE LANE.
HARE COURT
Church Yard Court
The Church Yard.
The Master's House.
Mitre Court
Ram Alley
Mitre - Court Buildings.
THE TEMPLE CHURCH.
The Master's Garden.
Exchequer Office.
GARDEN belonging to the ALIENATION OFFICE
Alienation Office
King's Bench Walks
Farrers Building.
Middle Temple Cloisters
LAMB BUILDING COURT
Lamb Building.
TANFIELD COURT.
Pump Court.
Twisden Building.
Inner Temple Cloisters
Hall Staircase
THE HALL
Library, Parliament Chambers, & Sub treasurer's Residence.
Pecks Building.
Kitchen, &c.
THE TERRACE.
Elm Court.
FIG-TREE COURT
KING'S BENCH WALKS.
CROWN - OFFICE - ROW.
Crown Office Row.
Sloping Bed of Flowers
PAPER BUILDINGS.
HARCOURTS - BUILDINGS.
Middle Temple Lane.
Grafs - Plat.
King's Bench Office. 2 sets of Chambers beneath.
Garden. Garden.
Garden belonging to the Masters of the Bench.
THE GARDEN.
WHITE-FRIARS' PRECINCT.
MIDDLE TEMPLE.
Temple Stairs.
Buildings belonging to the Inner Temple.
Buildings belonging to the Middle Temple.
Buildings } in common to both Societies.
Ground }
RIVER THAMES.
Scale of Feet.

Portraits

Master Shields

Thomas Inskip, by Augustus John RA.

A comparison of the catalogues of the Inn's collection of portraits made in 1915 and 1982 reveals the substantial damage suffered during the Second World War. Over 150 paintings were lost. Fortunately the Inn still retains a large collection of portraits of its famous, favourite and most successful members. Sitters include monarchs, all the Inner Temple Lord Chancellors, Lord Chief Justices and holders of every rank of judicial office, including the first female High Court Judge, Dame Elizabeth Lane. Fearless advocacy is represented by Marshall Hall and the arts by A P Herbert, the author of *Misleading Cases*. However, in contrast to those of the great and the good, there is the fine portrait of John Herbert by Carlo Maratta. Herbert was admitted in 1664 and was described by Walpole in his *Anecdotes of Painting* as 'a great virtuoso who was called the rough diamond'.

Also of particular interest are the portraits of the four so-called fire judges, Sir John Vaughan, Sir Orlando Bridgman, Sir Thomas Tyrrell and Lord Nottingham, which hang in the Hall Gallery. Following the devastation caused by the Great Fire of London in 1666, twenty-two of the chief judges of England were charged by the Court of Alderman of the City of London with resolving the numerous boundary and tenancy disputes which had arisen. Out of gratitude for their work the court commissioned John Michael Wright to paint their individual portraits for £60 apiece. These portraits had a peripatetic existence within the Guildhall until in 1952 the court decided to present them to interested bodies or individuals. Hence their presence in the Inn's collection.

Although many other portraits have come as gifts or bequests, it is clear that commissioning portraits has been a tradition since the seventeenth century. In 1694 £50 was paid to Sir Godfrey Kneller, a leading painter of the day, for two full length oils of William III and Queen Mary which were then 'set up in ye Hall' where, in its rebuilt state, they can be viewed today. Kneller's fame was obviously in the ascendant (or he had a good agent), as in 1703 he charged the Inn 'four-score pounds' for a portrait of Queen Anne in which she stands crowned wearing the Order of St George. Kneller is just one of many illustrious artists whose works are represented in the Inn; Allan Ramsay, George Romney and John Hoppner were the equals in their day to De Lazlo, Sir Oswald Birley, Augustus John, Sir Herbert Gunn and Sir John Lavery in the last century. Lavery's portrait of Lord Darling, renowned for

Lord Woolf by Andrew Tift.

his acerbic wit in court, might not be to everybody's taste. It shows the judge wearing a black cap and on the reverse it bears the inscription, 'Condamnation a Mort. Dedicated with the painter's compliments to the hanging committee' (of the Royal Academy).

This portrait was painted shortly after Darling had been a member of the Court of Appeal which had dismissed Sir Roger Casement's appeal against his conviction for treason and his sentence of execution. The power over life and death probably explains the expressions of austerity and severity which characterise so many sitters. This is particularly evident in Augustus John's three-quarter-length portrait of Thomas Inskip (1876–1947), who in turn became Solicitor-General, Attorney-General, Lord Chancellor and Lord Chief Justice. Painted in 1940, Inskip looks distinctly unamused. Maybe John's reputation as a philanderer required a necessary degree of public disapprobation.

Today a lighter touch can be brought to the Inn's commissions. The recent portraits of the five judges by Jane Mendoza, of Lord Irvine by James Lloyd, of Lord Rawlinson by Keith Breedon RP and of Lord Woolf by Andrew Tift capture their subjects in relaxed and friendly mood.

As Gainsborough observed, the painter's eye is what the lawyer's tongue is to him.

Tom Shields QC is Master of the Pictures.

'The Black Cap'; *portrait of Lord Darling by Sir John Lavery.*

Silver

Master Deby

Most people would expect the Inns of Court, like the City Livery Companies and Oxford and Cambridge colleges, to have gathered together a large collection of silver over the centuries. There have, however, been both additions and disposals. Additions have come mainly from gifts by Treasurers and other Benchers, with pride of place going to Master Schiller who was Treasurer in 1942 and bequeathed to the Inn in 1947 a very high proportion of the present collection.

The Inn itself must have purchased items of silver from time to time but the Inner Temple records make little reference to silver. There is, however, an entry in the contemporary account book recording the joint purchase with Middle Temple of what must have been a very splendid cup to give to James I in 1608 as a 'thank you' for the Royal Charter. Alas, the cup was pawned in Holland by Charles I and never redeemed, and has not since been traced.

On the debit side, silver is sometimes sold or melted down. All the silver (except church plate) was melted down in the Civil War, and changes of fashion doubtless led to pieces being remodelled; items were also sold when money was needed, in particular in the last century to fund student scholarships.

In this article I can only refer to some of the more interesting items in the collection. The piece we have had for the longest time is a silver-gilt chalice, which is one of a pair. They were supplied by Terry in 1609, the year after the Royal Charter, and the account book reads: 'To Terry, a goldsmith, for two new communion cups for the Temple Church, abating of the exchange of one old one, 13li 12s 2d; the Middle Temple paid the one half, 6li 16s 1d.'

Probably our most famous cup is one dated 1563. Scholars have argued whether it portrays a poppy, a pomegranate or a gourd, but it is clearly a melon, a fruit which had at that time recently been introduced to this country. In 1999 it was displayed at the Museum of London in the Exhibition 'London Eats Out' as an ornament to a table set with a feast of 1565. In 2001 it was displayed at the British Museum at an exhibition of Dürer, as its design clearly shows influences from his work. The Victorians were fond of copying older pieces of silver and we also have a good copy of this cup which was made in 1898.

Silver-gilt cup and cover, 1563.

A particularly beautiful piece is the silver-gilt Grace cup made in 1620. It is engraved '1588 McLeod of Lewes' and is said to have been made from silver salvaged from an Armada galleon wrecked off the island of Lewis. Another remarkable item is a large

Charles II silver-gilt tumbler cups, 1671 or 1673.

The Dolben porringer, 1678.

Britannia silver-gilt tazza, 1720.

rosewater dish and ewer made in 1670 and given to the Inn in that year. The dish has a very fine engraving of a Pegasus on it and was long used at important dinners. We also have an excellent copy of this, which was made and given to the Inn in 1878.

Then there is a pair of Charles II silver-gilt tumbler cups. They were usually made as part of a canteen for travellers. With their matted surface (effected by hammering) they could easily be thought to be modern but they date from 1671 or 1673. They are very attractive, not least because the neck of one of them can be inserted into the other, something which most people find irresistible.

The Inn has a good collection of porringers (which were always intended to contain drink and not porridge). The gem of our more recent acquisitions (in 1992) is a silver-gilt porringer of massive proportions made in 1678 by Robert Smythier for the City of London to give to Sir William Dolben on his giving up the Recordership of London. It cost £59 1s, an indication of the gratitude they felt for his services which is duly engraved on the porringer. It has been said to be as near to perfection as one could hope to find in a piece of silver. Dolben was a member of the Inn, a Bencher and Reader in autumn 1677.

A more recent acquisition is the so-called Sherlock Cup, which was purchased jointly with Middle Temple in 1725 at a cost of £49 9s 6d and was presented to the Master of the Temple, Dr Sherlock, in appreciation of his services. Dr Sherlock succeeded his father as Master in 1704 at the tender age of twenty-six. He remained at the Temple for forty-nine years; during the latter part he was also Bishop of London. Sherlock left the cup to his nephew, Thomas Gooch, and it remained in the family until the sale in 2000. It was then again bought jointly by the two Inns and is held in turn, year by year, so that the host Inn at the annual Amity dinner can place it in front of the two Treasurers.

Then we have a silver-gilt tazza (salver with a foot) engraved with the Royal Arms of William and Mary and those of Charles Montagu, Earl of Halifax. A number of such finely engraved salvers were made in the late seventeenth and early eighteenth century. It was the custom for the Chancellor of the Exchequer to retain as a perquisite his silver seal of office on the dissolution of Parliament. This was defaced and a salver made from it with the representation of the seal engraved on it. Halifax ceased to be Chancellor of the Exchequer in 1699 and died in 1715. This salver is dated 1720 and is apparently a replica of one made for the earl in 1687.

Our recently most famous piece is a Dutch silver layette basket of 1645 by Breghtel. Layette baskets had regularly been made from willow rods, but for a period of about thirty years in the seventeenth century in Holland they were made for the nobility from silver. In this basket the flat pierced sides reproduce the willow basketwork

Dutch silver layette basket, 1645.

The 'Nugee' silver pepper mills, 1996.

with vines weaving through and forming the handles and are finely engraved, whereas the pierced bottom is embossed and reproduces the crowned arms of Orange (for Prince William II) impaling those of Stuart (for Mary, daughter of Charles I) supported by the lion of Holland and the unicorn of England. It is decorated with vines and peacocks for fertility and marital fidelity, but there are also monkeys and weasels seeking to feast off the grapes, which are a symbol of chastity and virginity. The basket may have been given to Mary by her aunt and godmother, Elizabeth the 'Winter Queen'. It was given to the Inn in 1925 by Marshall Hall and other Benchers. There are only seven of these baskets extant and this is the oldest, the biggest and the best. It was displayed at an exhibition in The Hague in 2006.

The collection is strong in seventeenth- and eighteenth-century work and reasonably supplied with nineteenth-century work, ending with the Gilbert Marks rose bowl dated 1897, but there is a distinct dearth of new English silver thereafter until 1996 when Treasurer Nugee commissioned four pepper mills from Rod Kelly. He is the leading English expert on low relief chasing, and the pepper mills are decorated with scenes from the Temple. They go very well with our magnificent Victorian salts in the form of a flying Pegasus.

It was then decided to celebrate the millennium by commissioning a silver centrepiece. Half a dozen leading silversmiths were invited to submit designs, and eventually Rod

Victorian silver Pegasus salt cellar.

Millennium silver centrepiece by Rod Kelly.

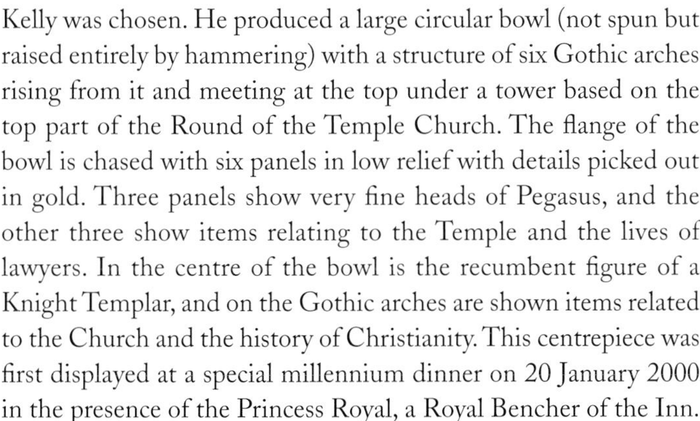

Kelly was chosen. He produced a large circular bowl (not spun but raised entirely by hammering) with a structure of six Gothic arches rising from it and meeting at the top under a tower based on the top part of the Round of the Temple Church. The flange of the bowl is chased with six panels in low relief with details picked out in gold. Three panels show very fine heads of Pegasus, and the other three show items relating to the Temple and the lives of lawyers. In the centre of the bowl is the recumbent figure of a Knight Templar, and on the Gothic arches are shown items related to the Church and the history of Christianity. This centrepiece was first displayed at a special millennium dinner on 20 January 2000 in the presence of the Princess Royal, a Royal Bencher of the Inn.

At the same time we commissioned a pair of candelabra from Anthony Elson. They are tall with a central stem and four branches pitched at such a level that diners can see and be seen under them. The design echoes features of the Temple Church and is surmounted by a Pegasus standing on a symbolic representation of the conjunction of the planets Jupiter and Saturn, thought to have been the most likely explanation of the Star of Bethlehem.

In an article at the time I wrote: 'They were much admired then and subsequently, but it is felt that we need to acquire another pair for the Bench Table for their full splendour to be seen, and that four smaller ones for the adjoining tables would add greatly to the array.' The first part of that wish was fulfilled in 2002 when a further pair was commissioned to celebrate the Queen's Golden Jubilee, and now the second part is fulfilled by the commissioning of four more to celebrate the 400th anniversary of the Royal Charter, one for each century.

John Deby QC is a retired barrister and Master of the Silver.

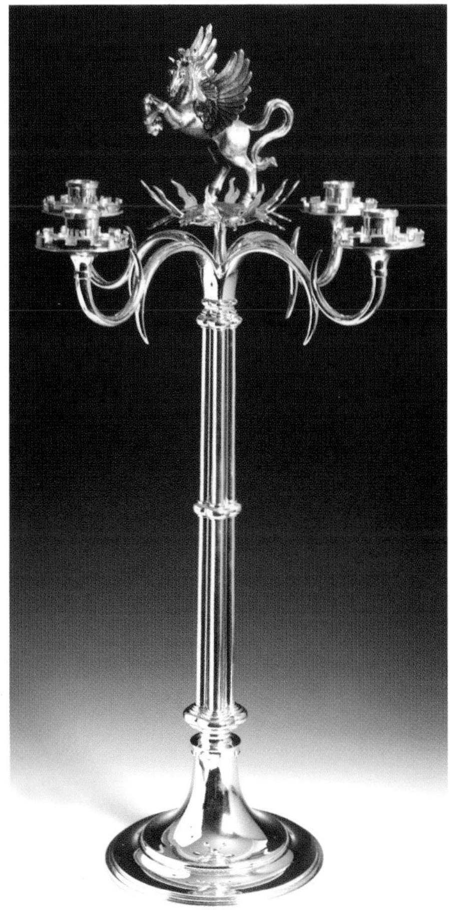

Silver candelabra by Anthony Elson.

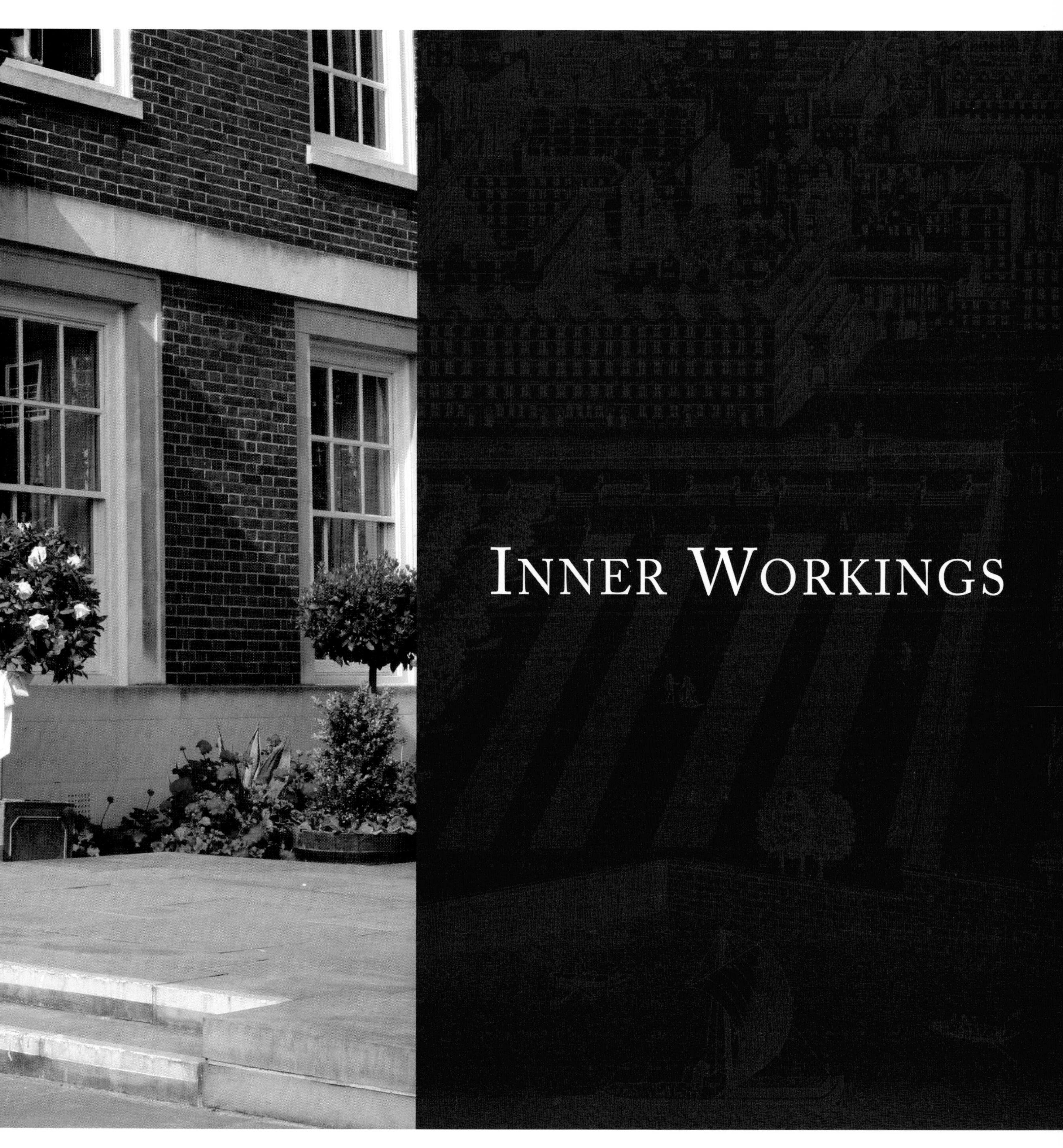

Inner Workings

Getting Things Done: The Inn's Governing Bodies

Master May

'Master Lerego, a Bench Table'. Thus the Treasurer invites acquiescence from the junior Bencher present to open a meeting of the governing body of the Inn. The convention is said to have arisen to ensure that a small cabal of senior Benchers did not take decisions which should be taken by the whole Bench. The distinction among members of the Inn between Benchers and barristers goes back to at least the fifteenth century. Students called to the Bar of a simulated court at moots took their places outside the Bar until in due course, having given a lecture or reading, they took their place on the Bench as Benchers. There is a record of a Treasurer in 1484. The office of Reader arose from the obligation to give lectures or readings.

Master HRH The Duke of Edinburgh, as Treasurer in 1961.

The Inn owns the freehold of its property between Fleet Street and the river by Royal Charter of King James I by Letters Patent dated 13 August 1608 granted jointly in trust to the Benchers of Inner and Middle Temple. There have been later adjustments of the boundary between the two Inns of Court. Inner Temple owns most of the property within the Temple east of Middle Temple Lane and also the southern half of the Temple Church. The Charter obliges the Inns to maintain the Temple Church in perpetuity, and to hold its property for the accommodation and education of those studying and following the profession of law. The Inn performs, with Middle Temple, its obligation to the Church by subvention, by maintaining the Master's House and paying his stipend and by membership of the Church Committee.

There are currently more than 10,000 members of the Inn of all categories. The number on the Inn's electronic records is, at the time of writing, 9899, but that is not the complete membership. The membership consists of Benchers, barristers and students. There are 396 Benchers; 4229 barrister members, of whom 708 are employed barristers and 430 overseas barristers or members; 2264 non-practising members; and 2486 student members. On average the Inn calls approaching 400 students to the Bar each year.

Inner Temple is an unincorporated association whose constitution is based on the gradual evolution of long-standing custom. Essential constitutional business is conducted at a Parliament, and the records of the Inn's Parliaments go back to the beginning of the sixteenth century. The business of a Parliament, surviving to the present day, includes the election of the Treasurer and Reader, the calling of students to the Bar and the confirmation of the appointment of the Sub-Treasurer. By the middle of the sixteenth century, the Masters of the Bench were established as the effective governing body of the Inn, and so they have remained.

The Executive Committee in 2007.

The Benchers meet to conduct business at a Bench Table, and the Inn's constitution is from time to time expressed in the 'Acts of Parliament and Bench Table Orders of the Honourable Society of the Inner Temple'. There have been Bench Table Orders since at least the second half of the seventeenth century. The present edition is an entirely modern document, most recently amended to make changes of detail to the process of election to the Bench of Barrister Governing Benchers.

There are seven categories of Masters of the Bench: Royal Benchers, Honorary Benchers, Governing Benchers, Academic Benchers, Senior Benchers, Overseas Benchers and Supernumerary Benchers. Once elected, a Master of the Bench normally remains a Master for life. The majority of all Benchers are Governing Benchers.

At present, Master HRH The Duke of Edinburgh and Master HRH The Princess Royal are Royal Benchers of Inner Temple and the Inn is immensely honoured that they are. Master HRH The Duke of Edinburgh was Treasurer of the Inn in 1961. The Bench Table Orders provide that, when a Royal Bencher accepts the office of Treasurer, the Bench may make necessary arrangements, including the election of a Deputy Treasurer.

Honorary Benchers are elected having regard to the services which they are able and willing to perform for the Inn and for the management of the affairs of the Inn. The Inn benefits enormously from the experience, services and support, provided gratuitously, of its distinguished Honorary Benchers in a wide variety of matters. These include financial, investment and property management, the care and management of the archives and relations with universities and other academic institutions, with the judiciary and legal professions in other jurisdictions and especially the Commonwealth. Honorary Benchers do not attend a Parliament or Bench Table, but may be elected to any committee or sub-committee.

Academic Benchers are distinguished teachers of law who are elected having regard to their willingness and ability to maintain the Inn's contacts with universities and their students.

Senior Benchers are former Governing Benchers from the end of the year in which they reach the age of seventy. They do not generally attend a Parliament or Bench Table other than a Call Day Parliament and are not generally members of committees or sub-committees. Supernumerary Benchers are former Governing Benchers who have asked to step down from being Governing Benchers but do not wish to resign. They do not take part in the Inn's business.

Governing Benchers are, as the name implies, those who govern the Inn and play their part in the management and functioning of its affairs. The essential qualification for election as a Governing Bencher is that the candidate, being a member of the Inn, is able and willing to take a significant part in the management of the Inn's affairs. Election as a Governing Bencher is therefore anything but a mere honour or sinecure. There are three categories of Governing Bencher: Barrister Governing Bencher, Judicial Governing Bencher and Other Governing Bencher. The additional qualifications for election as a Barrister Governing Bencher are that the candidate is in practice at the independent Bar or in employment, has shown ability and distinction as such and has taken a significant part in the affairs of the profession. The additional qualification for election as a Judicial Governing Bencher is that the candidate has been appointed to full time judicial office. Other Governing Benchers are members of the Inn who do not exactly fall into the other two categories. There is a minimum number of Barrister Governing Benchers designed to ensure that they comprise a majority of the Inn's Governing Body. This is constitutionally important to make sure that Judicial Governing Benchers do not dominate the management of an institution most of whose members are barristers or students. Governing Benchers are expected to attend Parliaments and Bench Tables, to attend meetings of committees and sub-committees to which they are elected, to dine in Hall regularly on occasions when students attend and to help the Inn in other ways including those relating to education and training.

Benchers' original voting box.

Of central constitutional importance is the process of election of Barrister Governing Benchers. There is a Selection Committee, whose chairman is normally the Reader, but without a vote. A majority of the voting members of the committee are Barrister Governing Benchers. The committee undertakes a screening process only of barrister members of the Inn who put themselves forward, with the support of Governing Benchers, for election to the Bench. The screening is to select those candidates who fulfil the qualification criteria, of which the willingness and ability to take a significant part in the management of the Inn's affairs is the most important. There is a requirement to have regard, among other factors, to the Inn's equal opportunities policy. Those selected go forward for election to fill available vacancies by ballot of all Governing Benchers. There is a recently introduced and highly successful process of electronic voting on the internet, one consequence of which has been a gratifying increase in the number of votes cast.

Thus, although the governance of the Inn is not a full democracy, nor is it a self-perpetuating oligarchy. The members of the governing body are too numerous for a small group to predominate. The governing body elects its new members. But candidates propose themselves with the support of a sponsor and go forward to the ballot provided they fulfil the qualifying criteria and there are vacancies. The selection committee and the Governing Benchers each have a voting majority of barristers, who are those likely to be most in touch with the barrister members of the Inn.

The Treasurer presides over the affairs of the Inn and is in practice akin to an executive chairman. The Treasurer is elected at a Parliament in Trinity term to serve for the following year. Normally the Bencher elected as Treasurer is the Bencher who was elected as Reader for the preceding year, and thus election as Reader normally determines who will be Treasurer in the following year. Executive continuity now also requires the election in the second preceding year of a Reader elect, who becomes a member of the Executive Committee. By this means, those who become Treasurer will have had two years of progressive introduction to what is in practice an onerous office. The Reader has to be under the age of sixty-nine at the beginning of his year of office; and thus the Treasurer has to be under the age of seventy at the beginning of his year.

There is an elaborate procedure in the Bench Table Orders for nomination and election of the Reader. But in recent years there has been no contested election for Treasurer or Reader. This is consonant with the way in which the Inn operates generally. Decisions at all levels, at Bench Table or in Committees, are taken

Roger Ward, the Head Porter, in formal attire

by a process of reasoned consensus and are rarely confrontational. There is constitutional provision for voting, but a formal vote is rarely taken. In the result, the Inn is governed in large measure harmoniously by a process of democratic osmosis. If political theorists might regard this as questionable, those concerned know that it works; and they appreciate the huge value of a process which gets things done with a minimum of confrontation.

The majority of members of the Inn are barristers who, as students, were called to the Bar by the Inn. Students are admitted to the Inn upon payment of a fairly modest prescribed fee, the amount of which has not changed for more than forty years. The purpose of being admitted as a student is to proceed to qualify for call to the Bar. There is an Admissions, Calls and Student Discipline Committee, with a review panel, whose function is to screen students for admission and call to the Bar to see that they are fit to be admitted or called. For example, those applying for admission are obliged to disclose if they have criminal convictions. Serious offences, especially of dishonestly, may result in rejection. A single offence of, for example, fare dodging on public transport may well be overlooked if it is openly admitted and genuinely regretted. Once they are duly qualified, students are called to the Bar upon the proposal of a Governing or Senior Bencher. The impressive call ceremony, which used to be in Hall, now takes place, when there are numerous students to be called, in the Temple Church. The students are called individually and presented with their call certificate by the Treasurer, who then addresses them and their families. The address is a mixture of congratulation and good wishes, with obligatory emphasis on the fundamental duties of barristers to their clients and to the court.

The main business of the Inn is conducted by a series of committees and sub-committees. The Treasurer and Reader are ex-officio members of all committees and sub-committees of the Bench. The principal committee is the Executive Committee whose membership includes the chairmen of the other main committees, the Masters of the House and of the Staff, the Bench and Bar Auditors, seven elected Governing Benchers and three other members of Hall nominated by and from the Bar Liaison Committee. There is a Finance Sub-Committee answerable to the Executive Committee and an Investment Sub-Committee concerned with the Inn's investments.

The other main committees are the Education and Training Committee, the Estates Committee and the Library Committee. The chairmen of these and other sub-committees are normally Barrister Governing Benchers, and the majority of their members have to be barristers practising in independent practice.

The pinnacle importance of the Education and Training Committee is illustrated by the fact that there are numerous committees or sub-committees within its overall responsibility. Their names signify their functions. They are the Scholarships Committee, the Education and Training Policy Sub-Committee, the Student Affairs Sub-Committee, the Pegasus Scholarship Trust, the Cumberland Lodge Committee, the Advocacy Training Sub-Committee, the Pupil Masters' and Pupil Mistresses' Sub-Committee and the Inn's representatives on a variety of educational and training bodies. Cumberland Lodge is an elegant residence in Windsor Great Park where the Inn is privileged to be able to hold weekend training courses for students. There are similar courses held at Latimer House in Buckinghamshire and Highgate House in Northamptonshire.

The Estates Committee manages the Inn's buildings and property and is responsible for letting professional and residential chambers. It performs the vital function of conserving the Inn's main source of income.

The Library Committee, whose chairman is known as the Master of the Library, manages the Inn's magnificent Library and its information technology facilities so as to achieve the best and most efficient services that can be provided, with the resources available, to judges, barristers, pupils and students. The Archives Committee manages the Inn's archives.

There are then numerous Masters of Activities responsible for the House, the Cellar, the Garden, the Car Park, the Staff, the Pictures, the Silver, the Trusts, the Insurances, the Archives, the Students' Debating Society, the Moots, Drama, the Revels, Qualifying Sessions, Equal Opportunities, Health and Safety, Sponsors, Clocks and the Inner Temple Yearbook. Many of these are assisted by a Governing Bencher and members of Hall nominated by the Bar Liaison Committee.

King's Bench Walk.

The Bar Liaison Committee consists of members of the Inn who are members of Hall and is constituted as determined by members of Hall. The Bar Liaison Committee nominates members of Hall to the various committees and other functions as provided by the Bench Table Orders.

All these committees, sub-committees and offices are complemented by a compact and dedicated employed staff, of whom the effective chief executive is the Sub-Treasurer, who engages and supervises members of staff and who attends Parliaments and Bench Tables. The Sub-Treasurership is an ancient office going back at least to the middle of the sixteenth century. The Sub-Treasurer is also, surprisingly perhaps, a local authority as explained opposite. Another ancient office is the Head Porter, who wears a brown and gold gown on ceremonial occasions and in the Temple Church, and carries an ancient ceremonial staff of bamboo with a silver head including a silver Pegasus, the emblem of the Inn. Under the Sub-Treasurer is the Deputy Sub-Treasurer and the other heads of Departments who, with their staff, administer the business of all the various committees, sub-committees and activities.

What emerges from this catalogue of rather dry structural detail is a modern educational institution whose senior and qualified professional members devote a large amount of their gratuitous time and energy to the education, welfare and vocational training of the Inn's students. The measure of it is that a glance at the full list of those concerned shows that the numbers of Benchers and barristers who serve in this way must approach 300. To give but two examples, there are thirty-nine members of the Scholarship Committee, apart from the Treasurer and Reader, who administer and award the Inn's scholarships and bursaries; and thirty-five members of the Pupils' and Students' Affairs Sub-Committee. Some members serve on more than one committee. But this is a massive resource of unpaid service directed in large measure to the education and training of future generations of barristers here and overseas. The employed staff are efficiently small in number and the whole is an effective institution which mercifully is not bureaucratic.

The Rt Hon Lord Justice May is the Reader of the Inn and will be Treasurer in 2008.

Within the Bounds: the Inn as a Local Authority

Master May

The street lighting in Inner Temple is by gas light. The lamps are now lit by automatic device, but until quite recently they were lit each evening by a lamp lighter using a torch on a traditional long pole. The reason for this independence from external means of illumination is that the Inn, in the person of the Sub-Treasurer, is in some respects its own local authority. So is Middle Temple.

This strange anomaly originates in the Middle Ages. The full history to 1972 may be found in Lord Silsoe's fascinating book *The Peculiarities of the Temple*. In bare outline it is as follows. The ownership of the land which is now the Temple, including the Temple Church, was acquired by the Knights Templar in 1162. The following year, a Papal Bull *'omne datum optimum'* of Pope Alexander III secured privileges and liberties for the Knights Templar and their property anywhere in the world. The enduring effect of this was that the order and its property were under the direct authority of the pope without episcopal intervention. The present 'Round' Church was consecrated in 1185 by the Patriarch of Jerusalem on a visit to King Henry II. Upon the suppression of the Knights Templar, the Knights Hospitaller acquired the land including the Temple Church in 1324 and it remained in their hands until the Reformation. During the fourteenth century, the Inner and Middle Temple became established as Inns of Court upon land formerly owned by the Knights Templar. At the Reformation, the ownership of the land and ecclesiastical authority over the Temple Church was acquired by Henry VIII. The Temple Church thus became a royal peculiar and continues to enjoy that status, that is a church outside episcopal jurisdiction. The Master of the Temple is appointed by the sovereign on the advice of Inner and Middle Temple, in whose care the Church is by the Royal Charter of 1608. By the Charter, the two Inns acquired the freehold of their present property.

In parallel with the ecclesiastical separation of the Temple Church, the Inner and Middle Temple, although they are part of London, are not within the ordinary local authority jurisdiction of either the City of London or the City of Westminster. The Temple stands astride the dividing line between those two authorities at Temple Bar, but is within the formal jurisdiction of neither. The tale of how, over five centuries, the Temple resisted incorporation into the City of London is long and detailed. But it did resist it. There were two colourful occasions, in 1555 and 1669, when the Lord Mayor of London attempted to assert the authority of the City by entering the Temple with his sword of office born erect, only to be beaten back by young members of the Inn. Sadly, relations between the Temple and the City remained cool for upwards of 400 years. The Lord Mayor never during those centuries dined in the Temple, until 1992, when Master Griffiths, as Treasurer of the Inn, helped to effect a long overdue prandial reconciliation.

Lighting the gas lamps: photographed from his chambers in the winter of 1961 by Donald Trotman.

So it is that the Sub-Treasurer is a local authority for some purposes of local government. By the Temples Order 1971, the Inner and Middle Temple are defined as local authorities with the same powers and responsibilities as Inner London Boroughs except in relation to housing. The Sub-Treasurer of Inner Temple and the Under-Treasurer of Middle Temple may delegate certain functions to the City Corporation, and the Inns have agreed that the City Corporation should be the charging authority for the Community Charge. The 1971 Order provides for some functions to be exercised by the Common Council of the Corporation of London within the Temple. Examples were dog licensing (now abolished) and regulation of milk from diseased cows. The City Police police the precincts of the Temple in liaison with the Inns' security staff. The Sub-Treasurer and Under-Treasurer retain some local authority functions. These include environmental protection, licensing, paving and lighting (hence the gas lights), planning (except for development plans and listed buildings), public health and safety, refuse collection and water supply and protection of badgers. It is not clear, however, that the Inn has a resident badger at the moment; but foxes have been spotted.

Life in the Inn

Riots, Mayhem and Murder

Ever since the middle of the twelfth century, when the Knights Templar established themselves on their new and larger site on the north bank of the Thames, the Temple precincts have been jurisdictionally outside the authority of the Mayor and Corporation of the City of London; the two legal societies which occupy the site remain to this day separate local authorities. This 'peculiar' status has led in the past to a certain tension which at times has boiled over into violence.

The first known dispute occurred in 1556, when the Lord Mayor was invited to the autumn Reader's feast and insisted on attending preceded by his swordbearer carrying the sword erect. This was the norm when the mayor processed in state within the City, whereas the sword was reversed when he went outside its bounds, and was understandably taken on this occasion as an attempt by the mayor to assert his authority over the Inn. Detailed records of what happened are now lost, but it seems that some of the young members took matters into their own hands and pulled the sword down.

The same thing happened over 100 years later in 1669, when Sir William Turner announced his intention of attending Christopher Goodfellow's Lent Reader's feast 'as Lord Mayor' and with the sword borne erect before him. George Jeffreys – later of Bloody Assize fame, but then a recently called member of the Inner Temple – was sent to reason with him but to no avail. Sir William was determined, and despite being informed, as he approached the Hall, that he would not be permitted to enter unless he lowered his sword, he persisted. He was met outside the Hall by a large crowd of members, many of them armed with swords under their gowns. A considerable melee ensued, which left the swordbearer bruised, several of the mayor's servants with black eyes and the sword itself damaged, with some pearls lost from its scabbard. The furious Lord Mayor retreated, but then complained bitterly to King Charles II who referred the matter to the Privy Council. The Inn's case was argued by Sir Heneage Finch, the Solicitor-General, and the king, who was sitting in person, avoided making a decision by referring the matter to be tried at common law. It seems that the City, at this stage, thought better of taking things any further and no more was heard of it – though the City authorities did not immediately give up any thoughts of asserting their authority over the Temple. When in 1679 a devastating fire broke out in Pump Court and was spreading rapidly, the members refused to accept the mayor's help when he arrived again with sword held erect, and stopped their fire-fighting to beat the sword down, whereupon the mayor retreated to a tavern and sulkily dismissed a fire engine which he had summoned. On both sides on this occasion, it seems, the issue of jurisdiction outweighed the dangers of a major fire, with the opportunistic mayor seizing the moment and the members of the Inner Temple placing independence above their buildings – though whether the mayor could have helped is a moot point.

Sarah Malcolm.

The independent status enjoyed by the Temple extended beyond its boundaries too – to the properties on Fleet Street which the Knights Hospitaller, who had been granted ownership of the Temple itself after the dissolution of the Order of the Knights Templar in 1312, also owned. Exemption from both secular and ecclesiastical jurisdiction had been granted to the Hospitallers by the king on the orders of the pope, and this status survived the dissolution of the monasteries in the reign of Henry VIII. The whole area had consequently become a refuge and a sanctuary for those fleeing debts and other legal penalties. It became known as 'Alsatia', a reference to the disputed territory of Alsace-Lorraine on the French-German border, and was notorious for lawlessness and mayhem.

This was a strange juxtaposition: the community of lawyers in the Temple found itself living cheek by jowl with a lawless community of miscreants. Houses and shops in the Fleet Street area were subdivided into small tenements, the neighbourhood swarmed with ale-houses and brothels and it boasted a theatre in which a number of Shakespeare's plays were performed in the early years of the seventeenth century. Like the theatres on the south bank of the Thames, the Whitefriars theatre found that there were advantages in being outside the reach of the civic authorities.

Some of the Temple's neighbours, however, were more respectable, and it was for the convenience of these people that the Inner Temple agreed to the construction of gates allowing passage through the Temple to Fleet Street and to the river. However, the use of these passageways by the more disreputable inhabitants of Alsatia

was the cause of ongoing friction, leading to restrictions on the hours when the gates would be open and also, at times, to them being totally walled up. The residents, however, did not take this lying down, and constantly broke the gates open again – actions which led to scuffles and even riots. The worst of these occurred in July 1691.

On that occasion, the Benchers had ordered that 'the little gate leading into Whitefriars be forthwith bricked up', and when that wall was demolished, that the work should be done again. On this second occasion, there were violent confrontations between the servants of the Temple who were trying to carry out the building work and the Alsatians, who threw the bricks down just as soon as they were put up. In desperation, the Benchers resorted to outside help and summoned the City Sheriffs to protect the bricklayers, but they too were assaulted. The riot lasted several hours, with shots fired and property damaged, and it was only when the king's guards intervened and arrested the ringleaders that peace descended. One of the leaders was eventually hanged for his part in the insurrection.

A year later, the locals successfully petitioned for the gates to be opened again under strict control; and the riot also resulted, in 1697, in an Act of Parliament which finally brought to an end the immunity which the inhabitants of that part of London had enjoyed for nearly 400 years. It is something of a mystery why the Temple had countenanced that immunity for so long. It is arguable perhaps that the lawyers felt a degree of fellow-feeling with their unruly neighbours in their desire for independence from outside interference. Or perhaps there were certain advantages in the near proximity of loose women and cheap ale.

The Temple was not immune also to crime within its precincts. In 1733, a notorious triple murder took place in the Inner Temple when, in the course of a burglary at a set of chambers in Tanfield Court (on the site of the present Library building), an elderly widow, Mrs Lydia Duncomb, and her maid Betty Harrison were strangled in their beds, and another young maid's throat was cut. Sarah Malcolm, a twenty-two-year-old laundress (charwoman) at the Temple who had worked in the household and was known to have made a social call there on the evening prior to the murders, was accused of the crime. She had hidden some bloodstained linen and a silver tankard belonging to Mrs Duncomb at the home of another employer and a large amount of money was found concealed under her cap. There was a strong suspicion that others were involved in the crime but no one else was ever charged. Malcolm admitted having planned the robbery but strenuously denied involvement in the murders. She was found guilty, however, and in recognition of the public outrage provoked by the crime she was sentenced to be hanged as close to the scene as possible, in Mitre Court, rather than at the normal place of execution at Tyburn.

Reconstruction of 1691 riot.

Living in the Inn

Reminiscences of a resident

Master Butler-Sloss

Master Butler-Sloss exercising her dog Maggie in the garden.

Joe and I have lived in the Inner Temple for forty-eight years. We were married in September 1958 and were offered the top floor of 8 King's Bench Walk, 3 Pair North, and moved in in early 1959. The flat had the bath in the bedroom but the Inn's carpenters put up a partition which also provided a little area where we placed our daughter's cot when she was born in October 1959. Two or three years later we moved to 10 King's Bench Walk, 3 Pair North, just before the birth of our elder son in 1962.

When we first moved to 10 King's Bench Walk, our neighbour at 3 Pair South was Mrs Kilham-Roberts who had an Ethiopian cat, whose food she used to cook. She was going through a divorce from her husband and was somewhat depressed. We used to worry about her and tried to keep an eye on her. On one occasion as we were going out we saw that her black door was closed but smoke was coming from underneath and from the sides and, as it gathered in volume, we became concerned and rang the fire brigade. They arrived in force, broke down the black door and the inner door and found that our neighbour was out and the cat's food was burning on the stove. In the meantime we went out with Joe carrying our baby daughter over his shoulder, to the cheers of the crowd who had gathered below.

We started with one flat but, at the request of our neighbour and with the Inn's approval, we knocked through the wall to the other flat and took over one large room. When Mrs Kilham-Roberts moved to Rome, we were nicely placed to take over the whole top floor, where we remain today.

We had our own much more serious fire which, while we were all away at the beginning of August, swept through the roof and demolished it completely without touching the roof at number 9 or at number 11. We were away for several months and were housed temporarily by the Inn at 2 Crown Office Row. That flat was about to be converted to chambers as soon as we could return home. I well remember the head clerk and Patrick Medd QC, head of chambers, each coming to call on us to inquire when we would be leaving.

We brought up three children in the Inn and they loved it. We had to cope with carrycots, pushchairs, bicycles and later school trunks up sixty-eight stairs and no lift, but we managed. My father, Sir Cecil Havers, a Bencher of the Inn, visited us regularly but was daunted by the stairs. He said he would walk up the stairs if we invited him for dinner but not if it was only for a drink.

Sue Darling, the wife of the late Gerald Darling QC of Middle Temple, and I ran a nursery school in the choir boys' practice room in the Temple Church. Her two children and my two elder children went to it, together with other children from the Temple and about six children from Gray's Inn, the two children of the head gardener, Geoff Sleeman, and the son of the Italian proprietors of Mick's Café in Fleet Street. The wonderful nursery teacher we employed was superb with the children but disapproved enormously of the barrister parents, all of whom she felt to be a bad influence on her delightful pupils.

I dropped out of managing the nursery school when my elder children went on to school, but returned to help when my younger son was two. This time I shared the duties with Rachel Waller, wife of Waller LJ from Gray's Inn. We still had the excellent nursery teacher. Unfortunately the choristers had cottoned on to the fact that she had strict views on behaviour and particularly on bad language, and they began to leave her rude notes. It came to the point that, with great regret, Rachel and I abandoned the Temple Church and set up the nursery school in the Hall of the Inns of Court Regiment in Lincoln's Inn where there was no bad language to upset Mrs Willenbrock.

As a family we used the Temple garden a great deal and played football and cricket and had children's parties. One Guy Fawkes evening, we had a bonfire in the bottom of the pond (no fish then) and fireworks. We insured the Inner Temple buildings against accidental fire for £100,000! On one or two occasions on a very hot summer's day our children, with others, stripped off and swam in the pond; and at one splendid summer garden party the Treasurer, I believe it was Peter Crowder QC, had a regimental band and all the children formed a procession and marched behind the band.

After my father died, my three brothers and I (my middle brother was Lord Havers, also a Bencher of the Inn) gave the fountain in the pond in memory of him with a Latin inscription now embedded in the brickwork surround of the pond.

Some years ago, when there was concern in London about IRA terrorism, we went on a Sunday to visit friends near Oxford who gave us produce from their garden to take home. About 10.30 that night we heard a noise outside the door but no one knocked. We went to look and saw an oblong package wrapped in a Sainsbury carrier bag. We decided not to touch it and called the duty porter who called the police who called the bomb squad, and we were bundled into a police car and taken to wait at Snow Hill Police Station. We left in such a hurry we had no money with us and the duty sergeant lent us 50p to buy coffee in the canteen. Two hours later we were taken home. The police were laughing and I asked what was in the package. It was the rhubarb we had forgotten to take home.

Living in King's Bench Walk we have a very good view of firework displays on the river, as well as the Lord Mayor's show and the London Marathon. We can also see the Royal Air Force fly pasts which go over Buckingham Palace. On one memorable occasion we saw the space shuttle which was being flown over London.

All our grandchildren come and play in the garden as their parents used to. I am very happy to see families with young children now living in the Inn. It is a good place to bring up children and a happy place to live.

The Rt Hon The Baroness Butler-Sloss of Marsh Green GBE is the former President of the Family Division and was Treasurer of the Inner Temple in 1998.

Growing up in the Inner Temple

Richard Compton Miller

I became a law student in 1966; but my connection with the Inner Temple began some ten years earlier when my parents, Sir John and Lady Compton Miller, moved into 2 Crown Office Row. We were one of the first families to return after the Inn was rebuilt following extensive war damage. It all looked wonderfully pristine, much as it would have done when Christopher Wren (allegedly) built 6 King's Bench Walk in the seventeenth century. The Inn allowed fewer cars to park then and the pedestrian-only quadrangles and alleys were great (and safe) for a child growing up in London. It was blissfully quiet too.

Filming in the Inner Temple.

King's Bench Walk in the 1950s.

A plaque on the outside of our building proclaimed that the writer Charles Lamb had once lived on the site. Sometimes when I was feeling naughty I would climb onto the flat roof which ran above the whole of Crown Office Row, carrying my catapult. Hiding behind a chimney I would take aim at the barristers as they strolled through the echoing quadrangle beneath. My ammunition was dried peas 'borrowed' from my mother's store cupboard. Luckily my aim was very poor! Barristers were easy to spot in those days, as they all wore bowler hats and carried brollies, even in summer.

One drawback of Temple-living was that I had no children of my own age to play with. But I was fascinated by the strange rituals of the Temple. Every evening a man on a bicycle would arrive to light the Victorian gaslights. He carried with him a long prong, like a pogo-stick, which he also used to extinguish them next morning. During term time the under-porter, Mr Pink, wearing his ceremonial rig, would blow a horn round the bounds of the Temple at dusk. My father explained that this was originally done to summon the barristers and bar students to dinner, some of whom might be wild-fowling on the Southwark marshes. They would hurry back, using the ferrymen that plied their trade along the river. You can see how busy the Thames then was in some of Canaletto's canvases.

At home Pedro, my feisty black and tan chihuahua, would sit on the window shelf overlooking the pavement watching the people go by. He would growl and bark wildly when the pug belonging to our neighbour Lord Spens, a former Chief Justice of India, passed beneath. I would take him for walks around Fountain Court and other Temple landmarks. But he was never allowed in the garden!

My mother found it difficult living in the Temple because shopping was so inconvenient. If you ran out of bread or milk you had to visit the Lyons tea-room opposite the Law Courts. During the week there was an old-established family-run grocers, Green's, in Fetter Lane. The nearest supermarket was the gloriously old-fashioned Sainsbury's in Blackfriars Road, which was demolished in the 1960s to make way for their headquarters. Harrods and Fortnum & Mason vans were frequent visitors to the Temple, making deliveries to residents either too elderly or too grand to do their own shopping. My father frequented El Vino in Fleet Street, not for wine but for the soda that he enjoyed with his evening whisky. It was my job to take back his empty soda siphons and reclaim the deposit.

My father loved the Temple and had lived in King's Bench Walk before the war. He would sit in the garden, a dignified figure in his green trilby and tweed jacket, reading *The Times* and composing poetry. For me the Temple Garden was like having your own private St James's Park. We used to hold picnics there and candle-lit dinner parties. At weekends it was almost empty, the perfect place to revise for my contract and tort exams.

One Saturday I awoke to find the entire Inner Temple car park transformed into an eighteenth-century London street scene, with horse-drawn carriages, bewigged men in frock coats and women in silk dresses carrying parasols. It was the film set of *Tom Jones*, directed by Tony Richardson and starring Albert Finney and Susannah York. Any chance of me becoming a film 'extra'? Not on that movie, but many Bar students helped make ends meet by joining the film extras' union in Marloes Road, Kensington.

Our flat was ideal for my law studies. While other students had to commute from digs in Kensington, Chelsea and less salubrious neighbourhoods, I was on the spot. I studied in the Middle Temple Library, just twenty-five yards away from Crown Office Row, because it opened half-an-hour before the Inner Temple. I went for lectures at the College of Law in Chancery Lane, a five-minute stroll away. Had I not lived in the Temple and had such a generous father would I have spent three long years reading for the Bar? Probably not, given my real ambition was to be a journalist. Every Saturday I walked down Fleet Street to the 'Black Lubyanka', the famous Art Deco offices of Lord Beaverbrook's newspaper empire, where once a week I became a cub reporter on the *Sunday Express*.

After passing my Bar exams in 1969 I did a year's pupillage with Desmond Perrett, who later became a Circuit judge. His chambers were two floors beneath our flat and so I could wake up at 8.30am after a night of heavy partying and be at work by 9am. But it was time to move on, to leave the Inner Temple and pursue the career that I had always dreamt of. Writing claimed me, just as it had done Charles Lamb who was born and brought up in Crown Office Row 200 years before.

Richard Compton Miller was called to the Bar at the Inner Temple in 1969. After doing his pupillage in 2 Crown Office Row, he pursued his real love, journalism.

Life on the *Da Vinci Code* Trail

Joanne Brown

I've lived at the Inner Temple for the past six years. My chambers are two doors down from the flat so it's my place of work as well. The top floors of the building are residential and, as a member, you're entitled to apply to live here. I'm just one of the very lucky ones. The buildings form a square between Fleet Street and Embankment, with a central garden full of sun-dials and fountains. It isn't somewhere that the public has easy access to, so you're privy to a secret part of London.

The Da Vinci Code has, of course, opened this place up to lots of people who come to see the Temple Church featured in the book. People stop me and ask about it all the time. At the weekends, when I unlock the gate, there are people trying to get in behind me. My twin boys get their photo taken by Japanese tourists.

There's a sense of a lost world about this place. The same people have worked here for years, and there's a whole sense of community. We had our wedding celebrations here fifteen years ago, and a naming ceremony for the boys in the Inner Temple garden. I held my fortieth birthday party in one of the function rooms – we've had all our significant life events here.

We live on the third floor, and you walk past the doors of chambers on your way up. The boys might keep their tricycles on the stairs, but this is an office, a working building. You're in the legal world all the time, but I like that. I don't find it difficult to switch off. The benefits outweigh any disadvantages. I can stop work and be home in five minutes. We have enormous flexibility – I see my children significantly more than many working mothers.

The twins are London boys – the marathon goes along Embankment at the bottom of the Temple, and we can see our home from the London Eye. I asked the boys what they liked about living here and they just said 'London'. I asked if they wanted to keep on living here, and one said 'I'd like to live here on my own'.

Our building was built in 1782, and the living room floor is a pure slope. When we moved in, we put our dining table by the windows and watched all the plates slide off. But it's very secure. There's a great thick door to the flat with huge bolts and locks. Just like the chambers downstairs, we have our family name painted over the door to the flat, and the first time I saw that I was very excited.

Even though we rent, I feel no sense of transience. I plan to live here until I can no longer make it up the stairs. How many people get the chance to live in a place like this? So central, but beautiful and secure and quiet? It's a huge privilege.

Joanne Brown is a practising barrister and resident of the Inn.

Joanne Brown and family.

A Day in the Life of the Treasurer

Master Schiemann

When I became Treasurer in 2003, Elisabeth and I moved into a flat in Hare Court. We discovered a new life. This beautiful little corner of London is a beehive of activity for most of the hours of the day.

I wake to the sound of the bells of St Clement's. One of our porters – Roger, David or Dennis – is already doing his rounds, just checking that the place is as he left it the night before and opening up various locked doors and gates. Chambers are being cleaned by ladies from all over the world. Dustmen come and remove the rubbish bags left by those who have cleaned. The milkman and the paper man leave their offerings at the bottom of each staircase. Food is being delivered to the kitchen. A light can be seen in chambers here and there illuminating someone with his nose in a pile of papers or some learned tome.

Rooftops, looking towards the Royal Courts of Justice.

Quite often one of the Inn's many committees has a meeting arranged for 8 or 8.30 which everyone involved knows will be over at the latest by 9.30. The Finance Sub-Committee will discuss whether to give its blessing to the sale or purchase of some property; or whether or not the bid by the Library Committee for more books or by the Scholarships Committee for more scholarships should be financed; or whether the price of lunches should be enhanced so as to enable both desires to be met. These morning tasks are made the more agreeable because the inner man has not been forgotten – Charles or Vicky have arranged for one of their staff, many of whom have been with us for years, to make some coffee and produce some fruit and croissants.

Meanwhile, outside the Church a notice board appears telling the outside world that 8.30 every morning is when a twenty-minute Matins is said by the Master and whoever else feels that this is a good start to the day.

In the Hall the staff are clearing up the debris from a twenty-first birthday party the night before and making everything spick and span for lunch. Out in the garden Les is tending the Inner Temple Rose. He has won the Riverside Trophy presented by the Worshipful Company of Gardeners in each of the last three years. So walking round the garden is always a joy.

I go to my room to find a full in-tray. There will be cheques to sign, suggestions by committee chairmen to consider, minutes of committee meetings to note or approve, agendas for forthcoming meetings to decide, letters to read, draft or sign and so on. In all this my task is made infinitely easier by help from various quarters. The cheques will already have been approved by the Head of Department or his deputy and by the Sub-Treasurer, one of whose many gifts is anticipating by a note the very question that I wish to ask; the letters may well have been drafted by the chairman of the relevant committee or by the Sub-Treasurer. When I come across something where I have any doubts which the Sub-Treasurer does not put to rest, I can discuss it with the appropriate Head of Department, the relevant committee chairman, or the Reader and

The Temple Church from Hare Court.

the Reader-designate or indeed put it before the Executive Committee or Bench Table. The sense of working together as part of a team of barristers, judges and staff is undoubtedly satisfying.

The amount of things done by one or more members of this team is astonishing. When I was chairman of the Scholarships Committee I thought I had some idea of what the Education and Training Department under Yeshim were involved in. I did not know the half of it. Not only do they work weekends marshalling scholarship candidates but they also spend evenings and weekends supervising and organising events at Cumberland Lodge, Highgate House, Latimer House and the Inn itself, seeing that students and the younger barristers learn from their elders the gentle arts of examining witnesses, preparing skeleton arguments and dealing with difficult judges. The staff do far more than they are contracted to do and scores of barristers and judges regularly give of their time to teach others and serve on committees. The Inn owes them a lot – but I hope and suspect that they get as much out of it all as they put in. The end result is that we have a sense of community which I think is stronger than it used to be when I joined the Inn.

To work surrounded by graceful buildings and spaces is a privilege and a joy. Of course, all those buildings need maintenance. The Surveyor's Department, in addition to planning and supervising large building projects, has a highly skilled staff of plumbers, electricians and carpenters, each with an apprentice, who turn out to deal with the routine tasks and inevitable emergencies and challenges to which such an estate as ours gives rise – and not just during working hours. Many of them have been here for years; at least one is working with his father. We can be proud of them.

At my desk in the Law Courts there are e-mails waiting to be answered and then I can get down to concentrating on the latest piece of litigation. While I am quietly exchanging thoughts with counsel, back at the Inn things are moving in the kitchen.

On a typical day this is just part of what we get through: 50 ducks, 200 salmon cutlets, 10 legs of lamb, 100 kgs potatoes and vegetables, 100 eggs accompanied by 200 rolls and 12 loaves of bread. The kitchens are modern and spotless. Each of the staff has his appointed task and everything moves in a preordained rhythm towards lunch. The staff eat before barristers and judges come across from the courts and then greet us with a smile and with food which is the envy of the other Inns. Martin, our head chef, will tell you on exactly which tree in what field the cow used to scratch her back before she gave her all to grace our tables. Like everyone else, so far as I can see, he takes a justified pride in his work. I enjoy lunch so much that I usually miss the concert which is taking place in the Church whilst organ enthusiasts eat their sandwiches there.

Food and conversations over lunch with friends or perhaps a distinguished visitor set me up for an afternoon in court or doing papers of one sort or another. Just time to have a quick word with anyone who has a problem which they want to discuss with me while we're there. Occasionally I'm five minutes late for court because of this but I hope I'm forgiven.

Meanwhile, in the Library they are poring over some new piece of software and helping some barristers in a hurry find what they want; and Clare Rider the archivist is busy answering a query about the history of the Inn. In the garden, manure is being delivered for the roses. In the kitchen the washing up is proceeding apace. A leaking roof is being mended and somewhere else a tap stops dripping. Rooms are being prepared for two or three committee meetings taking place at 5 o'clock. Potential staff are being interviewed. The Collector is explaining pension arrangements to someone about to retire. Sounds of singing can be heard from the Church. All round us conferences are taking place. Between 6 and 6.30 the place gradually gets emptier and then starts filling up again, perhaps with those who have been to a memorial service, perhaps with diners or party goers or those attending a Bar Music Society concert. Sometimes I'm amongst them, sometimes I'm working, sometimes I'm at a concert elsewhere and return to an Inn temporarily hushed.

As we stroll around in the darkness there is the reassuring figure of Dennis and his dog, Floyd, guarding this jewel in the centre of London.

The Rt Hon Lord Justice Schiemann is a Lord Justice of Appeal and was Treasurer of the Inn in 2003.

The Inn's Charitable Functions and the 'Little Temples'

The records of the Inner Temple can illuminate in unexpected ways London life in the past. The prosperous inhabitants of the Inn at that time lived cheek by jowl with neighbourhoods teeming with considerably more socially deprived folk, a closeness which could not but afford daily examples of poverty and want. The Inn was usually aware of its duty towards those less fortunate, particularly when it had a direct responsibility; in 1816, for example, a payment of £20 was made to a bricklayer, Robert Thacker, who was badly injured when he fell from scaffolding around the Hall that collapsed. But it also accepted responsibility for anyone who suffered a misfortune while within its precincts; the costs of looking after, or conveying to hospital, anyone who broke a limb or went into labour while within the walls were borne by the Society, as indeed were the burial costs of people drowned at Temple Stairs.

But nowhere is this social conscience displayed more strikingly than in the Inn's care of foundling children in the eighteenth century. The abandonment of babies and young children by parents who could not, or would not, care for them was one of the nastier aspects of life then. Thomas Coram established his famous Foundling Hospital in 1741 after becoming angry at the numbers of dead and abandoned babies he saw in the streets whenever he walked through the city. And the Inns too were seen by many desperate parents as a similar refuge. The first reference to a child abandoned in the Inner Temple occurs in the accounts for 1617–18 and the last in 1830.

The Inn did its best to avoid this responsibility. Watchmen were ordered to examine every basket or bundle brought into the Temple by night 'to prevent the dropping of any child which may become chargeable to the Society'. If parents intent on abandoning a child managed to evade the watchmen, every effort was made to trace them and return the child. But some children inevitably had to be accepted, and were put into the care of the Inn's servants who received an allowance for their upkeep and entered into a bond to perform their fostering duties. The children remained in care until they were of an age when they could be put out as apprentices, at which point they stopped being a charge on the Inn.

Many – inevitably in that era of high child mortality – quickly died, so it was a priority to baptise them as soon as possible. This duty fell to the Head Porter who arranged for baptism in the Temple Church, as well as burial in the churchyard when that was necessary. After 1675 the custom arose of giving these little foundlings the surname Temple, with the Christian names chosen by the foster parent.

After 1754 the Inn decided to put its fostering activities on a more regular footing and appointed Mary Wharry as a sort of Foster Mother General. She remained in the Inn's service until her death in 1799. The number of children in her care varied, sometimes amounting to as many as a dozen, and the records show considerable sums paid to

Sir Francis Page (1661–1741); portrait attributed to Jonathan Richardson.

her for their maintenance. In general, each child was allowed 3s 6d a week for food, washing and clothing, with medical costs paid separately. Mrs Wharry seems to have been a kindly soul, and sought to keep some of the girls with her longer than the Inn was usually prepared to countenance: one Mary Temple had managed to stay until she was twenty years old, far older than others who could often be put out to work at the age of ten. Another girl, Ann Temple, was found to be seventeen years old or more, and was told that she would have to leave the Inn's care; but they were good enough to allow her three guineas for new clothes so that she would be presentable when she went out into the world.

Some responsibilities lasted longer than others, and were more costly. In 1728, there is a reference to a payment of £5 to a Mr Sparham 'for his cure of Ann Temple, a poor child maintained by this Society (her thigh having been broken by Mr Baron Page's coach)'. This was Sir Francis Page, a member of the Inn; it is assumed that the child was playing within the Inn's precincts when the accident occurred. Ann Temple clearly did not recover fully, since there is a further record three years later of payment for six and a half weeks' nursing 'before she went out as an apprentice' – as it happens, to a family named Page who had entered into a bond with the Society to indemnify it for any further charge for Ann Temple. It is not obvious what the relationship was between this family and Sir Francis Page, but he was clearly still involved with the child since a doctor he called in to treat her again the following year had to apply to the Inn for payment of his bill. This was 'for medicine for a girl maintained by this Society who was hurt by the coach of Mr Justice Page by prescription of a physician called in by Mr Justice Page'. Although the Inn was no longer liable for any payments for Ann Temple, on this occasion they did pay the £5 bill after Sir Francis apparently refused.

…id for makeing Thirty Cliffords Cloathes	£ s d
Three Shirts	0 : 1 : 0
Three Peticoats and stays	0 : 1 : 6
Clouts	0 : 0 : 6
two Frocks	0 : 1 : 4
two bed Gowns	0 : 1 : 0
two pin Cloaths	0 : 0 : 4
Three Muslin Caps	0 : 1 : 0
Three Night Caps	0 : 0 : 9
Tapes	0 : [illegible] : 0
Bonnett & Rib:	0 : 3 : 0
	£ 0 : 11 : 5

Bill for 'Clifford's Inn cloths' to clothe foundling children cared for by Clifford's Inn, 1707.

The Quit Rents Ceremony

No doubt in the annals of territorial squabbles, that between the Mayor and Corporation of the City of London and the Honourable Societies of the Inner and Middle Temple can only be reckoned as relatively trivial. Yet a memory of that particular tiff rears its head every year when Her Majesty's Sheriffs of the City of London have a little business to do. There is rent to pay for a piece of wasteland in Shropshire called 'The Moors' and for a tenement at St Clement Danes, Middlesex, called 'The Forge'. Surely the easiest method of paying these rents would be a cheque posted on the due date each year? But it's not as simple as that: the rent for 'The Moors' consists of the presentation of a blunt knife and a sharp knife, and that for 'The Forge' is made up of six horseshoes and sixty-one nails. These Quit Rents – whereby the tenant is 'quit' of rents and other feudal services – are a token payment in kind for freedom from all services, and are rendered by HM Sheriffs on behalf of the Corporation of London to the Queen's Rememberancer.

This annual Quit Rents ceremony takes place in the Court of the Lord Chief Justice. The knives for 'The Moors' are tested by bending a hazel rod over the blunt knife which is then broken over the sharp knife. They have been rendered for over 750 years; the earliest recorded mention of them is in the Shropshire Serjeant's Diaries for 1211 in the reign of King John. The rents for 'The Forge' are first recorded in 1235 during the reign of Henry III, and when the horseshoes and nails are presented they are counted to ensure that the total is correct. The nails and horseshoes are themselves over 550 years old since they are kept in the Rememberancer's Office and loaned to the Corporation of London to be rendered again the following year.

Why then is there a dispute about this ancient ritual? The matter goes back to 1765, when the Lord Mayor and the Sheriffs appeared in the Temple precincts in full regalia on their way to pay the rents, and stones were thrown at them by some of the young members of the Middle and Inner Temples. No doubt memories still rankled about attempts by previous Lord Mayors to assert authority over the Temple. Subsequent mayors and sheriffs therefore desisted from trespassing on Temple property – until, that is, 1982, when the Sheriffs wrote to the Treasurer of the Inner Temple and the Masters of the Bench applying for consent to their passage on foot through the Inn to the Law Courts for the ceremony, after travelling by barge from Tower Bridge.

Part of this request was that, if any stones were to be thrown, they should be directed at the Common Serjeant of London rather than at Her Majesty's Sheriffs. The Treasurer replied that 'steps will be taken to ensure that the student members of the Honourable Society of the Inner Temple who, it is understood, cast stones on the recent previous occasion referred to, will be kept to their book learning and studies during the period of the passage of Her Majesty's Sheriffs through the land of the Honourable Society.' He went on to point out that the Serjeant was currently an honourable Master of the Bench of the Inner Temple so any stones thrown at him would result in disciplinary action. The procession has continued ever since.

RULES AND ORDERS

To be observed and performed by the PORTERS, WATCHMEN, and WARDERS belonging to the Two HONORABLE SOCIETIES of the TEMPLE.

ORDERED, that the HEAD and UNDER PORTERS attend regularly throughout the Day, to keep the *Temple* free from all
Beggars, Criers of Old Clothes, &c. to prevent Nuisances, and to preserve Peace and good Order therein; and to enable them to do so, it is RESOLVED, that the Porters shall not (upon any
pretence whatsoever) go on Errands or Messages out of the *Temple*, except upon the business of their respective Societies.

THAT they attend at their respective Gates every Night, alternately, from 10 o'clock until 6 o'clock in the Morning, from Lady-day to Michaelmas-day; and until 7 o'clock, from
Michaelmas-day to Lady-day; and that each, on the Evening preceding the Night of his Attendance, shall place the several Watchmen (who are to attend him for that purpose at Dusk) at
their respective stands; and shall visit, twice at least in each Night, every Watchbox, in order to ascertain the Vigilance of the Watchmen; and also to prevent any person not belonging to
the *Temple*, whose business shall not be satisfactorily explained, from entering the *Temple* after 11 o'clock at Night.

THAT each shall make a Report in Writing, to the Under-Treasurer, (on the Morning subsequent to the Night of his Attendance) of all transactions, as well as of the conduct of the
Watchmen, during the preceding Night; stating, also, whether the Lamps continued properly lighted throughout the Night; which Report is to be entered in the Book kept for that purpose.

THAT they take particular care that the several Gates are shut, and also locked, at the appointed periods.

THAT neither of them be allowed to perform the Night Duty by Deputy, unless by the special permission of the Under-Treasurer. Any of them who shall make a false Report to the
Sub-Treasurer, shall forfeit, for the first Offence, one Week's Wages; and, for the second, be dismissed from his Office.

ORDERED, that the EVENING WATCH come on their stations every Evening at Dusk, and continue to walk their Rounds every half
hour until 11 o'clock, or until they are relieved by the Night Watchmen. That the *NIGHT WATCH* come on duty at 11 o'clock, to relieve the Evening Watch, and remain on duty
until 6 o'clock in the Morning, from Lady-day to Michaelmas-day; and until 7, from Michaelmas-day to Lady-day. That the *WATCHMEN* proclaim the time of the Night every half
hour, commencing at 10 o'clock; and that each Watchman shall go to the top of every Staircase in his District twice during his Watch, in order to drive out of the *Temple* all such loose
and disorderly persons as shall be found lurking in the Staircases, or strolling about; and shall also examine every suspicious Basket or Bundle that may be brought into the *Temple* after
Dusk. That they attend in person, unless special permission be given to the contrary, in which case one of the regular supernumerary Watchmen shall attend as Deputy; and that no
Watchman continue on Duty for the Night, after having watched during the Evening, except it shall be necessary, through the neglect of the man who ought to relieve him, which neglect the
Porter (on duty) shall report.

THAT any Watchman found sleeping on his station, shall forfeit One Shilling; and that if, on any pretence whatsoever, a Watchman shall neglect his Duty, by being absent from his
station, he shall forfeit one full Week's Pay for the first Offence, and for the second Offence (besides such Forfeit) shall be dismissed, and never employed again. That any Watchman drunk
on his station, be liable to a Forfeit of one Week's Pay, and, on a repetition of the Offence, to Dismissal.

ORDERED, that the WARDERS attend every Day throughout the Year, from the time the Watch quit their stations in the Morning until the setting of
the Watch in the Evening; and that they take especial care to turn out of the *Temple* all Beggars, idle and disorderly people, Criers of Old Clothes, &c. and to keep peace and good order
within the Confines of the *Temple*.

THAT they shall be subject to the same Regulations and Penalties as the Watchmen hereinbefore mentioned, and shall not be permitted to go with Errands or Messages out of the *Temple*,
except upon the Business of the Society.

THAT the Porters, Ticket Porters, Watchmen, and other Servants of the House shall assist the Warders in quelling any Disturbances; and, in case any of them refuse so to do, when
required, that such Porter, &c. shall (on Complaint being made to the Bench) be dismissed.

ORDERED, that the House Porters, Warders, and Ticket Porters shall take particular care to prevent the Entrance of (or turn out of the *Temple*) all Beggars, Criers of Old Clothes,
and persons crying Articles for Sale, or making a Noise.

THAT no Horses be fed or exercised in the *Temple*, nor any Carriage permitted to remain on the Crossings.

THAT any Person detected in depositing any Ashes, Rubbish, Dust, or Filth, (except in the Places appropriated for such purposes) or committing any other Nuisance in any Court or
Passage within the *Temple*, be prosecuted; and that a Reward of Five Shillings be paid to the Informer.

THAT Copies of this Order be painted on Boards, and placed in some conspicuous Parts of the *Temple*.

ORDERED, that on every SUNDAY EVENING (throughout the Year) all the *GATES* in the *Temple* be shut and finally closed at Dusk; and that no Person or Carriage be allowed
to come in or go out of the *Temple*, except at the Great Gate at the top of the *Inner Temple Lane*, and the Great Gate at the top of the *Middle Temple Lane*, which Gates are to be opened,
as occasion may require, for the Entrance or Exit of Carriages or Persons resident or having Business in the *Temple*.

... be admitted by the Porter until

ORDERED, that the MIDDLE TEMPLE LANE GATE be shut every Evening (except on Sundays, as before sta
12, after which hour no Carriages shall be allowed to enter, except those of Benchers, and Members of Parliament residing in
Porter admit proper Persons all Night. That the Carriage Gate and Wicket shall not be opened before 6 o'clock in the M
Michaelmas to Lady-day.

THAT the INNER TEMPLE LANE GATE be shut every Evening (except on Sundays, as before stated) at Dusk, an
shall be set; but that the Porters admit proper Persons all Night. That the Gate shall not be opened before 6 o'clock in the
Michaelmas to Lady-day.

THAT the MITRE COURT GATE be half shut every Evening (except on Sundays, as before stated) at Dusk, and prop
be finally closed and locked, and the Key then taken to the Chief or Under Porter attending at the *Inner Temple Lane Gate*.
from Lady-day to Michaelmas, and not before 7, from Michaelmas to Lady-day.

THAT the GATE next RAM ALLEY be shut and finally closed every Evening (except on Sundays, as before stated) at
in the Morning, from Lady-day to Michaelmas, and not before 8, from Michaelmas to Lady-day.

THAT the WHITE-FRIARS GATE be shut every Evening (except on Sundays, as before stated) at Dusk. That Carri
after which hour no Carriages shall be allowed to enter, except those of Benchers, and Members of Parliament residing in th
(at that hour) taken to the Chief or Under Porter attending at the *Inner Temple Lane Gate*. That the Carriage Gate and
Lady-day to Michaelmas, and not before 7, from Michaelmas to Lady-day.

THAT the WATER GATE be completely closed on every Sunday, and also on Christmas-day and Good Friday; and
That this Gate shall not be opened before 7 o'clock in the Morning, from Lady-day to Michaelmas, and not before 8, fro

THAT NEW COURT GATE, leading to DEVEREUX COURT, be shut every Evening (except on Sundays, as be
persons be admitted until 12, at which hour the Gate be finally closed and locked, and the Key then taken to the Chief or
the Gate shall not be opened before 6 o'clock in the Morning, from Lady-day to Michaelmas, and not before 7, from Mich

THAT the GATE next PALSGRAVE PLACE be completely closed on every Sunday, and also on the first Day of ever
That the Gate shall not be opened again, from the time of its being shut at Dusk, until 7 o'clock in the Morning, from Lad

ORDERED, that a Copy of these Regulations be constantly placed on a Board in the Treasurers' Offices, (and i
Members of each House; and that they be requested to give Information to the Under-Treasurer of the Society to whic
may come to their knowledge, who shall forthwith communicate such Information to the Bench, if the same shall happen i

June, 1822.

Printed orders for porters, watchmen and warders, 1822, above; right, Dennis Moffat, one of today's porters, at the Bencher's entrance.

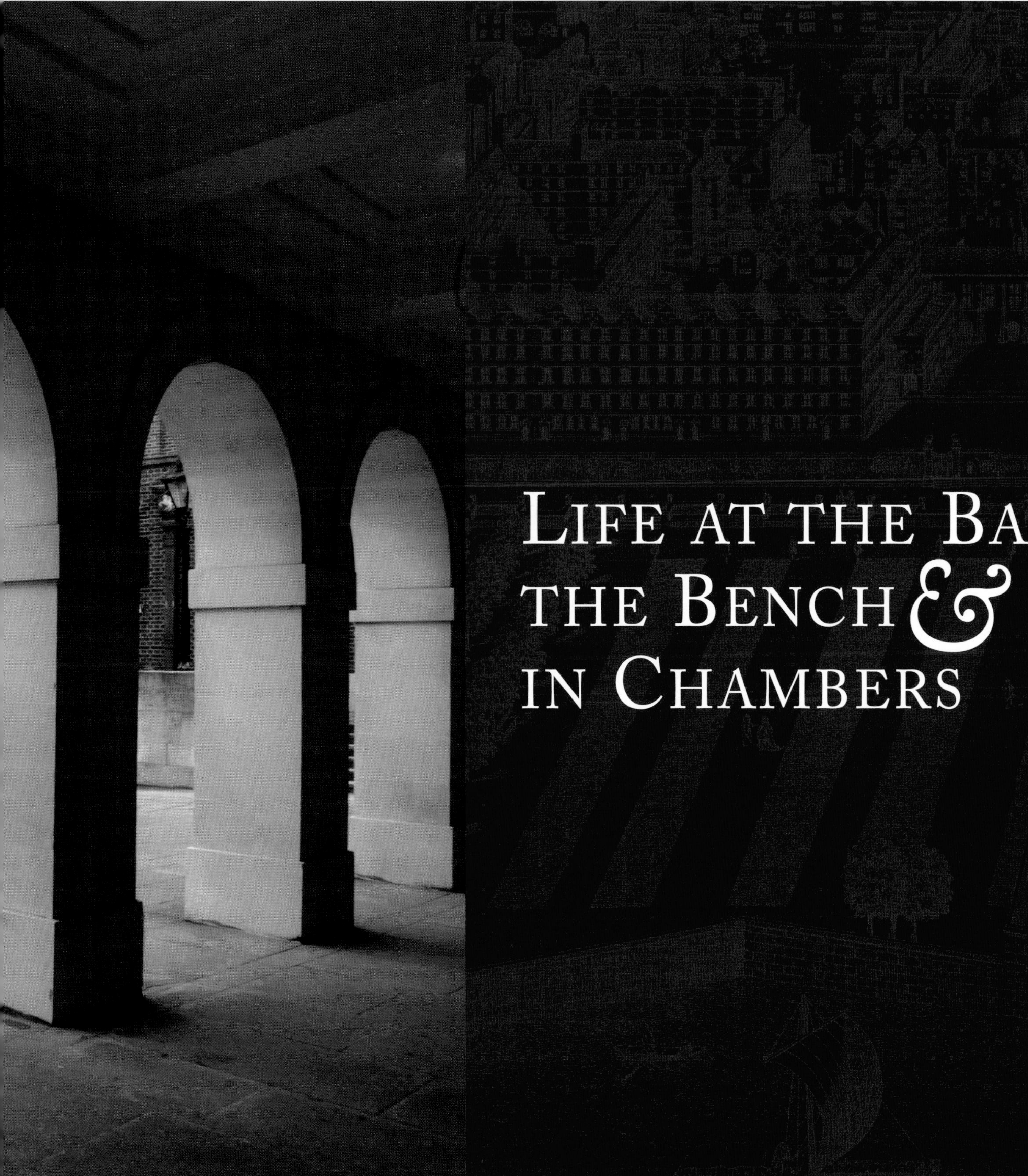

Life at the Bar, the Bench & in Chambers

The Independent Bar

Members of the Inner Temple have contributed many memories and reminiscences of their experiences while training and being called to the Bar, and later during independent practice.

I first remember the Inner Temple in the 1920s. My father was a partner in the oldest solicitors' firm in the Temple, at 7 King's Bench Walk, which had been established there since the 1820s. Every Saturday my mother and I used to be driven to the Temple to pick up my father from the office. I remember the office well, particularly the sealing wax machine with its spirit lamp and conical funnel; you pressed a lever and a blob of wax fell onto the paper, to be quickly impressed with the seal.

During the war, when bombs were falling all around, my father retreated to the basement, but when the war ended the firm grew bigger again and eventually also took over number 6. My brother had by now joined the practice, and the firm stayed there until he died in 1986 and the long association with the Temple ceased after over 160 years. Meanwhile, however, I maintained the family connection by being called to the Bar in 1951, and for over twenty years practising in various parts of the Inner Temple. And then one of my sons was called in 1989 and now has a busy practice in London and on the Western Circuit. Soon, over three generations, my family will have had an association with the Inner Temple stretching over 100 years.

Michael Meredith Hardy

Wood engraving of the Round in 1931 by Michael Meredith Hardy's aunt, Viva Talbot, a former pupil of Robert Gibbings.

In the late summer of 1946 I was demobilised from the Royal Corps of Signals after seven years in the Army. I scarcely knew any other way of life, and found myself in London wondering what to do next. I had begun in 1938 to read law at Oxford, so back I went to the old familiar place and in two years sat for the degree of BCL which in the ordinary way was supposed to need four years of study. We 'old sweats' worked very hard and played very little, anxious to get degrees in as short a time as possible.

The next obvious step was to pass the Bar examinations. No grant was available to study for these, so it was plain to me that I must get a job somehow and earn a living while I read the necessary books. As most of my army career had been concerned with electrical equipment of every kind it seemed sensible to apply to Ferranti Ltd, a famous firm of electrical engineers in the north, and they immediately gave me a job. I began to work there and in the evenings I studied to pass the Bar examinations.

In due course, I applied to the Inn to be called. I was sent a lengthy form to complete, the last question in which was: 'Have you ever been employed in trade or industry?' or words to that effect. I naively replied that I had been, and in fact still was, employed by Ferranti Ltd. The Benchers were outraged. How could one possibly call to the Bar a young man who had not only been but was at the moment employed in TRADE. I received a curt note from the Treasury Office so informing me. I felt very angry and wrote to the Sub-Treasurer explaining that as an ex-serviceman with a small family I had to earn a living of some kind while studying for the Bar examinations, and anyway I did not think that my employment at Ferranti Ltd could sensibly be described as TRADE. No good.

Word of this rejection came to the ears of my Uncle Wilfrid, who by then was a Bencher and was later to become Treasurer of the Inn. He was extremely indignant, not so much on my behalf, but because his pride was injured by the thought that any nephew of his should be refused admission to the Bar on the ground that he had been engaged in TRADE! He must have gathered together a small lobby of Benchers to get the decision revoked. And so it was that six months later I was called to the Bar.

It seems remarkable today that the Benchers of the Inn should regard honest employment in industry as a disqualification for the Bar. But it must be remembered that in 1950 most of the Benchers would have been born towards the end of the nineteenth century and their numbers had not been reinforced by younger men during the five years of war. They were in fact Victorians or Edwardians, so their prejudices were both numerous and insuperable. My Uncle Wilfrid, for example, never sat as a judge unless he was wearing a stiff starched shirt and collar. He had brought to him on the Bench at three o'clock precisely a tray of tea, comprising teapot, milk jug, sugar bowl and biscuits, lest he be wearied by counsel's submissions. Unembarrassed by the lack of refreshment provided for everyone else in court, he poured and stirred and rattled the china while the case proceeded.

Master Clothier

I remember that in 1944 no one was allowed to enter if they were in business. At that time, I was doing important work as a research scientist, but this was not considered to be 'business' and I was given special dispensation to commence my studies. I was permitted to take the preliminary examinations one at a time, and whenever I had time I went to the Old Bailey and other courts to observe and learn. I was called to the Bar in November 1950 aged thirty-four but I never went into chambers as I could not afford to give up my job as I had a wife and small child to support.

Charles Simons

It must be fifty years since I was called to the Bar; fifty years – it sounds like one of Lord Goddard's more merciful sentences! And I have to admit that I enrolled at the Inn for the most ephemeral of reasons. It was my tutor who inspired me: a gifted teacher with a clarity of mind which would certainly have taken him to the very top of the legal profession had he so wished, but he had chosen instead the academic life and the delights of teaching law to the young at Oxford. Perhaps surprisingly, given his cloistered existence, this unworldly but kindly man also took it upon himself to steer those placed in his charge towards careers which he judged were best suited to their talents. It was a role for

Orlando Gibbons, barrister, in his chambers in King's Bench Walk.

which he was wholly ill-equipped. 'In your case,' he said, 'you must either do nothing for a living, or failing that become a solicitor – or there is of course the Bar. But there you would start with a serious disadvantage, for you have no possible influence: no brother a partner in a litigious firm, no relation a clerk in chambers… and there would also be the terrible chore of trundling up to London to eat dinners on as many as six evenings a term for as long as three years.'

Well, to a native of the Celtic fringes of distant Northumberland still on the nursery slopes of life, here dangled before me were the bright lights of London, brought within range on no fewer than six occasions in each term and moreover with the blessing of the university authorities. And at about that same time it so happened that the Viscount Simon, one-time Lord Chancellor and a considerable ornament of the Inn, came to All Souls to judge a student moot. It took but that one evening to persuade me that if I was to give the Inns of Court a whirl, the Inner was the Inn to join.

Thus, and quite by chance, I came to the Inner Temple. It was a move I was never to regret. I was called in the Trinity term of 1956 along with six others, by the then Treasurer, Lord Birkett. Thus were laid the foundation stones for the next twenty-three years of my life at the Bar, followed by twenty-two years more of comparative solitude in the isolation of judicial office. Each of those years I remember with affection although I have to own that I then relinquished the post and sought retirement long before the allotted day. There is always a danger that the law will dominate the man if he stays too long. Now in retirement there is a little time for my other interests; and, most importantly, my treasured membership of the Inn continues.

MASTER ORDE

When I was a student at the Inn, prior to my call in June 1951, a group of us produced a small magazine for which we sought contributions from eminent Benchers giving their recollections of their first year at the Bar. Following publication of a number of distinguished contributions, I decided to write to the Prime Minister, Clement Attlee, who was of course a Bencher and whose portrait hangs in the Inn today. By return I received a tiny postcard, headed 10 Downing Street, SW1, with the following handwritten message: 'Dear Hirst, I remember nothing about my first year at the Bar. Yours sincerely, C R Attlee'. This was duly published to conclude the series. No wonder Mr Attlee was famous as a man of few words!

SIR DAVID HIRST

I was called to the Bar by the Inner Temple in 1951 and practised for a few years in London and on the Western Circuit. But in 1955 I gave up practice at the Bar for employment in the City. Later I decided to become a solicitor, for which purpose I had to be disbarred. I was admitted as a solicitor in 1963 and practised contentedly in that capacity until my retirement at the beginning of the new century.

Recently I met the Sub-Treasurer socially and, in the course of conversation, inquired whether it was open to me in my retirement to rejoin the Inn. He very good-naturedly undertook to look into the matter, and ultimately came back to me with the reply that he could find no record of my ever having been disbarred and would reactivate my membership. It would therefore appear that, according to the records, I have been a member of the Bar for the past fifty-five years, for forty-one of which I have also been a solicitor. I am not in favour of fusion, so it is with mixed feelings that I find myself in the forefront of the movement in that direction.

CHRISTOPHER (NICK) CRACE

Call night in Inner Temple Hall, 7 February 1961 with Lord Monkton presiding as Treasurer; Judge Trotman is standing sixth from the left at the back.

Looking back through fifty years at a place 5000 miles away is not an easy matter. The difficulties interposed by time and distance; an ageing memory; former friends and colleagues who cannot be accounted for; names forgotten. Then there is the retarding nostalgia of remembering the youthful past…

Leaving the sunny little village of Golden Grove, Demerara, in British Guiana (now Guyana), I travelled to London in October 1956 where, on a cold Michaelmas morning, I duly 'signed, sealed and delivered' a written Obligation by which I was 'held and firmly bound unto The Right Honourable Lord Justice Birkett, Treasurer, Arthur Moore Esquire, QC and G B McClure, two of the Masters of the Bench of the Honourable Society of the Inner Temple in fifty pounds of lawful money of Great Britain …'. You can imagine how overawed I was to be signing a bond to which the great Birkett was the principal signatory.
Student lectures supervised by the Council of Legal Education were held at Stone Building in Chancery Lane and the Old Hall in Lincoln's Inn, and provided a unique opportunity for meeting young people from almost all the Commonwealth countries and fostering future Commonwealth relations. Here too were foundation training programmes for the courtroom through debates, moots and advocacy contests, and the activities of the Inns of Court Students Union. My active involvement in all these, including arranging dances and sherry parties, led to my election as President of the Union for 1958/9 which made life around the four Inns considerably more enjoyable. Needless to say, these activities were not compatible with attending lectures regularly and writing exams successfully.I remember that cricket, after hard negotiating with the Benchers through the Sub-Treasurer, was eventually practised and played in the Inner Temple Garden. One of the Benchers recalled that many years ago, Norman Yardley (later captain of England), while a student member of the Inn, and his team had done the same thing in the same place. This fortuitous discovery of precedent, a doctrine so embedded in the legal psyche, allowed the learned Benchers to relent.

I cannot forget the rededication of the Temple Church, on Friday 7 November 1958. I was nearly excluded, or more aptly expelled, from these historic proceedings. Awaking late that morning, and having to launder the only shirt worth wearing to the Church, precious time was wasted which could have been better spent in timely travel between Archway and Temple stations. Consequently, my late appearance at the Church after evading a gatekeeper and several heavy-footed policemen created an unwelcome stir and murmuring among the gathered crowd, who were expectantly awaiting the imminent arrival of the royal party. As I slunk through the door to the students' section of the congregation, I felt the bewilderment of the Treasurers of the Inner and Middle Temple as they prematurely emerged to greet Her Majesty and His Royal Highness.

We are eight Inner Temple Members in Guyana and not likely to increase. Two of us have become Supreme Court Judges. As we all grow older with the Inner Temple, let us concur with Browning: 'The best is yet to be/The last of life for which the first was made'.

Judge Donald Trotman

The motorist provided a staple diet for the young common law barrister: in particular the careless and the dangerous driver. The briefs to defend them came in bundles, paying three guineas each, to be distributed largesse-like by Ernest, the clerk. It was to his entire discretion that the solicitor entrusted the allocation of this bounty: its final direction was all in Ernest's gift. This was my first awareness of the clerk's daunting power: an administrator, who had usually worked his way up from teaboy, he was remunerated by a handsome percentage of all fees earned by barristers in chambers. Responsible for the negotiation of fees with solicitors, he was the contact man and could direct and manipulate the flow of work largely as and to whom he pleased. He could make or break, and it was as well to be on the right side of him.

It was not a glamorous existence. Mr Pickwick had been rightly told: 'What fine places of slow torture barristers' chambers are for the young lawyer: the waiting – the hope – the disappointment – the fear – the misery – the poverty'.

There were unnerving interludes when nobody sought my services and, when they did, the trek was eternally round magistrates' courts. It was cold and wet in winter, hot and dusty in summer, and too often the time wasted awaiting hearing in these soulless places was intolerable: all pent-up energy for conflict seeped inexorably away and by three o'clock was almost wholly spent.

Yet soon a little written and advisory work came my way. When I was engaged on this in chambers, there was lunch in Hall at the Inn and always a contemporary for companionable chat at a table to which those of a like age gravitated and where the motherly waitress came to know and to spoil us all. Notes were compared, and the behaviour, prejudices and foibles of the newly encountered magistrates and judges discussed. The most recently reported utterances of the House of Lords too were subjected to a precocious, if often telling, scrutiny. There was the light-heartedness of youth but, at the same time, a great and essentially idealistic, forward-looking sense of purpose and ambition; and an extraordinary appetite for long hours of hard work in order to get on.

John Gray

I started my pupillage with R Graham Dow on 1 January 1959. James Stirling had recently become head of chambers, taking over from the Hon Victor Russell. Through neglecting to eat the necessary number of dinners I could not be called until later that year but tried to make myself useful in the meantime by doing routine paper work and attending court to take a note. On one such occasion I was asked to attend an undefended divorce and then to go to Chelsea to Victor to report upon how things had gone. He was a trustee of one of the parties.

The case was called on last before the luncheon adjournment in one of the many small offices which had to serve as court rooms to cope with the massive numbers of post-war divorces. The case was one of adultery but the evidence, even to my untutored eye, was about as bogus as it could be. The place was the Dorchester Hotel; the woman named was a resting actress; there was none of the customary evidence of the presence of clothing lying about the bedroom to suggest that the parties, whose heads were seen over the bedcovers by the floor waiter, were either naked or in nightclothes.

I could see that my account of proceedings was paining Victor somewhat and that my hint at collusion was not being well received. I turned to happier topics. The arrangements for the children of the family were declared excellent and the petitioner had looked delightful in a black coat and dress with a, then fashionable, pillbox hat. However, the old man's interest in such details appeared non-existent, so I asked him if there was any particular detail which he might like to hear about. 'Indeed there is,' he replied. 'What about that dreadful Miss Totty No-Drawers [the woman named]? Had she the shameless impudence to be present?' In the bus back to the

Temple I realised that I had for a moment been carried back to the late Victorian era and that such expressions were probably commonplace in the 'naughty nineties' when Victor was called to the Bar. Indeed, true it was that both Victor and his twin brother were godsons of Queen Victoria.

KEITH TOPLEY

The following is an extract from a piece first published in February 2002 in Counsel*:*

John Kennedy was still in the White House; Harold Macmillan was still in Downing Street; Margaret Thatcher was only a very junior minister; and Tony Blair had only just started at his prep school. The Queen was celebrating the tenth anniversary of her accession. Members of the Bar in independent practice numbered fewer than 2000, and only 5% of these were women. The Bar was not as yet a graduate profession – that came much later – and there was no requirement even to attend Bar School.

At that time there was very little junior work around. My taxable income in my first full year of practice was barely £500. Even allowing for inflation it was not a living wage and I only survived through the generosity of Inner Temple scholarships. Others spent evenings teaching, and one fellow pupil paid his way by doing all-night stints on the international telephone exchange. He is now a very successful silk.

Criminal legal aid was in its infancy, and we were regularly sent out on the first day of Assizes or Quarter Sessions, without any work at all, in the hope that we might pick up a dock brief at £2 4s 6d or even a court legal aid at £11. I fondly remember chairmen and deputy chairmen of Quarter Sessions trying hard to persuade a defendant that it would be so much better if he had legal aid rather than a dock brief, knowing that I would at least be able to pay for lunch and my rail fare on the proceeds.

The divorce Bar, as it was then called, relied extensively on undefended divorces; many a mortgage was paid for by a single day of undefendeds once a month. But the rate of turnover could be very variable. Some judges could barely get through half a dozen a day. Others could easily top twenty or thirty.

Those were the days of 'corrective training' and 'preventive detention', of 'kite briefs' and 'soups', of 'going special' and 'straw juniors'. It was no easier to get started then than it is now – though for rather different reasons. But the Bar has always been a high risk and a high reward profession. Those are its attractions.

MARTIN BOWLEY QC

A memory from 1963: Ted Laughton-Scott, a much loved member of the Bar, appeared in Reading Crown Court before another great character of that time, Judge Duveen, and against a third contemporary character, Old O'Malley, a Bencher of the Inn. Old O'Malley was, perhaps, the last practitioner to wear a bowler hat throughout the day, seated behind his desk in chambers. He was about ninety and had only a limited understanding of the changes in style which had overtaken advocacy since his early days. He was representing a driver who had crashed his car into Ted's client's car and the case proceeded in standard form, until Old O'Malley rose to cross examine, at which point he said to Ted's client, 'I put it to you that you are a liar, a thief and a rogue.' Ted rose, in astonishment, to object to this unmerited attack but Claude Duveen, who had a fine sense of the appropriate, waved a hand at him and said, 'Sit down, Mr Laughton-Scott, sit down. Nobody interrupts Mr O'Malley.'

JOHN BEVERIDGE QC

In the last ten years, I have found that a fair proportion of my work has been in London and I have therefore spent many nights in the barristers' accommodation in Paper Buildings. To my regret, this reasonably priced accommodation has now been replaced by accommodation that is, I am sure, much more luxurious but also much more expensive and – more importantly, I suspect – much less fun (for the single occupant).

The point is that the barristers' accommodation in Paper Buildings comprised two bedrooms with a shared bathroom, sitting room and kitchen. On my sojourns there, I met many (and varied) members of the Inn and others – students, overseas lawyers, High Court Judges and the Inn's head chef

as well as members of the Bar – some already known to me and others whom I met for the first time. The company more than made up for the occasional problem – such as the door handle in the windowless bathroom breaking when I tried to open the door from the inside, leaving me to contemplate starvation before a fortuitous rescue.

Of course, sharing a bathroom is not always straightforward and I remember one evening when I had to discuss the morning bathroom rota with a High Court Judge (now a Lord Justice of Appeal), who explained to me that he intended to have a lie-in until 6am. I was able to assure him that I did not foresee any prospect of our paths crossing on the way to the bathroom in the morning!

Anthony J Engel

In 1966 I set sail on the SS Marconi from Singapore, eventually reaching the Inner Temple some weeks later after a train journey from Genoa to London. I was enticed to take up law because the entrance qualifications were then rather relaxed – a minimum of five O-levels would almost certainly secure your admission if you also happened to have an acceptable amount in your bank account. I chose the Inner Temple at random – I thought there were too many schoolmates choosing Lincoln's Inn and the Inner Temple sounded rather a comfortable place. There were quite a number of Chinese in the Inner Temple, and many more of my classmates came from different parts of the world, including a good friend from British Guyana. Dinners were of course compulsory and I still think it was a wonderful opportunity to meet your fellow students whom you might never otherwise come across. It created a fellowship between the Bench and the students which is still a cherished relationship in all Commonwealth countries that I have visited.

My favourite place then was the Library. It was an ideal place to study and a cheap lunch was available across the way in the common room. I was called to the Bar in 1969 after having to wait a few extra months as I had to be at least twenty-one years old to be awarded the title of barrister at law (Inner Temple). A few years later, after I had taken a Diploma in International Law at Cambridge, I decided to practise in Hong Kong instead of Malaysia.

Cheng Huan

In 1986 I set up the Inner Temple Bar and Police Liaison Committee, which set out to establish high level links between the Home Office, the Bar and the Metropolitan Police. A number of Inner Temple members spent time with various units of the MPS in and around London, including the TSG riot squad patrolling Holloway, SO19 (the armed units) at their training base in Essex and front line area cars in various London boroughs. A number of us also lectured at the Detective Training College in Hounslow on rules of evidence, and the Inner Temple hosted a hugely successful reception, attended by Commissioners, ministers, law lords and Masters, and was variously described as a significant step forward in promoting a better working relationship between the Bar and the MPS.

MARK BROWNING

I was at the CLE during the academic year 1981/2. It was a rather strange and impersonal place. I joined the Inner Temple, which turned out to be a total contrast to the CLE – friendly, open, welcoming. I made some good friends at the student dining tables. From time to time there were lectures and moots after dinner, and one which stands out even now was a terrific apologia on behalf of Peter Rabbit delivered by the late Sir Christopher French during a Benchers' moot. Call night in July 1982 was a powerful experience and I have a crystal clear memory of it today. I did my pupillage with Sir Peregrine Simon at 1 Brick Court. That was a really fantastic time, when the late and very great Bob Alexander QC was head of chambers and Burly was chief clerk. When I was a student, I was fortunate to be awarded the Profumo Scholarship by the Inner Temple which kept the wolf from the door. Later, I remember one occasion during pupillage when I did some work for Bob Alexander which would have merited £30 if anything (those were different times) but he gave me a cheque for £250, an unbelievable amount of money but it was the only £250 I had right then and somehow he had known that.

PENELOPE HAMILTON BIRD

In 1987 Master Havers was appointed Lord Chancellor and the Benchers arranged a dinner in his honour for Wednesday 28 October, which I was to attend. On the previous Monday he resigned and I was appointed to succeed him. I suggested that if he concurred we should proceed with the dinner, and he readily agreed. The only change required was to add my wife's name to the list of guests, which already included Carol Havers. None who were present will forget the moving speech which Michael made on that occasion and the characteristically generous way in which he referred to my wife and me. The menus had been printed some weeks before and fortunately carried only the title 'Dinner given by the Benchers of the Inner Temple in honour of the Lord Chancellor'.

LORD MACKAY

Three Lord Chancellors: Lord Mackay (centre) with Lord Irvine (right) and Lord Falconer (left).

I was called to the Bar at the Inner Temple in Hilary term 1984. I was an unpaid pupil in 3 Paper Buildings having been introduced to those chambers by an Australian magistrate in Hong Kong where I was previously a criminal law solicitor advocate. This Hong Kong magistrate was called 'Bluey Wilson' and had spent some time in a Japanese prisoner of war camp on the Burma Road with Patrick Back QC who was then head of chambers and Leader of the Western Circuit. I dined in the Inner Temple as much as possible, and was fortunately invited into the Benchers' retirement room more than once after dining, where I was privileged to meet and converse with the late Lord Denning on more than one occasion. He told me a story about his time at the junior Bar when he owned an Austin Seven and would drive it all over the Western Circuit. Once he found himself under suspicion from the Somerset police who were investigating a burglary in which an Austin Seven had been used as the 'getaway car'. It was of course a case of mistaken identity; but he was not very pleased at having his collar felt.

ALAN R WALTON

Like many of my generation, I left school at the age of fifteen with no qualifications and it was by means of an Access to Law course that I gained a place as an LLB student at the University of the West of England in 1992. I was close to fifty when, as very much the 'senior' of my year, I began my degree course. Thanks to the intelligence and good nature of my younger class mates I had the most wonderful time for three years. I enjoyed it so much that I stayed on for postgraduate education as a 'Bar Finalist'.

At the conclusion of the course I, together with two young friends, Nicole and Nick, sat the Bar Final examinations in London, We all failed and so began again, dining in gowns that were sometimes too long or too short, eating food that reminded me of my RAF days, sharing less than luxurious accommodation during dining, swotting and fretting, crying into our beer in the students' bar and suffering the occasional consequential headache. We need not have worried. We all failed again. As I progress through my sixth decade, still a student member and an occasional visitor to the Pegasus Bar, I am privileged to be part of the Inner Temple and I am grateful to a community that has allowed me to be part of something rather special. There is an agreeable irony in being a pensioner student.

PETER GREY

The Inner Temple has become a home from home very quickly since I became a member in March 2003. I remember signing the famous book alongside some great legal and other famous names throughout history who have been members, and considering myself very lucky to be in the position I was in. Nothing has changed in those three years. I have joined an elite crowd of splendid individuals who found the time and courtesy to welcome in new members like myself at a time when the concept and very nature of the Bar was changing. This is where the Inner Temple came into its own for me. Although my time at Northumbria University certainly prepared me for practice, the Inner Temple helped make me the type of person who could become one with the Bar. The Educational Days with members of LAMADA made me more open to what was to come, encouraging me do things I would not normally do with close friends, let alone in public! The weekend in Windsor was also a learning curve in how students, pupil barristers, silks and judges could interact together. It put away any thoughts that the Bar was not a modern profession but also had those private and traditional parts that make it so unique in our society. The Inner Temple is a modern organisation steeped in history and tradition, and long may it thrive.

IAN BRANDON

Inner Temple has always had a strong tradition of inclusion regardless of social, cultural or economic background. When it was announced that gay men and lesbians would be able to take part in a ceremony which provided us with the same legal rights as heterosexual married couples, Mark and I knew that it was very important to us to hold our celebrations there. On that magical day – 10 June 2006 – ours was the first ever civil partnership ceremony to be held at the Inn. The moving ceremony in the Parliament Chamber was followed by a reception in the garden and then a sumptuous banquet in the Hall, with guests from all corners of the globe, followed by fireworks in the garden and dancing until midnight. Our memories are blessed in the knowledge that, in marking the happiest day in our lives, those who joined us in our celebrations were also helping us to make history.

S CHELVAN

I attended a lecture given by John Mortimer, my particular favourite person, about ten years ago, in which he compared the Commercial Bar to the Criminal Bar. He said, 'you go to the Commercial Bar – human beings had swindled other human beings to the point of penury – and you would have thought that a punch up would have been in order. Instead, there they all sit, staring at each other with gloomy faces. In contrast, go to the Old Bailey. One human being is accused of killing another human being, and what do you find in court? Laughter!'

WINSTON ASANTE

This is a picture of Dorien Lovell-Pank QC playing 'drunk jenga' at this year's Inner Temple Latimer House Advocacy weekend. It sums up the way the Inner Temple and its members do so much for the younger members of the Bar, in a way that has no pretension, no condescension. The members are a constant support and inspiration to those of us at the junior end of the Bar; they have not forgotten what it's like to be a lowly baby barrister.

RHIANNON LLOYD

The Employed Bar: From the Front Row to the British Boardroom

Master Webb

Few activities are, in my experience, more thrilling than securing the confidence of a client, understanding the drama that has brought him to a court and presenting a view of that drama on his behalf with force and honesty. It can be a cathartic process for the client, a pleasure and a skill for the advocate and it allows for the orderly resolution of human conflict in many cases. The stillness of the court, the authority of the judge and the submission to a common law binding all those taking part adds an element of comfort and certainty, much envied in those countries where it cannot be enjoyed.

That is not, however, necessarily the whole story of being a barrister. Dispute resolution, whatever its useful and indispensable form, has two dessicating features. The first is that the events under discussion have, necessarily, already occurred. An archaeology of the facts must always be the opening chapter. Secondly, the resolution must always be solved according to a certain, even if hard to ascertain, template, such as a statute, the common law or an individual's judicial discretion. These features, when eternally combined, can produce an effect of ennui in the eternal practitioner: an ennui which sometimes displays as simply that, sometimes perhaps as a slight pomposity or even, in extreme cases, a feeling on behalf of the advocate that Nanny knows best.

Once these symptoms occur, it is time to move on. 'We pass this way but once.' The skills of the Bar are deployable in some industries outside the Bar, and while the practising Bar have on occasion viewed the employed Bar with apparent disdain – I saw this quite clearly while helping with the Clementi review – this is, in my experience of both, a mistake.

Master Webb.

I was ten years a silk in private practice and have been for eight years General Counsel at British Airways and a director of the London Stock Exchange. I also sit on the Board of the BBC. Each period has been as stimulating as the other; at the LSE we have had half a dozen hostile bids in eighteen months – each time the stock price has risen, the advisors have enthused, the 'business model' has been re-encrypted and the stakeholders (customers, staff and shareholders) have all benefited, at least so far! At the BBC we have a wholly new corporate structure, a new licence fee; blogs, podcasts and the net. A world turned upside down, where the public broadcasts to us in much the same way as we do to them. The interactive button is truly a two-way street and the videocam artist is today's Fellini.

At BA we have erected the London Eye, we have had the trauma of 9/11 when aircraft were first used as missiles and weapons of war, and when we turned round several aircraft in the air on their way to America, the grounding of Concorde, two unlawful bouts of un-balloted secondary industrial action and, continuously over the last eight years, over 600 flights a day to over 100 airports, long haul and short haul, frills and no frills. We now look forward to T5 in a few months time and a new long haul fleet after that.

Big events in the business world, and even routine ones, such as the carriage round the world of over thirty million passengers a year, brings challenges, and real time challenges, which can be at least as absorbing as the discovery of the true meaning of section 4(A)(ii)(b) when applied to events of the recent (and sometimes not so recent) past before a Tribunal similarly so focused, and guided, or misled as the case may be, by Precedent, whether binding or merely 'helpful'.

And so I would close with one of English literature's earliest and most balanced sentences, from St Augustine: 'Do not despair, one of the thieves was saved; do not presume, one of the thieves was damned.'

There is life for barristers both within and without the practising Bar, and good fun it is too! The practising Bar need not despise the employed Bar, nor need the latter display more chips than fish. It would be good if the governance of the Bar, and of the Inns, could lead the field in the recognition of that truth.

Robert Webb QC was Head of Chambers at 5 Bell Yard 1988–98 and is now General Counsel at British Airways.

THE INNER TEMPLE AND LIFE AS A JUDGE

Master Rix

Fleet Street runs like the River Styx between the Temple, to its south, and the Royal Courts of Justice, to its north. The comparison with the Styx, the river across which the gloomy ferryman Charon ferried departed souls into the underworld, should not perhaps be pressed too far, although Fleet Street is itself named after a subterranean river. Even so, when a barrister leaves his chambers in the Temple to take up an appointment on the High Court Bench, he is often said to be going 'over the road', and in some sense he is like a departed soul, exchanging the earthly beauty of the Temple with its courtyards, gardens and human life for the austere and closeted after-life of the judge behind locked doors in a vast Gormanghast palace which professes not humanity but dominion.

'In a way', as Lord Denning used to say when he wanted to commit himself in the course of argument neither to agreeing nor to disagreeing. My simile is only made for the purpose of contrasting what might be with what really is. The change upon crossing the road to become a judge is profound, but Fleet Street does not separate; it joins together. The pleasures and benefits of the Inn are not lost but appreciated all the more, and the life of the judge is satisfying and absorbing, largely for the very reason that he, or she, remains, through the Inn, a part of the world. Fleet Street, after all, is not a river but is like the Rialto; it is a bridge.

I would like to try to explain this, first by saying something about the life of a judge, and secondly by placing that life in the context of membership of an Inn like my own, the Inner Temple.

A judge may no longer participate in the life of his earlier profession, let us say at the Bar, but the collegiality of the Bench goes beyond compensation and is a jewel in its own right. Although the work of a trial judge is solitary, for he, or she, sits alone on the Bench of his court, nevertheless he is surrounded by colleagues with whom he has the most cordial of relations and on whom he is able to rely for the utmost help. Moreover, in the Court of Appeal, where I now sit, since most cases require a Bench of three, that collegiality extends into every area of work. We have our individual responsibilities, but our search for analysis, understanding and solutions proceeds multilaterally.

I am often asked how life on the Bench compares with life at the Bar, and whether I miss my old profession. A career at the Bar is a wonderful job, but its many satisfactions are replaced by pleasures which I think are still more considerable. The barrister has to advise, but the judge has to decide. The barrister has to advocate, but the judge has to solve. The barrister has to advance the interests of his client, but the judge has to conduct a hearing fairly and to find a solution which will not only do justice in the instant case but also point the way to justice in other similar cases. Whereas the barrister by and large knows where he wants to go, what constitutes success for the client, the judge does not have that guide, but has to discover for himself where he wants to go. The barrister assists the court in finding, analysing and even developing the law, but the judge has the ultimate responsibility of stating it. Whether in the give and take of argument, or in extemporaneous judgments, or in the more carefully considered writing of reserved judgments, the judge is soon made aware of the way in which lawyers and their clients can take comfort or sorrow in a single word or phrase. These heightened responsibilities give to the work a new sense of absorbing interest and satisfaction.

The judge also of course has to find the facts, although generally speaking that is the role of the trial rather than appellate judge. The facts can often be harder to determine than the law. Again, the roles of barrister and judge differ. The barrister has to distance himself from his own witnesses, other than his client, and generally lives in terror of what they will turn out to say; while with the opposing witnesses he is locked in the combat of cross examination. In many ways the barrister is either too distant from or too close to the action. The judge, on the other hand, is first and foremost an observer, even if he may ask a few questions himself. The whole of life comes before him. His role is not to extract the evidence but properly to understand and evaluate it. He needs a very human eye and ear.

Master Rix.

In this life of the judge, what, if any, is the role of the Inn? All barristers must be called to the Bar by an Inn, and once a member, always a member. Translation from Bar to Bench still leaves the new judge a member of his or her Inn. It might be thought that this is undesirable: that institutional arrangements should be put in place to prevent any unnecessary meeting between advocates and judges, and that therefore one of the consequences of becoming a judge would be that the judge would have to leave his Inn. However, in this country that has never been adopted as a principle. On the contrary, judges have continued to play a full role in their Inns and it has been thought not only right but desirable and even necessary that they should do so.

This is because of the general belief that one of the most important functions of an Inn is to provide a meeting ground for all ranks of those who are concerned in the interface of the court process. The would-be advocate starts as a student barrister, qualifies and is called to the Bar, progresses in the profession as his practice matures, may become a Queen's Counsel and indeed a leading member of his profession and may then either remain to guide the profession or progress to the Bench. In civil law countries where the Bench is an entirely separate profession from that of advocacy, and is entered upon at an early age, matters may be different; but in common law countries this progression is an organic development. At each stage, the student, young entrant, maturing advocate, Queen's Counsel, senior advocate and judges of all levels, however different from one another in their personal lives, come together to learn from each other. The students, including the many who come from overseas, both from the Commonwealth and elsewhere, bring their youthful modernity, their novel learning from the universities and their insights into a world which is many decades younger than that of senior practitioners or judges. The practitioners bring the practical concerns of their profession and the experience of daily exposure to the problems of litigants; and also, for passing to the students and younger members of the Inn, the ethos and standards of their profession as well as considerable help in the form of advocacy training and continuing education. The judges bring their own standards and a mature viewpoint from the other side of the court room. Each group learns from the other. All are on view.

I have always enjoyed the atmosphere of the Inner Temple, but in the past nearly fourteen years as a judge more than ever. It is always a pleasure to cross the road from north to south, whether it is for my daily lunch in Inner Temple Hall, or for a committee meeting in respect of some aspect of the Inn's governance, or for a lecture from a distinguished barrister or judicial colleague or other eminent speaker, or for a dinner with, say, university lecturers or European lawyers, or for a student dining night or Call Night, when the students or new entrants take centre stage.

There are some of my colleagues who regularly eat lunch at their desks. But that is not for me if I can possibly help it, even if it means an earlier start or later finish to the day. I find it necessary to leave my room at the Royal Courts, for however brief a period, to cross the Rialto of Fleet Street, to breathe in the day and snatch lunch at the Inner Temple. As for committee meetings, they are now on the wane, for their apogee was in 2005 when I had the great good fortune and inestimable honour to be Treasurer of the Inn; but they still continue, and that too is a privilege as they bring me face to face with issues of governance. And it is always an undiluted pleasure to meet with students, who represent the future. Indeed, Call Nights in the Temple Church, when I as Treasurer did the calling and had the opportunity of addressing the new barristers, were to my mind the most significant events of my year.

Whenever I am in the Inn, I look with pleasure at its portraits of judges of other periods, far off or more recent. Some faces are more appealing than others. Some are kindly, some stern, some unforgiving, some intelligent, some, surprisingly, without the light of reason in their eyes. Perhaps that was the fault of the artist. Fortunately, no one will ever want to have my portrait painted.

The Rt Hon Lord Justice Rix was Treasurer of the Inn in 2005.

LIFE ON CIRCUIT

Master Williamson

In 1685 Judge Jeffreys went out on the Western Circuit to dispense the King's justice, at what became known as the 'Bloody Assize'. What he was doing was fulfilling a function (perhaps over-zealously) which High Court judges were required to do then and continue to do to this day. London has always been regarded as the source of judicial wisdom, 'where it's at', and Circuit succumbs to the justice brought down from above, on Commission.

Circuits, the areas outside London, are the way the country has been split up for the administration of Justice. They are the South Eastern, the Western, the Wales and Chester, the Midland, the Northern and the North Eastern. From time to time the boundaries of the Circuits have been redrawn. The Northern Circuit covered the whole of the north of England until 1876 when the North Eastern Circuit was formed to the east of the Pennines. Even now when a Bar Mess is held by barristers of the Northern and North Eastern Circuits together, it is deemed to be a mess of the old Northern Circuit. The Leaders and the Juniors of the mess speak in unison rather than yield superiority one to the other.

In recent times the Midland and Oxford Circuit have lost Oxford to the South Eastern Circuit. Winchester also was at risk of being swallowed by the South Eastern Circuit, but this was resisted successfully by their Presiding Judge of the day Mrs Justice (as she then was) Hallett. Thus it is clear that the nature and delineation of the Circuits are the creation of central administration and always were.

In times past it must be the case that no barrister actually permanently practised on Circuit, though the successful barrister might have his country seat and be a Recorder for a town or city well away from London. Some barristers must have been more inclined to visit some Circuits rather than others, if they left London at all. One pictures the Judge travelling from Assize town to Assize town on Circuit, staying in lodgings, followed by the barristers staying in lodgings nearby. Hence, at the end of the day, barristers got together in an Inn and had dinner, a Bar Mess. Even in my day at a Bar Mess, the Leader would ask 'all those who have enjoyed the comfort of their wives on Circuit' to stand up. The culprits would be 'congratulated' ie fined in sums which doubtless helped to pay for the wine.

Life on Circuit has become much more regularised for the Bar with the establishment of chambers out of London, and with a reasonably steady supply of work. Prior to 1971 this would be some Assize work, Civil and Criminal, Quarter Sessions where crime was dealt with by a Recorder or County Sessions, and the County Court. I recall the arrival of the High Court Judges in Leeds for the Assize. To begin there was a service in the Leeds Parish Church and the Judges would then appear in Court One in Leeds Town Hall wearing full court dress including full bottom wigs. There was the reading of the commission of 'Oyez and Terminer and Goal Delivery'. Each of Her Majesty's Judges was then announced in turn and acknowledged, eg 'Raymond Hinchliffe Knight'. Then the business would begin. Even as a most junior barrister I generally managed to get a plea in front of a red judge; something that does not happen now.

By the time I was practising in Leeds, not only had Circuit life been long established but it was jealously protected from a professional point of view. Counsel from London was regarded with the greatest suspicion. A silk coming up from London who was not a member of Circuit was said to be going 'Special'; and if he had a junior from London, there was a requirement that a junior from the Circuit should also be briefed. The silk clearly had to pay some sort of fee to Circuit. As the North Eastern Circuit seemed to be rather short in the necessary talent, London silks came quite often and the Circuit cellar bulged with an embarrassing amount of silver and wine as a result. There came a time, unsurprisingly, when this practice was regarded as unacceptable, and silks and juniors were able to raid the North Eastern Circuit with impunity.

Of course the Bar was much smaller in the 1960s than it is now, but there seemed to be enough to do. Lists on Assize were fixed by the clerks, and the powerful clerks were the ones who clerked the most successful and busiest barristers, the top silks. The clerk's job

Master Williamson.

was to ensure that the lists were fixed through the length and breadth of Circuit – Newcastle, York, Leeds and Sheffield – so that the busy and successful remained busy and successful. The top barristers were of course the silks who were members of Circuit. They had as juniors been members of a London set who maintained their Circuit connection on taking silk, or they had been juniors practising in chambers on Circuit, who on taking silk were obliged to leave their local set and join London chambers.

This rule was eventually relaxed following some quite vituperative debate, but it was another rule which could not survive.

The same top silks were of course the Recorders of the major towns and cities and, needless to say, their Quarter Sessions did not sit during the time of the Assize. I have appeared in Bradford Quarter Sessions on the day after Boxing Day. There were of course deputies or assistants who sat in courts adjacent to the Recorder or even in the Recorder's place. They were often steady senior junior barristers, the type one would expect until recently to be the mainstay of the Circuit Bench.

Thus, following the 1971 Courts Act, it came about that many who had sat as deputy or assistant Recorders now became appointed in the permanent posts of Circuit Judges. Crown Courts were created and County Court Judges found that in future they would share their status and their work with other judges. In effect Circuit Judges were to try civil and criminal matters, though individuals try to have their preferences for work respected, so that some do no civil and others do little crime. A further development through the years has been for certain Circuit Judges to try serious crime, including murder, and for Circuit Judges on occasions to try in the County Court complex cases involving a lot of money. Thus the division between High Court and Circuit Judges' jurisdiction is often blurred. An area which has developed considerably is Family Law and on Circuit much of the work falls on the Circuit Judge or District Judge. There is much to do. Certain centres have also gained a Mercantile Court, which again can keep work away from London.

The organisation of the Courts has of course become much more formalised, with the Civil Service now thoroughly in charge. Each Circuit has a Circuit Administrator and a Regional Administrator, each with a support staff. The Courts are run by Court Managers, lists are fixed by Listing Officers (notoriously one of the worst jobs, but a path to promotion). Court Clerks and Ushers are all Civil Servants in the employ of the Department of Constitutional Affairs. In overall supervision of the Circuit's court business are the two Presiding Judges, High Court Judges appointed for four years in two year stages so that the Judge when first appointed is the Junior of the two for two years and then graduates in turn to be the Senior Presider. This means there is a High Court presence always on Circuit, and the only Circuit the Presiding Judge has anything to do with during the term as Presider is the one Circuit to which he/she is appointed.

In the North Eastern Circuit, Scarborough, Rotherham and Pontefract were among the towns which lost their Quarter Sessions but did not gain a Crown Court. York, once a proud Assize City, is now a two-court centre which rarely, if ever, attracts a High Court Judge. On the other hand, Teesside Crown Court where Middlesbrough Quarter Sessions used to be is now a Class One Centre.

With so much movement by barristers from centre to centre and from London out onto Circuits, many members of the Bar have learned the attractions of life on Circuit. Circuit for the Bar is the centre of information and activity for the profession. Through the Circuit Leader and the Circuit committees there is representation on the Bar Council. Circuit arranges and conducts training for pupils and advocacy training. In any activity it is loyalty to the Circuit which is the motivation. One is rarely moved to ask a Circuiteer which Inn he or she belongs to; it is not relevant. There is a Grand Court each term to discuss policy issues and if necessary to elect the Circuit Junior. A great event on the North Eastern Circuit is

Christmas Mess at the Merchant Adventurers' Hall in York. In excess of 200 members of the Bar will eat and drink together, sing carols together and enjoy the entertainment of the revellers.

Of course, what is obvious to many who may have hankered to be in the centre of things in London is the life-style advantage. It has always been the case that housing is less expensive and mobility about the Circuit that much easier. So one can have a pleasing house and be back every night from any corner of the Circuit to enjoy being at home. For the family, schools provide a better and less expensive choice, and in many ways life is much more normal. On a recent visit to Norwich Crown Court I was reminded how a local Bar, away from the relatively hot-house atmosphere of the Temple, the Royal Courts of Justice, the Old Bailey and even El Vino's, can have a most enjoyable professional life. It is said that a third of the Bar now practises outside London. I am confident that proportion will grow.

Developments in certain cities confirm my belief. Manchester already has two Crown Court centres: Crown Square and Minshull Street. There are plans for a major County Court centre in Manchester, which will no doubt draw work from the whole of Greater Manchester and perhaps beyond. In Birmingham, I believe, a permanent High Court presence is planned. There must be other developments in other parts of the country, but if Southampton's Cricket Ground is to be granted Test Match status, what next?

Stephen Williamson QC is a practising barrister with 4 King's Bench Walk and 7 Park Square chambers and Treasurer of the Inn in 2007.

Margaret Killerby draws our attention to the following:

A Parliament held on 8 February in the year 43 Elizabeth I 1600/1, Daveys Treasurer, it is Ordered that:

> *'Whereas divers and many gentlemen, fellows of this House and society, are very negligent and slack to go abroad into the City of London and other places in cloaks and hats, and some booted, and spurred, and weaponed, and some unweaponed, and otherwise unseemly attired and arrayed, contrary to the ancient orders of this House and government of the same, and also do wear long hair, very indecent and unseemly for gentlemen of their profession, it is now at this present Parliament, Ordered and decreed that no gentleman, which is now or at any finis hereafter shall be fellow of this House and Society, shall wear any long or unseemly hair or be otherwise unseemly attired and arrayed.'*

Now in the Easter Term in the year 16 Elizabeth II 1966, Silsoe Treasurer, it is Ordered that:

> *'The Order of 43 Elizabeth I should be read again by members and students of the Society, gentlemen and ladies, and that gentlemen members are unseemly attired and arrayed if they wear no tie at lunch or dinner and that lady members should not ape the clothing of gentlemen members.'*

Lord Silsoe in 1966 as Treasuer.

Music & Recreation

Lord Robert Dudley and the 1561 Revels

Clare Rider

Lord Robert Dudley, by Steven van der Meulen c1560.

In 1561 the Inner Temple had good reason to be grateful to Lord Robert Dudley, favourite of Elizabeth I and her Master of the Horse. As a result of his personal intervention with the Queen the Inner Temple retained its sovereignty over Lyon's Inn, one of its three associated Inns of Chancery, which was in danger of falling to the Middle Temple. The Middle Temple had been deprived of Strand Inn, one of its two Inns of Chancery, when it had been requisitioned in 1549 by Lord Protector Somerset, in order to build Somerset House on the site. A case for the transfer of Lyon's Inn, which was the smallest and furthest west of the Inner Temple's three Inns of Chancery, was made to the Lord Keeper, Sir Nicholas Bacon, by the two Lord Chief Justices of the royal court, both former members of the Middle Temple. The Benchers of the Inner Temple 'considering the earnestness of the said Chief Justices' made 'humble suit' to Lord Robert Dudley 'as to our chief refuge'. As a result of Dudley's intervention, Elizabeth not only sent her ring as a token to Sir Nicholas Bacon, but also spoke to him in person, ordering him 'to cease and no further proceed or meddle in the same matter, but to suffer us to continue our said ancient and just possession to the readings of the same three Houses of Chancery'. Being a member of Gray's Inn, which was 'of ancient amity, familiarity, and friendship with this our House', Bacon was apparently pleased to oblige. Lyon's Inn, now buried under the modern Aldwych, was to remain in the ownership of the Inner Temple until its demolition in 1863.

The Benchers of the Inner Temple were delighted, and promised that Dudley's favour to the Inn would remain as a 'perpetual memory to our successors', and that his coat of arms should forever adorn the Inn's Hall, an undertaking honoured to this day. They also granted special admission to Lord Robert Dudley and his kinsman, John Dudley, in 1561, and to Robert's brother, Lord Ambrose Dudley, in 1562, and granted Lord Robert (later to become Earl of Leicester) a plot of land within the Inn on which to construct his own chambers. A further sign of the Inner Temple's gratitude to Dudley was his election as Lord Governor of the Christmas revels in 1561, a rare instance of the appointment of an outsider to the principal role in the Inn's Christmas and New Year festivities. The annual Christmas revels were at the heart of the Inner Temple's social calendar and, indeed, participation in the entertainment, feasting, dramatic interludes and dancing was a compulsory part of the law students' training. However, the 1561 revels were exceptional in their scale and cost, borne by the

Opposite: Robert Dudley's arms in the west window of the Hall.

members by means of a special levy. Rarely did the Inns of Court entertain so lavishly, and seldom do we have a written description of events. Gerard Legh's account of the 1561 revelry in his contemporary 'bestseller', *The Accedence of Armorie*, offers a unique observer's insight into the occasion.

Legh's account, a curious mixture of narrative and illusion, introduces us to the Court of Prince Pallaphilos, lieutenant and devoted champion to the Goddess Pallas (an allegory for Queen Elizabeth), in whose honour the entertainments were to take place. Lord Robert was to act as Prince Pallaphilos ('lover of Pallas'), the 'Constable and Marshal' of the revels. In one of the principal scenes, the Prince entertained 'ambassadors' from the other Inns of Court and Inns of Chancery to a grand feast, at which were served 'tender meats, sweet fruits and dainty delicates, confectioned with curious cookery'. Also present were 'royal councillors and officers' played by the prominent members of the Inn, including Richard Onslow as 'Lord Chancellor', Anthony Stapleton as 'Lord Treasurer', Christopher Hatton as 'Master of the Game' and no fewer than four 'Masters of the Revels'. The Prince then selected twenty-four knights to form the Order of the Pegasus and initiated them in a fictional version of the garter ceremony, enjoining them to serve the Goddess Pallas and to sacrifice to her in her Temple (the Temple Church). Then followed examples of knightly pursuits demonstrated by the members of the Order of the Pegasus, armed with allegorical armour and shields, and each with a collar of double Ps and a pendant Pegasus round his neck. It is surely no coincidence that, as Master of the Queen's Horse, Dudley adopted the Order of the Pegasus, with the device of the flying horse as its arms. This is the first recorded instance of the employment of the Pegasus symbol by the Inn and it has been suggested, with some foundation, that this is the reason for its subsequent adoption as the Inn's emblem.

In addition to the general entertainments, the Inns of Court traditionally commissioned plays for their revels, the most notable example being Shakespeare's *Twelfth Night* performed at the Middle Temple. In the Inner Temple, the renowned playwright Arthur Broke provided some of the dramatic interludes for the 1561 Inner Temple revels. He was granted honorary membership of the Inn for his pains, his pledges on his admission being fellow dramatists, Thomas Sackville and Thomas Norton, both members of the Inner Temple. Sackville and Norton also played a significant role in the 1561 revels, co-authoring a play entitled *Gorboduc* or *The Tragedy of Ferrex and Porrex*, which was performed in the Inn at New Year festivities and shortly afterwards, in January 1562, before Elizabeth I at the royal court 'by the gentlemen of the Inner Temple'. Legh does not seem to have been present at these performances, and unfortunately the interludes written by Broke for this occasion have not survived. However, we are fortunate that Sackville and Norton's play was subsequently printed in two editions, an unofficial version in 1565 and an authorised version in 1571, both available to the modern reader and described by an anonymous observer.

¶ The Tragidie of Ferrex and Porrex, ſet forth without addition or alteration but altogether as the ſame was ſhewed on ſtage before the Queenes Maieſtie, about nine yeares paſt, vz. the xviij. day of Ianuarie. 1561. by the gentlemen of the Inner Temple.

Seen and allowed. &c.

Imprinted at London by Iohn Daye, dwelling ouer Alderſgate.

Title page of the 1571 edition of The Tragidie of Ferrex and Porrex *or* Gorboduc *by Sackville and Norton*

The play recounted the legend of Gorboduc, King of Britain, who divided his realm during his lifetime between his two sons, Ferrex and Porrex, against the advice of his principal advisors. The elder son, Ferrex, aggrieved at being denied half his inheritance and suspicious of his younger brother's ambitions, set about raising soldiers to defend himself against Porrex. On hearing of Ferrex's military preparations, Porrex sent his own troops against his elder brother and had him killed. Queen Videna, to avenge the death of her favourite elder son, brought about the murder of Porrex. The people, moved by these cruel and unnatural deeds, rose in rebellion and slew both king and queen. In the vacuum of power, the nobility united to destroy the rebels. However, since the succession remained uncertain, the nobles soon divided and fell into civil war, in which both they and most of their offspring were destroyed, leaving the throne open to foreign claimants. At the end of the tragedy, Eubulus, wise counsellor and former secretary to King Gorboduc, predicted 'the woeful wrack and utter ruin of this noble realm' for want of an established heir. Having drawn a bleak picture of murder, rape and pillage, Eubulus brings the drama to an end on a more optimistic note:

> *Of justice, yet must God restore*
> *This noble crown unto the lawful heir:*
> *For right will always live, and rise at length,*
> *But wrong can never take deep root to last.*

After all that has occurred, his optimism is unconvincing. Interestingly the play, which predates those of Shakespeare, appears to be the first truly English tragedy, independent of a classical theme, and the first English drama composed in blank verse.

However, the 1561 revels were not envisaged purely as entertainment. Running throughout the masquing, drama and feasting was a propagandist theme, aimed at Elizabeth I, who was procrastinating on the subject of her marriage. The message could scarcely have been clearer: wed a suitable English husband and produce an heir to prevent the country falling into future chaos. Displaying Lord Robert Dudley's handsome figure and talents at their best and emphasising his desirability as a partner, the revelry was clearly intended to favour his own suit to the Queen. Although not present at the Inner Temple, Elizabeth I would surely have received a detailed report of events there and Dudley's pivotal role in them, and she could hardly have missed the message embodied in the text of *Gorboduc* when it was performed before her at the royal court. However, this sustained attack proved fruitless, for the Queen was to die unmarried and childless in 1603.

The Inn might have been unsuccessful in promoting Dudley's marriage suit, but it continued to honour its undertakings to its patron, allowing his heirs to continue to nominate occupants for his chambers, and ensuring that none of the Inn's members acted professionally against him or his family and that his arms remained in the windows of the successive Inner Temple Halls. However, arguably Dudley's most lasting legacy is the Pegasus emblem which continues to be displayed throughout the Inn. While some have ascribed its origins to the Knights Templar's seal of a horse with two riders and others to the misrepresentation of a broken tile of a knight on horseback in the Temple Church, the surely most convincing argument for its adoption is as a tribute to the Master of the Queen's Horse, the 'chief patron and defender' of the Inner Temple.

The west window of the Hall.

Extract from Gerard Legh's description of a feast in Inner Temple Hall in 1561

He [the herald] brought me into a long gallery that stretcheth itself along the hall near the Prince's table where I saw the Prince set, a man of tall personage, of manly countenance, somewhat brown of visage, strongly featured and thereto comely proportioned in all ligaments of body. At the nether end of the same table were placed the ambassadors of divers princes. Before him stood the Carver, Server and Cup-bearer, with great number of gentlemen waiters attending his person, the Ushers making place [for] strangers of sundry regions that came to behold the honour of this mighty captain. After the placing of these honourable guests, the Lord's Steward, Treasurer, and Keeper of Pallas' Seal, with divers honourable personages of that nobility, were placed at a side table near adjoining the Prince on the right hand. At another side were placed the Treasurer of the Household, Secretary, the Prince's Serjeant of Law, the four Masters of the Revels, the King of Arms, the Dean of the Chapel, and divers gentlemen pensioners to furnish the same. At another table on the other side were the Master of the Game and his Chief Ranger, Masters of the Household, Clerks of the Green Cloth and Check, with divers other strangers to furnish the same. On the other side against them began the table [of] the Lieutenant of the Tower, accompanied with divers Captains of Footbands and Shot. At the nether end of the Hall began the table [of] the High Butler and Pantler, Clerks of the Kitchen, Master Cook of the Privy Kitchen, furnished throughout with the soldiers and guard of the Prince. All which, with [a] number of inferior officers placed and served in the Hall, beside the great resort of strangers, I spare to write. The Prince so served with tender meats, sweet fruits, and dainty delicates, confectioned with curious cookery, as it seemed wonder, a world to serve the provision. And at every course the trumpets blew the courageous blast of deadly war, with noise of drum and fife, with the sweet harmony of violins, sackbuts, recorders and cornets, with other instruments of music, as it seemed Apollo's harp had turned their stroke. Thus the Hall was served after the most ancient order of the island, in commendation whereof I say, I have also seen the service of great princes in solemn seasons and times of triumph, yet the order hereof was not inferior to any.

MUSIC AND MASQUES

Andrew Ashbee

From the fifteenth century onwards attendance at one of the Inns of Court became something of a rite of passage for most sons of gentlemen. Often their fathers had arranged their admission before they spent some time at university; then they came on to the Inns to gain some understanding of the law before taking up authority over their country estates. Sir John Fortescue asserted in the mid-fifteenth century that young men went to the Inns of Court not merely to learn law but also to 'learn singing, and all kinds of music, dancing and such other accomplishments and diversions (which are called revels) as are suitable to their quality, and such as are usually practised at court. At other times... the greater part apply themselves to the study of the law.' His giving pride of place to cultural activities over study of the law is perhaps unintentional, but for some no doubt they took priority. The royal court was the other draw, with its opportunities for social contact and preferment. Many courtiers used the Inns as a stepping stone between university and court, and the Inns themselves were always keen to promote an aristocratic image.

Searches through the archives of the various Inns produce little hard information concerning the cultural life of their members. This is not surprising, since culture was extracurricular and so had to be supplied (and paid for) by the members themselves. One exception was payments to musicians for their services at the two main times of revels – feasts and music with dancing of the post-revels. The first was for All Saints (1 November) and Candlemas (2 February) and the second was for the Christmas festival. In this the Inns were echoing practice at the English court, where the Revels Office was responsible for providing the entertainments during the revels season, which also began on All Saints Day and took in the traditional feasts around Christmas and up to Twelfth Night, Candlemas and Shrovetide (the Sunday, Monday and Tuesday before Ash Wednesday). Plays took place in the afternoons, but music and masques were evening activities.

Within the four Inns just twenty-seven named musicians have been found in the records before 1642 – not a large haul over 200 years. During the sixteenth century these generally comprise a number of harpers (who also had a long and distinguished place at the English court). There is no written harp music by these men and it is believed their principal occupation was to perform improvised songs and ballads of 'old adventures' in the troubadour tradition. It is not clear what the duties of these musicians at the Inns were. Were they employed to play during meals, or afterwards, their small retainer of 40s a year being supplemented by donations from the assembled company? Presumably they were able to perform for dances too.

In the second half of the sixteenth century groups of between two and four minstrels were engaged. Some were very obscure and otherwise unknown, but others were members of the City of London waits – among the most accomplished musicians of their time. The waits were also automatically admitted as members of the City Musicians' Company. At the Inner Temple the house musicians received 40s for playing on All Saints Day and Candlemas Day and a further 13s 4d for Guy Fawkes Day. Before 1607 it is said they stood in the 'gallery in the hall', but this was replaced by a 'music room': painted walls or screen with a cloth over and curtains. No picture of either structure is known.

Just four musicians are named at the Inner Temple, the earliest of whom is a 'Mr Hall' in 1583. Nothing more is known of him. The next is John Hopper, who is recorded as the leader of the house musicians from 1615 to 1617. He became a bass violinist at the English court in 1621 and he was among the fourteen violins who played in *The Triumph of Peace* in 1634. The leader in 1637 was Henry Field, described as 'an ancient servant of this house'. Presumably, then, this was a regular engagement for him. Field was a London wait, serving from 1619. In 1629 he was paid by the Middle Temple 'for playing upon the treble violin', and in September 1634 he was one of those performing the city night watch on wind instruments. Earlier that year he had appeared as one of the Blackfriars theatre musicians in the second music chariot in the procession preceding the Inns of Court masque *The Triumph*

Inner Temple students' drama society production of Henry VIII's Wives.

of Peace. William Saunder(s), named in 1642, is first heard of in 1624 as a theatre musician in the King's Company, but by 1634 he was playing in the City waits, having 'for many years exercised and played… by their good approbation in service of this city in the time and absence of Francis Parker occasioned by reason of his sickness'. After the Restoration in 1660, Saunders petitioned for a place in the King's Musick and was supported by several of the court musicians. They testified that Saunders 'is a very able person both for his knowledge in Musique and for his performance on the Sagbutt and is very fitt and able to doe Service on the said Instrument in his Maties Chapell Royall; And that he is very usefull and serviceable for the base violin, a part which there is much want of in his Maties Band of violins; and also that the said Saunders is a man of sober life and Conversacion.' He got the job and served until his death in 1674.

So the records of music and musicians at the Inns are minimal, often consisting of an annual payment only to unnamed persons for services at All Saints, Candlemas and Christmas. Where musicians are named this is so infrequent that it is of little help in tracing any continuity of performance by them. Records prior to the mid-sixteenth century suggest that the Inns generally retained a single musician, sometimes identified as a harpist, and they hired small consorts for the Grand Feasts. A clearer picture emerges between the latter part of Elizabeth's reign and the Interregnum, with waits and theatre musicians predominating at the various revels. An important question is: what happened the rest of the time? The simple answer is that we don't know, because nothing is recorded in surviving documentation. However, family papers and diaries show that the Benchers themselves made music while at the Inns and hint that musical life there extended beyond the times of the revels.

The account books of the L'Estrange family of Hunstanton, Norfolk, show that after school at Eton, Nicholas L'Estrange attended Trinity College, Cambridge, for two years before spending time at Lincoln's Inn from 28 October 1624. His brother Hamon became a fellow-commoner at Christ's College, Cambridge, in October 1623, where he continued his music (singing?) lessons at 6s 8d per month. He too went to Lincoln's Inn from 16 June 1626 and both men made music there:

June 1626	for his [Hamon's] admittance into the Dancing Schoole	£1 0s 0d
	for his general and speciall admittance into Lincoln's Inn	£9 10s 0d
	for a voyall [viol] case 15s and for bringing it home 2s 6d [Nicholas's, from London]	17s 6d
August? 1626	to Mr Taylour the Musition	£3 6s 8d

A Middle Templar (William Freke) also paid 6s a month to be taught the viol by 'Mr Taylor, my musician'. 'Mr Taylour' was almost certainly Robert Taylor, the court musician and city wait, so £3 6s 8d was perhaps a year's fees. We know that Robert Taylor had a house at Lincoln's Inn. There was also 'Pietro' who taught the lute to John Petre of Ingatestone, Essex, at the Middle Temple between 1567 and 1570.

Residence in chambers was not compulsory (and was at a premium), and many Benchers rented accommodation elsewhere, in hostelries or private houses. Music tutors would visit them there to give lessons. The opportunity to make music with fellow students and professionals was readily available and one wonders whether informal playing of this kind ever became part of evening entertainments at the Inns. No doubt too the members could club together to hire players at will. Of course there is no collection of music manuscripts associated with the Inns such as can be found with other institutions like cathedrals and universities; students would take them home with them on departure. But one interesting manuscript has come down to us as British Library Additional MS 10,444, a collection of more than 160 two-part airs for treble and bass, owned and partially copied by Sir Nicholas L'Estrange. It is possible that this collection was made during his time at Lincoln's Inn and it comprises skeleton versions of dances from masques. It is the sort of thing that pupil and teacher could play together.

Bulstrode Whitelocke had been instructed at Eton and Merchant Taylors School, where the Master 'used his scholars… often to act in playes & publique shewes, to breed in them the better confidence, elocution, & behaviour. & Whitelocke had his part in them, he was also taught musicke, dauncing, fencing, & writing & was no unapt scholar in them.' Having been admitted to the Middle Temple, aged fifteen, he then went to Oxford. In November 1622, aged eighteen, he became a Bencher at the Middle Temple and studied the law seriously. But 'He also used dauncing, vaulting, fencing, riding the great horse… in musicke he grew a Master, & pleased his father therby who was much delighted in it.' He 'kept close to his study of the law' for the next two years. 'Yett he neglected not his musicke & exercises of body, wherin he gave his father contentment by constant attendance att his music meetings, in which both he & his children did beare their parts in vocall musicke.' Clearly not all Bulstrode's music making was at the Inns, but it did form a contemporary counterpart to his study of the law.

Schools of dancing and of fencing were on hand to supply the needs of the Benchers. There are a number of surviving documents written by them (and others) as memory aids for dance steps. Most are brief and fragmentary. An exception is a small book of *c*1500 now among the papers of the Gresley family of Derbyshire, containing twenty-six dance choreographies with French, Italian and English names. There is no evidence that it was connected with the Inns, but the fact that it seems to require male dancers only may indicate that it is linked to the 'grave measures' of the traditional Inn revels, which were danced round the Hall by men only until the mid-seventeenth century. Others include choreographies by a Lincoln's Inn student, Edward Gunter, written *c*1560s–70s, by John Willoughby in 1594 and by the Middle Templar John Ramsey *c*1607. Ramsey's 'Practise for Dauncinge' includes instructions for the eight dances which make up the core of the traditional 'old measures', a staple of dances at the Inns and at court. Bulstrode Whitelocke describes the Middle Temple revels in 1628:

> *Allholland day came, which by the custom of those societies is reckoned the beginning of their Christmas, in the evening the Mr entered the Hall, with about 16 revellers, proper hansome young gentlemen, habited in rich suits, shoes and stockings, hats and great feathers, the Mr led them in his bar gowne with a white staffe in his hand, the musique playing before them. They began with the old measures, after that they daunced the Branles, then the Mr took his seat, & the Revellers daunced Galliards, Corantoes, & French daunces, then countrey daunces till it grew very late… Sometimes to[o] Court Ladyes & other Grandesses did them the honor to come to the Revells, & were no small charge to the Mr, and being so much noted and frequented, there was a great striving for places to see them …*

Particularly important is the 'Butler Buggins Manuscript' of the 1670s in the Inner Temple Library. Butler Buggins was Master of the Revels at the Inner Temple in 1672 and again in 1674–5 and his manuscript describes the Inner Temple revels. Royal College of Music MS 1119 incorporates the 'old Measures of the Inner Temple… as they were first begun and taught by Robert Holeman, a dancing-Master before 1640 and Continued ever since in the Inner-Temple-Hall'. Indeed the 1670s saw a revival of ceremonial dancing at the Inns (which had been interrupted by the Commonwealth) and this continued until the 1730s.

Revels were also a fixed ingredient in masques, which had developed from the disguisings and pageants popular at the early Tudor court. A Master of the Revels oversaw the entertainments there at festive seasons and a special post was created for him in 1545. There was also a 'Lord of Misrule' – an anti-authority figure – chosen to preside over the Christmas festivities. Words, music, dance and design all contributed to masques and were loosely based round an idea provided by the librettist/poet. Often this celebrated some event (like a marriage) or made a political statement, such as *The Triumph of Peace* (1634), which the four Inns presented (at the request of Charles I) to repudiate a Puritan attack on the licentiousness of the aristocracy by one of their members, William Prynne. Lords of Misrule had their place during Christmas festivities at the Inns too and the masque sometimes featured as a high point of the in-house revels. Not all were as lavish as the court productions, of course, and many were home-grown, presented by members. There was no fixed structure, but among the usual elements were (1) a procession, (2) an allegorical speech, (3) the antimasque – usually some rustic or extraordinary entertainment performed by professional actors, (4) banishment of the antimasque and transformation to the scene of the main masque, (5) main masque – classical or allegorical setting, (6) revels with the audience, (7) final peroration/dance on stage. Among the most elaborate (and costly) masques were those presented by the Inns for the court at Whitehall. The marriage celebrations of James I's daughter Elizabeth to Frederick V, Elector Palatine, in February 1613 included *The Memorable Masque of the Middle Temple and Lincoln's Inn*, followed by *The Masque of the Inner Temple and Gray's Inn*. The latter had to be postponed from its planned date because the king felt too tired. It was described by John Chamberlain in a letter to Alice Carleton:

> *On teusday yt came to Grayes ynne and the inner Temples turne to come wth theyre mask, wherof Sr Francis Bacon was the cheife contriver, and because the former came on horseback and open chariots, they made choise to come by water from winchester place in Southwark (wch suted well enough wth theyre devise, wch was the mariage of the river of Thames to the Rhine), and theyre shew by water was very gallant by reason of infinite store of lights very curiously set and placed: and many boats and barges wth devises of light and lampes, wth three peales of ordinance, one at theyre taking water, another in the Temple garden, and the last at theyre landing: wch passage by water cost them better than three hundred poundes. They were received at the privie stayres: and great expactation thayre was that went before them, both in devise, daintiness, of apparell, and above all in danncing (wherin they are held excellent) and esteemed for the properer men, but by what yll planet yt fell out I know not, they came home as they went wthout doing anything, the reason whereof I cannot yet learne thoroughly, but only that the hall was so full that yt was not possible to accoyde yt or make roome for them, besides that most of the Ladies were in the galleries to see them land, and could not get in, but the worst of all was that the king was so wearied and sleapie wth sitting up almost two whole nights before, that he had no edge to yt … but wthall gave them very goode wordes and appointed them to come again on Saterday. …'*

CIRCE AND ULYSSES
THE INNER TEMPLE MASQUE
PRESENTED BY THE GENTLEMEN THERE JANUARY 13, 1614. WRITTEN BY WILLIAM BROWNE OF TAVISTOCK AND NOW EDITED · WITH AN ESSAY ON WILLIAM BROWNE AND THE ENGLISH MASQUE · BY GWYN JONES
SEVEN WOOD · ENGRAVINGS BY MARK SEVERIN

Printed in Great Britain by
THE GOLDEN COCKEREL PRESS
1954

The Circe and Ulysses *masque in a 1954 edition.*

Clearly this was no small production. Sir Francis Bacon had been a Gray's Inn man and the poet was Francis Beaumont, formerly of the Inner Temple. It is likely that the performers were drawn from the best at court, as had occurred with the Middle Temple and Lincoln's Inn masque. Perhaps encouraged by their success, on 13 January 1615 the Inner Temple staged William Browne's *Circe and Ulysses* 'to please ourselves in private'. This proved to be the last masque written by a resident member of the society performing it. Only one song survives, but the libretto shows a freedom from masque convention, perhaps attempted because the performance was a private entertainment. Another home event was Thomas Middleton's *Inner Temple Masque or Masque of Heroes* (1619) in which the gentlemen at the Inn were joined by actors from Prince Charles's Men. It was billed as 'an Entertainment for many worthy Ladies'. No Inns of Court masques were created between 1621 and 1634, when James Shirley's The *Triumph of Peace* (mentioned earlier) was presented at Whitehall. Virtually all the musicians came from court. So successful was the show that the queen ordered it to be repeated a fortnight later. This was an exceptional event and cost the Inns £21,000 to produce. Normally masques were financed entirely by members below the Bar, but (as for the marriage celebrations in 1613) this required all members to be levied for a contribution to the costs. Five months before the performances Thomas Coke wrote 'No law studied in the Inns of Court; now all turned dancing schools'. Bulstrode Whitelocke had charge of the music and it is thanks largely to him that this is the best recorded of all masques.

Freedom to pursue a liberal education alongside study of the law was clearly an advantage of residence at the Inns and one which many seized avidly. For some sons of gentlemen music was an important element in their life and one which would not be discarded during their time in London.

Andrew Ashbee is a retired schoolmaster and a Trustee and member of the editorial committee of the Musica Britannica Trust with a particular interest in Tudor and Stuart music and musicians.

Dancing

Master Sedley

Cameo portrait of John Playford.

Although it has had in recent years to sell some of its most valuable non-legal books, the Inner Temple Library still has some eclectic delights on its shelves. Among them is a fourth edition, published in 1670, of John Playford's *The Dancing Master*. It came (though probably not directly) from Playford's bookshop by the porch of the Temple Church.

Playford was apprenticed in 1639, at the relatively advanced age of sixteen, to a stationer. But music was his first love, and within three years he had rented, at £2 a year, the shop or booth by the Church porch from which for the rest of his life he sold not only music books but instruments and medicaments (among them 'Doctor Turner's dentifrices and Sir Kenelme Digby's Sympathetical Powder'). Here musicians and music-lovers came, among them Henry Purcell, Dr Blow and Samuel Pepys, who bought a copy of *The Dancing Master* in 1662. Another of his customers, the poet laureate Nahum Tate, wrote an elegy for Playford's funeral in December 1686, when he died in his house in Arundel Street and was buried – or so it is thought – in the Temple Church.

The booksellers of seventeenth-century London were its publishers. The books Playford published during the Commonwealth show how little there is in the notion that Cromwell's England was a psalm-singing cultural desert. Late in 1650 the Stationers' Company gave Playford its licence to publish *The English Dancing Master*, which he did the following year. The adjective 'English' in the title, which had been dropped by the time of publication of the second edition in 1653, was not fortuitous. Every acknowledged dancing master in the country was French, and formal dancing was an elite pastime. The point Playford was setting out to make, and which his book memorably proved, was that England had its own popular dances which, with simple-to-follow notation, every fiddler could play and in which everyone could join. The book is prefaced by a key setting out the dance symbols, and each score carries instructions.

To judge by the quality of his books, Playford must have been a demanding publisher. His first printer was Thomas Harper, but by

Title page of the fourth edition of The Dancing Master, *1670.*

the time of the Inn's edition *The Dancing Master* was being printed by William Godbid, with whose widow or daughter Playford's son went into partnership, finally taking over the print shop. Playford himself, who had a print shop of his own in Little Britain, later in the 1650s introduced the use of horizontal strokes to join quavers and semiquavers, a device which was picked up by Dutch printers and has become a universal feature of music printing.

Although Playford published the works of many of the leading composers of his time, it is on *The Dancing Master* that his reputation rests, alongside his *Catch that Catch Can*, a collection of popular rounds and catches which he published in the following year. It was *The Dancing Master*, however, which went through numerous editions, first in the hands of his son, then (from 1709) of his successor John Young and then in the hands of a variety of publishers. By 1728 it was in its seventeenth edition. By 1850 it had expanded to three volumes, and over a thousand dances had at one time or another been included in it.

Playford's *Dancing Master* is the source of a number of tunes which would otherwise have been lost. Among them is that of 'The bonny broom', a song which Beaumont and Fletcher early in the century had heard milkmaids singing and which twentieth-century singers have been able, with Playford's help, to restore as a complete song. It is also a ready source of a number of popular melodies, including the Elizabethan tune 'Sellenger's round', a version of which is in the Fitzwilliam Virginal Book but which by the eighteenth century was being specified on penny broadsides as the melody for such texts as the ribald 'Fair maid of Islington'.

By obtaining appointment in about 1653 as clerk to the Temple Church, Playford became able, in addition to collecting burial fees and rents, to function as the Inns' bookbinder and to be secure in the tenure of his shop. A serious musicologist, he wrote and published a history of music which ran through ten editions before his death. After the Restoration, grumbling that 'all solemn musick is much laid aside, being esteemed too heavy and dull for the light heels and brains of this nimble and wanton age', he republished some of his own liturgical books.

In 2008 the Inner Temple celebrates the 400th anniversary of the grant of its Royal Charter. It may be that Playford and his *Dancing Master* will feature in the celebrations, for both his tunes and his dances (one of them is 'Pegasus, or the Flying Horse') bring to life a period of the Inn's and the country's history not far removed from that moment.

Music in the Temple Church

Ann Elise Smoot

Touching musical harmony whether by instrument or voice, such is the force thereof, and so pleasing effects it hath in that very part of man which is most divine, that some have been thereby induced to think that the soul itself by nature is or hath in it harmony.

Richard Hooker, Master of the Temple 1585–91

Were Richard Hooker to visit the Temple Church today, he would be gratified to hear the music that the congregation enjoys each Sunday. The Temple Church is known nationally and, indeed, internationally as a centre of musical excellence. The music that plays a vital part in the Temple liturgy each week is part of a tradition which extends back, in one form or another, to the twelfth century. The singing of services to plain chant had been a cornerstone of the Roman Catholic liturgy for centuries and polyphonic works based on chant were also heard in certain churches in the Middle Ages, although a number of priests decried them as being rooted in secular tradition and obscuring the sacred texts. It is impossible to know whether polyphonic music would have been heard at the Temple Church in its earliest years, but it is difficult to imagine an order as grand and prosperous as the Knights Templar not having portions of their services sung, and sung very well. The consecration of the Round on 10 February 1185, most likely attended by Henry II, and of the chancel in 1240 in the presence of Henry III, must surely have featured a feast of wonderful music to accompany the pomp and pageantry of such important events. By 1308 it appears that the Temple Church had a large choir, and that it included some young boys. The inventory of items taken from the Church on the dissolution of the Knights Templar included five books containing liturgical music, two cushions for the chanters' chairs, one book for the organs, indicating that the Church was in possession of more than one instrument, and most significantly, 'twenty-eight choir copes, and four little copes for the choristers'.

Choirmen in the Round.

Services continued in the Temple Church after the ejection of the Knights Templar, and there may have been a choir, albeit on a smaller scale, in addition to the organs. Although records from this time are scarce, a manuscript dating from the first half of the sixteenth century documents that Matins and Mass were 'solemnly sung' on festival days, while an entry in Inner Temple minutes for 1519 records an 'Order for a roll to be made containing the names of members of the Society, in order that from them may be raised 70s for new organs in the Church'. It seems that, even before they had been granted ownership of the Church, the Inns were taking an active interest in its musical welfare. The religious upheavals of the 1540s and 1550s seem not to have halted liturgical music-

Print of the chancel by Cattermole and Melville, 1840s.

making at the Temple and, certainly, choral singing must have been heard during the reign of Queen Mary, as the Treasurer of the Inner Temple was required to finance new books for the choir in 1553.

Surprisingly, there are no references to a choir during the reign of Elizabeth I, the only music referred to at this stage being the congregational singing of metrical (versified) psalms, first published in 1549. It is strange to think that the Temple's music became pared down during a reign often considered to be the golden era of English church music. Were the anthems and settings of Byrd and Tallis never heard here during this time? The lawyers spent vast sums of money on the repair of the Church after they were granted their Charter by James I; would they not have wanted a choir to enhance the services in this newly restored space? It seems not. There is no mention of choristers after 1557 and, even in the first years of the Restoration, it seems that the services in the Temple Church remained unadorned. Samuel Pepys, who was a keen musician and often bought music in John Playford's shop in the Church porch, regularly attended services there. Had there been any music of note at the Temple, he would certainly have mentioned it in his diary.

After this rather uneventful period in Temple Church music came a dramatic interlude, which has come to be known as 'The Battle of the Organs' – although 'The Battle of the two Inns' might be a more accurate description, for this incident seems to have been as much a 'turf war' between the two Inns as it was a competition between two organ builders. The 'Battle of the Organs' consisted of a lengthy and high-profile contest to determine which of two renowned organ builders, Renatus Harris and Bernard Smith, better known as 'Father Smith', would supply the Temple Church's new organ. The records of the Inner and Middle Temple do not agree on the sequence of events. The Middle Temple archives contain a statement by a surveyor named William Cleare, dated 8 May 1683, that he overheard the Treasurers of both Inns in September 1682 'give full ordre and directions unto Mr Bernard Smith the Kings organ maker to make an organ for the Tempell Church … and that then neither Remy Harris nor any other person

The Reader of the Temple Church with the choir at a commemorative service on 15 May 2001.

Whatsoever was ever mentioned to have any orders or Directions to make an organ for the Tempell Church'.

This account contradicts an earlier document in the Inner Temple archives, stating that Harris and Smith had each been asked to construct an organ and that the Inns would then judge 'which shall be the best organ both as to sound and price'. Did Middle Temple always have Smith firmly in mind for the job? Did Inner Temple introduce Harris into the equation after a verbal agreement had been made with Smith? It is difficult to know, but it seems that each Inn placed their money – literally – on one of the candidates, with Middle Temple giving advance payments to Smith and Inner Temple doing the same with Harris.

By 13 June 1683, Harris had completed his organ and was ready to set it up in the Church, complaining to the Inns when it appeared that Smith was not yet able to install his instrument. However, Smith's organ must have been completed soon afterwards, because in August 1683 Middle Temple made a payment to John Blow to test it and give his opinion. No decision was made in 1683 and the dispute rumbled on for two years, during which Smith and Harris probably continued to work on improving their respective instruments. On 22 June 1685, Middle Temple sent an Order of Parliament to the Benchers of the Inner Temple, proposing that the dispute might be ended quickly if only they would concede the superiority of the Smith organ. With the situation no closer to resolution, a committee was set up to appoint impartial judges. Written submissions were made by Smith and Harris to Judge Jeffreys, Lord Chancellor and coincidentally a member of the Inner Temple. However, it appears that the decision was not left solely to him but to a panel of judges. Tempers flared as the saga wore on, and there appear to have been incidents of sabotage. In May 1686 Harris petitioned the Inner Temple for money, in part to cover the expense of having to post watchmen to prevent damage to his instrument and in part to repair already inflicted damage. How the final decision was taken in 1688 in favour of Smith's organ is not known, but 'the tedious competition between the two organ makers', as it was referred to once by Middle Temple, was finally over, with the result going the Middle Temple's way. The turn of events must have seriously rankled Harris, though he may have enjoyed a degree of poetic justice: it is said that part of the organ he constructed for the Temple was used in the organ of Christ Church Dublin in 1697, where he had beaten none other than Smith to the contract.

Ill feelings aside, the Temple Church now found itself in possession of a splendid new instrument, and one which incorporated the newest trends in organ building – in fact, the Smith organ is England's first documented three-manual instrument. Having put in a state of the art organ, the Inns were also prepared to pay handsomely to employ someone to play it, and wished to attract the best players of the day. Francis Pigott was appointed in May 1688 and was paid a salary of £50 a year – a huge sum for an organist in those days.

While the organ playing in the Temple Church was undoubtedly of the highest quality, there was almost certainly no choir in the seventeenth and eighteenth centuries, and congregational singing was probably confined to the metrical psalm. Even the organ playing was not appreciated by all: the light and fast voluntaries so popular during this period did not meet with everyone's approval, a mere handful of decades after the heyday of Puritanism. But many congregants flocked to hear the playing of such virtuosi as the blind John Stanley, who became organist to the Society of the Inner Temple in 1734. Finally in 1827, two professional female singers were employed, who sang from the organ gallery. They were clearly a success, because in May 1828 it was decided to retain their services and to add a male singer, presumably a tenor as a bass was appointed four years later.

Temple Church music continued along these lines until the late 1830s, when the influence of the Oxford Movement – which had been building considerable momentum since its launch in 1833 – began to make itself felt at the Temple. However, Christopher Benson, the Master of the Temple since 1826, was evidently not a great lover of church music, disapproving in particular of any liturgical music in which the congregation could not participate. In a letter to the Benchers in 1843 he wrote:

> *When I first came to the Temple, it was to an unpretentious Church... in which all might join in the responses, and nothing was wanting to answer the demands of seriousness and piety but an improvement in the psalmody, which was miserably deficient from the improper appointment of a clerk who could not sing. To remedy this defect some male and females singers were unhappily introduced whose exhibitions in the Organ Gallery were offensive to many, though, at last, I had the pleasure of hearing members joining in this mode of praising God. This band of singers was afterwards employed in chanting various parts of the Service, and one psalm in which the congregation could, was superseded by an anthem in which they could not join – and that Anthem not so performed as much to gratify either devotion or taste.*

Stephen Layton (right), former Director of Music, with composer John Tavener (left).

It seems that the singers who had originally been employed to lead congregational singing were now singing other parts of the service on their own. The Benchers were apparently leaning towards a larger role for music in the Temple liturgy.

In 1840, the Inner and Middle Temple Benchers decided to embark on an extensive renovation of the Temple Church. Its closure set in motion the events leading to the establishment of a permanent choir. After considerable experimentation, the north aisle was settled on as the best place for the organ, previously located within the screen between the Round and chancel. It was reconstructed in a new organ chamber and various improvements were made, including the introduction of an octave and a half of pedals 'on the same scale of those in St Paul's Cathedral'. In fact, the Temple organ at this time was larger than the one in St Paul's, which must have gratified the Benchers.

The choir continued to be placed in the loft 'in two rows in front of the organist', rather than in the main body of the Church. However, it was of a type not seen in the Temple Church for centuries: a choir of men and boys. The Oxford Movement had reawakened an interest in traditional ritual and liturgy in the Church of England, and there could hardly have been a more favorable time for the Temple Church to reintroduce a surpliced choir. In 1842 there were very few such choirs in London and, in creating one, the Temple Church established itself at the forefront of modern liturgical thinking.

Originally the choir of men and boys had been contracted only to sing at the grand reopening service of the Church on 20 November 1842. The service attracted national attention and Turle and Goss, organists of Westminster Abbey and St Paul's respectively, attended rehearsals. Fortunately the Benchers decided to maintain a permanent choir thereafter, with some expressing a desire for daily sung services. The Master, Christopher Benson, was by no means happy with the renewed interest in church music that seemed to be thriving at the Temple, and at various points he attempted to stop certain portions of the service being sung. However, the Benchers' wishes prevailed and Benson was told politely, but firmly, that the choir was there to stay.

National interest in the renewed Temple Church continued, with several royal visits in 1843. The choir moved to stalls in the main body of the Church in 1843, and that year also saw another significant event: the first Sunday that a young organist named E J Hopkins came to play at the Temple, aged just twenty-five. Hopkins was a remarkable young man, who had already amassed a great deal of experience and demonstrated considerable energy and commitment to church music. He had been a chorister at the Chapel Royal, and unofficially one at St Paul's. When still a boy, he used to play voluntaries for his teacher, Walmisley, at St Martin's in the Fields. He would courier music for Thomas Attwood between the Chapel Royal and St Paul's, and played on occasion for services in Westminster Abbey. Turle obviously considered him sufficiently good to be trusted with these and it was he who recommended Hopkins for the position at Mitcham Parish Church, which he held immediately before his appointment at the Temple.

When Hopkins was eventually offered the Temple post on a permanent basis in 1844, the Benchers were shrewd enough to recognise his considerable gifts. Hopkins recounted that when the Under- and Sub-Treasurers of the two Inns informed him of his appointment, they reported the Benchers' feeling that, rather than offering two or three pages of terms and conditions, they 'need do no more than merely request that you will carry out your new duties in the manner that seems best to yourself'. Over the next few years, the Benchers also granted Hopkins several requests which would

Temple Church choristers.

have incurred a sizeable financial outlay, including a full pedal-board for the organ and a salary increase to enable more rehearsal time with the boys.

Hopkins presided over the Temple's music during a fifty-five-year period in which the choir became firmly established as one of the best in the United Kingdom. The Temple choir was a huge draw for visitors, enhanced by Hopkins' performances on the organ. This elevated reputation continued under Hopkins' successor, Henry Walford Davies, who was appointed in 1898 and counted Harold Darke, William Harris and Leopold Stokowski amongst his assistants. The choir's reputation continued to flourish subsequently, under George Thalben-Ball, and reached out to a huge new audience through the new technology of recordings – including the world-famous 1927 recording of chorister Ernest Lough singing Mendelssohn's 'O for the wings of a dove', which to date has sold over five million copies.

Hopkins, Walford Davies and Thalben-Ball devoted a vast proportion of their lives to the Temple Church; the music from 1843 to1982 was presided over by just these three men. Interestingly, all three were exceptionally young when appointed to the post of Organist and Director of Music; the Benchers clearly had a keen eye for talent and energy, and did not see youth as an impediment to success in such an important job. Hopkins was twenty-five when appointed, Walford Davies twenty-eight and Thalben-Ball twenty-seven. More recently, Stephen Layton (Director of Music from 1997 to 2006) was appointed at the age of twenty-nine and when, in 2004, the post of Organist and Director of Music was split into two positions, James Vivian was appointed as Organist at the same age, later, in September 2006, recombining the two titles when he took on both roles. A rare exception to this trend in favour of youth was the appointment of Dr John Birch in 1982, who served as Director of Music after a long and distinguished tenure as Organist and Master of the Choristers at Chichester Cathedral.

Building on the strong foundations laid by Hopkins and his successors, the Temple Church choir continues to be regarded as one of the best in the country; yet, not content to rest on its laurels, the Inns' Church Committee continues to move forward, endorsing new ideas and projects. A firmly established Wednesday recital series draws listeners from all over London and beyond to enjoy a range of traditional and more modern music, while support for new composition forms an important part of the Temple's philosophy. To celebrate the millennium, *January Writ* by eminent young composer Thomas Adès was commissioned by the Inner Temple, while 2003 witnessed a unique event in the history of the choir with the commissioning by both Inns of John Tavener's *Veil of the*

Temple. This unique all-night vigil will live on vividly in the memories of those fortunate enough to be part of it, while the work was subsequently performed in New York and in a concert version at the BBC Proms. Meanwhile, the Temple Composition Prize was established in 2001 and will be awarded for a fourth time in 2007, with the winning piece receiving its premiere in 2008. The Composition Prize attracts entries from composers all over the UK and abroad.

Concerts have been a part of the Temple choir's schedule since its foundation in the nineteenth century, and they continue to be much appreciated. A review in the *Daily Telegraph* described a recent concert as 'a performance of perfectly poised fluency, quiet intensity and consolatory contemplation'. In 2005, the musical calendar of the Temple Church was further enhanced by the introduction of Temple Cantata concerts, featuring soloists from the choir accompanied by a professional baroque ensemble, the Temple Players, founded by James Vivian and Joseph Crouch. In 2007 the Temple Players are joining the Temple Church choir, both in worship and in concert, and in 2008 a festival will take place to commemorate the 400th anniversary of James I's Charter, in which the Temple choir and Organists will play an important role, the musical centerpiece being a fully-staged performance of Purcell's *Dido and Aeneas*, featuring several men of the choir and the Temple Players.

Those Benchers who argued passionately for the introduction of daily sung services in the 1840s would be delighted to see that several evensongs and mid-week sung services are part of the Temple diary, offering spiritual refreshment to those who live and work locally and constituting a new form of outreach to the community. The Temple Church also continues to serve its regular congregation by conducting many weddings and memorial services throughout the year. However, the heart of the Temple Church's music remains firmly rooted in the weekly offerings at the Sunday services. The first priority of the choir is, and will always be, enhancing and supporting the liturgy in the Church. The Inns continue to be unstinting in their support of the choir, and provide generous scholarships towards the education of the boys, who rehearse four afternoons each week after school and on Sunday mornings.

The Temple Church is, and will continue to be, a remarkable place. It provides an oasis of calm in the middle of one of the world's most dynamic cities. Music is at the heart of its mission and David Lewer, a long serving chorister and choirman, quotes one former chorister as saying, 'the word "Temple" means infinitely more than just a church, a choir or a vicinity. It means an emotional experience… a world apart. And if ever a world had a soul, that world was Temple; and the soul of the Temple was *Music*.'

Ann Elise Smoot is a professional organist and freelance writer who lives in King's Bench Walk with her husband, James Vivian, Director of Music at the Temple Church.

I first came to the Temple as a chorister of the Temple Church in 1972, when I was ten years old. The choirmaster was the redoubtable Dr Thalben-Ball (later Sir George Thalben-Ball) who had been in post since 1923. We had choir practice five days out of seven every week of the year except during the long vacation and for one week after Easter. On Fridays, we had about an hour to play in and about the Inn while we waited for the 'gentlemen' of the choir (the adult voices) to arrive from their places of work for a late practice. We were given tea in the Niblett Hall, which then stood at the top of King's Bench Walk. In summer, we played in the Inner Temple Garden and in the winter, or when the weather was bad, we choristers had the run of some shabby, interconnecting rooms in the basement of Goldsmith Building, which we reached from the yard at the back of the Church. Here the main game was table tennis, but the back room had a more furtive atmosphere, suitable for illicit activity like letting off indoor fireworks.

We sang a full choral service on Sundays, and also did a trickle of wedding and memorial services throughout the year, for which we were paid extra, cash in hand. The music for weddings and memorials was always the same, and needed practically no rehearsal. The seating of the Temple Church was divided, then as now, into four quarters. The south side was for the Inner Temple, the north side for the Middle Temple, the eastern half of each side was for Benchers and the western half was for the public, with the front row marked out by a sign as 'reserved for barristers'. But there were hardly any barristers, or Benchers either. For probationer choristers, who had to take the collection, the best pick was the Middle Temple Benchers, because their quarter of the church would generally have only half a dozen people in it or fewer. The worst pick was the Inner Temple side allocated to the public because, since it was closest to the door, it was always full.

Since choir practice was always after school (except on Sundays), my abiding memory of the Inn at that time is as a dark place, lit by gaslight, and with a network of courts and passages which never entirely lost their mystery.

Martin Griffiths

The Inner Temple & the Wider World

THE ADMISSION OF OVERSEAS STUDENTS IN THE NINETEENTH CENTURY

Clare Rider

Since the seventeenth century, the Inns of Court have played a significant role in the development of the British dependencies abroad. The first successful attempt at overseas colonial settlement was largely financed by Middle Temple lawyers, who had been persuaded to invest their own capital in the Virginia Company, founded in London in 1606. The American colony in question, Jamestown in Virginia, did not provide the gold or other riches anticipated by the London investors. However, after a shaky start, the settlement survived and turned loss into profit with the establishment of tobacco plantations. Subsequently, many of the sons of the colonial gentry from Virginia, Carolina, Maryland and New England were sent to London to acquire legal knowledge and professional status, mainly to the Middle Temple, but also to the Inner Temple, Lincoln's Inn and Gray's Inn. William Paca, one of the signatories of the Declaration of American Independence, was an Inner Templar. Despite the loss of her American colonies, the British empire grew in size and complexity during the eighteenth and nineteenth centuries, and the sons of the colonial administrators and judiciary dotted around the world, from Africa to Hong Kong and Tasmania, were frequently sent home to London to acquire a legal education at the Inns of Court. When did these opportunities become open to the indigenous subjects of the British empire?

William Paca of Maryland (1740-99), signatory of the American Declaration of Independence.

From the admission registers, it seems that the first Asian member of the Inner Temple was Aviet Agabeg from Calcutta, a student of St John's College, Cambridge, who was admitted on 11 June 1864 and called to the Bar in 1868. He was followed, several years later, by Amanda Mohan Bose, Ali Ameer and Pathal Chandra Roy of Bengal (admitted in 1870), and then by Arraloon Carapiel and John Apcar of Calcutta and Grija Sanker Sen of Dacca (admitted in 1871). There may have been others. The number of Asian students continued to rise in the 1870s and 1880s and included Mohandas Karamchand Gandhi, who was admitted to the Inner Temple in 1888. Admissions to the other Inns of Court follow a similar pattern, with Lincoln's Inn claiming the first Indian student to join and become qualified: Ganendra Mohan Tagore, admitted in 1859 and called to the Bar on 11 June 1862. By 1885, 108 Indian barristers had been educated in England, encouraged by the Indian government, the Inns of Court and the Council of Legal Education, which granted concessions to Indian students to facilitate their training. Lincoln's Inn also recruited a number of indigenous students from further east in the nineteenth century, the first being Ng Achoy from Hong Kong, admitted in 1872 and called in 1877. Lincoln's Inn still retains a special association with India and Hong Kong.

However, identifying black African, American and West Indian bar students poses a problem, since the majority had adopted

Seretse and Ruth Khama photographed in London in 1950. Excluded by the British government from his Chieftainship in Bechuanaland because of his 'unfortuante marriage' to a white woman, he was subsequently knighted and became the first President of an independent Botswana in 1966.

European style names. We know from other sources that Alexander Kennedy Isbiter of Hudson's Bay, admitted to the Middle Temple in 1862 and called to the Bar in 1864, was part native American, and that Thomas Morris Chester, admitted to the Middle Temple in 1867 and called in 1870, was a black American, probably the first black American to qualify as a barrister in England. Similarly, without further evidence it would be impossible to detect that Christian Frederick Cole, the second son of Jacob Cole of Kissey, Sierra Leone, clergyman, was a black African. He matriculated as a non-collegiate student at Oxford University in 1873, was admitted to the Inner Temple in 1879 and was called to the Bar in 1883. Cole seems to have been the first black student to join Oxford University and his appearance at university events caused considerable interest. He is mentioned in the diary of Florence Ward, the younger sister of William Ward who was a close friend of Oscar Wilde at Magdalen College in the 1870s. Whilst visiting her brother during Commemoration Week in June 1876, she recorded in her entry relating to the annual Show Sunday Promenade in the Broad Walk, Christ Church, on Sunday 18 June: 'Saw Christian Cole (Coal?) (the nigger)'. While we would consider this an unacceptable remark, it must be taken in its historical context.

Two years later, the *Oxford Chronicle* of 29 June 1878, in its account of Encaenia, noted that, before the procession entered, 'Some amusement was caused by "Three Cheers for Christian Cole", a gentleman of colour, of University College, who had entered the Theatre a few moments previously and was standing in the area.' Cole became known in Oxford as 'Old King Cole', a nickname employed in a contemporary cartoon. While Oxford and Cambridge Universities seem to have started to accept black students in the 1860s and 1870s, the same period as the Inns of Court, it appears that the non-denominational University College London commenced almost thirty years earlier. London University's first (quarter) black American student, an emancipated slave called Moses Roper, was admitted to UCL in 1838, while Indian students appeared in the admission registers from at least the 1840s.

To understand the timing of these developments, it is necessary to look at the historical context of our colonial past, particularly in relation to India. In the decades preceding the Indian mutiny of 1857, the subject of the education of indigenous Indians had prompted debate. In acquiring sovereignty over India, the British had inherited a complex and multi-layered society. At the top of the hierarchy sat the previously independent princes and urban intelligentsia (concentrated in Calcutta, Madras and Bombay, the main bases of British trade), who were cultured and well educated. At the bottom stood the mass of the population, condemned in many cases to ignorant poverty. By negotiating with the princes, rather than toppling them from their thrones, the British had made powerful allies. However, there was no serious suggestion that Indians should play a part in imperial government until the 1830s, when the question was considered in the lead up to the passing of the India Act of 1833. Foremost in the movement for native recruitment to the East Indian civil service were Sir Charles Trevelyan and Thomas Macaulay, who were serving in India at this time. While many among the British establishment feared that the education and employment of Indians would threaten the British empire, Trevelyan and Macaulay argued the reverse, although appreciating that it would take some time to achieve true integration. Macaulay declared in a speech on the India bill in 1833:

> *I feel that, for the good of India itself, the admission of natives to high office must be effected by slow degrees. But that, when the fullness of time is come, when the interest of India requires the change… to refuse to make that change lest we should endanger our power… is a doctrine of which I cannot think without indignation.*

Central to this development was the education of the indigenous population. In arguing that this education should be in the English language and should follow the British tradition and syllabus, Macaulay wrote in his famous 'Minute of 2 February 1835 on Indian Education':

> *In one point I fully agree with the gentlemen to whose general views I am opposed. I feel with them that it is impossible for*

us, with our limited means, to attempt to educate the body of the people. We must at present do our best to form a class who may be interpreters between us and the millions whom we govern; a class of persons, Indian in blood and colour, but English in taste, opinions, in morals and intellect.

Although universities and colleges were subsequently established in a number of Indian towns and cities, the sons of the rich continued to be sent to England to receive a traditional education at the Indian civil service college at Haileybury, at the universities and at the Inns of Court. The majority were to return to their native country to pursue a career in the Indian civil service and judiciary. It is significant that the first Indian to return from England to serve in the Indian civil service, in 1864, was Satyendranath Tagore, a relative of Ganendra Mohan Tagore, the first Indian to be called to the Bar in London. The Tagore family of Calcutta were to play a significant part in the social advancement of their country, including promoting the liberation of women.

English common law was considered an important area of study, since it was in operation in all the British colonies, although it never entirely replaced native laws and customs. Moreover, training for the Bar had the added advantages of equipping students with advocacy skills and conferring status, prestige and potential wealth at home. It is no coincidence that many of the leaders of the early independence movements had been trained as barristers in England. These included Gandhi, Nehru, Seretse Khama, the first president of Bechuanaland (modern Botswana), and Tunku Abdul Rahman, founder of modern Malaysia; all of them were educated at the Inner Temple. While in Britain, they adopted the dress and manners of English gentlemen in line with their contemporaries. Mohandas Gandhi was no exception, though he also maintained a number of Indian practices and traditions in London, including his diet.

Meanwhile, the promotion of British higher education spread further through the Empire. Students from Japan and Hong Kong arrived in England soon after those from India, while the sons of African chiefs, merchants and clerics were admitted to the Inns of Court and universities not long afterwards. In the West Indies the situation was different. With the virtual extinction of the indigenous peoples, the black population was made up almost entirely from former slaves, who did not share the advantages of their eastern counterparts. However, after emancipation, an educated class emerged, some of whom were able to send their sons to Britain. Since former slaves tended to adopt the surnames of their European masters, it is difficult to assess when the first black West Indians entered the Inns of Court. Certainly they were in evidence by the 1890s. In 1899 George Christian of Dominica, the son of a former slave, was admitted to Gray's Inn, where he was called to the Bar in 1902. He was to play a significant part in the pan-African Congress held in London in 1900. He subsequently went to West Africa to assist in the establishment of the British legal system there.

Gandhi photographed soon after his arrival in London in the 1880s.

To return to India, a country in which the vast majority of women remained in subjugation, it is interesting to find evidence of surprisingly liberal views among the Indian intelligentsia in Bengal. Thus Cornelia Sorabji, a Parsee whose parents were Christian, was allowed to travel to England to matriculate at Somerville Hall in 1888. In 1892 she became the first woman at Oxford University to sit the examination for Bachelor of Civil Law, although she could not be awarded the degree to which she was entitled for another thirty years. After the passing of the Sex Disqualification (Removal) Act in 1919, Cornelia Sorabji was among the first women to be admitted to Lincoln's Inn. She was called to the Bar in 1923, the year after the first female barrister, Ivy Williams, had been called at the Inner Temple. She subsequently enrolled in the Calcutta High Court and worked assiduously to remove the disadvantages of purdah. Returning to England in later life, she remained in favour of British rule in India, as did the majority of Indians educated in England.

The history of British colonialism continues to give rise to controversy. However, the positive effects of western education should not be overlooked. Without their legal training, would Gandhi and Nehru have been able to negotiate for Indian independence so skilfully, and without major bloodshed? Although much has been made of the Benchers' decision to disbar Gandhi from the Inner Temple in 1922, his conviction for sedition in a British Court made this course of action inevitable. Nor should it be forgotten that, by admitting overseas students in the previous century, the Inns of Court had played a significant part in preparing the British colonies for independence.

Inner Templars Abroad

Master Schiemann

The English are often accused of being parochial and so we are in many ways. Yet the influence of our legal culture on the outside world has been and still is enormous. American legal culture is of course suffused with its English origins and Master Scalia, when sitting in the US Supreme Court alongside Masters Breyer and Kennedy interpreting the US constitution, will happily make reference to old common law cases although he rejects in principle the citation of cases from any other jurisdiction. The influence of English legal thinking in Australia, Canada, the Caribbean, Hong Kong, India, Israel, Malaysia, New Zealand, Pakistan, Singapore, a number of African countries and many others elsewhere is substantial. The same can be said of several international courts. If you look at our honorary Benchers many are distinguished foreign lawyers and we happily share what we each have to offer.

Master Schiemann.

If you had come into dinner in Hall fifty years ago you would have seen students from Ghana, Uganda, Malaya, Singapore, Hong Kong, Bermuda, Cyprus and various other parts of the Commonwealth. My recollection is that in those days those of us whose skin colour was white were in a minority. In many countries the title of barrister at law was prized not only by would-be legal practitioners but also by those with political ambitions. Many of the native-born Englishmen were particularly keen to share a mess with a couple of these Commonwealth students – sometimes because of a desire to know more about the world, but sometimes, I fear, in the hope that the strict observance by some of the party of religiously enjoined teetotalism left rather more wine for the rest.

This early training of Commonwealth students has left its mark on the world. Thus it comes about that Master Fuad became a judge successively in Cyprus, Uganda, Hong Kong and Brunei. Most recently the former Chief Justice of Nigeria, Master Belgore, has been elected an overseas Bencher. There are still many jurisdictions where to this day substantive and procedural aspects of English law and its underlying values are woven into the local legal fabric; indeed, to take a silly example, I would not be surprised if the wearing of wigs by, well, bigwigs survived somewhere in the outside world long after the English had decided to sport other uniforms. The commercial and shipping Bar has always had an international outlook and many barristers have earned more than a crust from cases with transnational elements. These cases are fought in courts or in arbitrations both in England and abroad. All this has a long history and still continues.

However, there have been some new developments in the last fifty years which have had the effect that in some ways the international influence of the Bar and Bench has increased and in others it remains strong. Thus it comes about that, to look simply at some Benchers of the Inner Temple who spring to mind as I write this piece in Luxembourg, we find that the late Master Richard May presided over the International Criminal Tribunal for the former Yugoslavia in The Hague where Masters Nice and Korner have also appeared. Other members of the Bar such as Master Plender appear before or act as members of panels of the World Trade Organisation. Master Sumption is in demand in various common law jurisdictions round the world and disappears for weeks at a time to make submissions there. Many members of the Inner Temple, such as Master Sedley, have appeared before or sat on the European Court of Human Rights (ECtHR) or, following the example of Master Vaughan, have addressed the European Court of Justice (ECJ). Master Higgins, the President of the International Court of Justice, is a Bencher of this Inn as is the British judge at the ECJ. Master Brittan became Vice-President of the European Commission, showing that Inner Templars are not only interested in law but can take in politics as well. Yet we have all taken with us traditions which we learned at home and have often found that these have been valued by our colleagues from other countries.

And so, while the last fifty years have seen a diminution in the number of students from all round the world who used to grace our tables, members of this Inn continue to play a part in spreading the values which we hold dear.

Links with Overseas

America

David P Carey, Brigadier General, US Army (Retired), Executive Director, American Inns of Court, writes: 'On behalf of the American Inns of Court, I heartily congratulate the Inner and Middle Temple on reaching yet another milestone in their history. The close association between the English Inns of Court and the American Inns of Court is remarkable; indeed, the American Inns owe not only their origins but also their rapid development to the English Inns.

'You might be surprised to know that only twenty-seven years ago, many leading American jurists and lawyers considered adopting the English Inns of Court as a model for reshaping the American legal landscape. However, the size of the United States, the method of education of lawyers and the organisation of the legal profession dictated a different approach from the successful English system. But the core principles of professionalism, ethics and civility remain undiluted, and also unchanged is the central mission of the Inns to pass on the best of the common law tradition from one generation of lawyers to the next in one great unbroken chain, from the Middle Ages to the twenty-first century.

'Our formal relationship was sealed in 1988 with a Declaration of Friendship signed in the United States Supreme Court by Chief Justice Warren Burger, on behalf of the American Inns, and the Right Honourable the Lord Bridge of Harwich, a Bencher and former Treasurer of the Inner Temple, for the English Inns. The purpose of the declaration was "to commemorate and celebrate the perpetual friendship and brotherhood between the Inns of Court, the Honourable Society of Lincoln's Inn, the Honourable Society of the Inner Temple, the Honourable Society of the Middle Temple, and the Honourable Society of Gray's Inn and the American Inns of Court Foundation and the chartered American Inns of Court. In token whereof we extend to each other our mutual pledges of amity as apprentices of the common law in the Old World and the New." These elegant words have taken on a special purpose as the cooperation between the English Inns and the American Inns has broadened.

'My personal bond with the Inner Temple was forged during the first occasion when I walked the stones of the Inner Temple. Behind the southern facade of Fleet Street was tucked a world I had known so much about that I could already imagine what I might see when I stepped through the arched entrance. My imagination did not do justice to the beautiful reality I discovered. With magnificent courts and quadrangles, its stunning terraces, its ancient Church, its gardens sweeping down to the Thames, this seemingly secret world was truly the centre of the legal universe, as I recall thinking.

'As I passed by the latest crop of eager young prospects – themselves only recently called to the Bar – I could not help thinking that their paths were clearly leading to success. Those paths, on which thousands of the best and the brightest of English barristers had walked, were also the paths that have contributed so much to the development of American law. Just as the stones speak out their encouragement to today's prospects, they also call out their encouragement to all those who share the values of our common law traditions. We American lawyers are grateful to our colleagues in the Inner Temple for our heritage and forever mindful of your continuing encouragement.'

Germany

Volker Heinz, in a speech given on 11 May 2001, celebrated the Temple Gift Foundation, established that year in order to mark reconciliation and friendship between Great Britain and Germany: 'The Foundation is about gifts offered from Germany to this country on the occasion of the sixtieth anniversary of the destruction of much of the Temple Church by Germany's Luftwaffe in May 1941. The gifts are offered in memory of Helmuth James Count von Moltke, a German attorney executed by the Nazi authorities, and behind them lies the lasting burden of the Second World War, a war prepared and provoked by a criminal political leadership in Germany. The atrocities committed by its government, its armies and police forces are likely to stay at the

The Temple Church with its memorial benches.

top of the international league table of barbarity for ever… That is one side of tragedy. Perhaps even more painful is the other: how could a sizeable portion of society in Third Reich Germany have elected, supported, even collaborated with such a government? No sensible German can ignore the moral duties arising from such a tragedy… the first, in my opinion, being to acknowledge it and the second to take continually a moral stance on matters civic and politic…

'Against this background, the Temple Gift was born earlier this year, when I saw pictures of the 1941 destruction of the Temple Church, and of the Inner Temple Hall, where, after its reconstruction, I had been called to the Bar in 1989. I recalled my first visit to the Temple in 1987 where, for the first time, I had been confronted with a plaque reminding us of the destruction of the Lamb Building which formerly stood in the centre of Church Court; the words "Destroyed by Enemy Action", without reference to the identity of the enemy, triggered in me feelings of both shame and respect. After seeing those gripping pictures I could not find an easy exit from my renewed feelings of shame. I realised that I wanted to deal with these feelings in a forward-looking way. With legal homes in Germany and Great Britain, I felt that I should make a contribution to the ongoing process of reconciliation and friendship between the former enemies. And I wanted to respond to Coventry's gesture towards Dresden where a British-funded large cross is now crowning the dome of the reconstructed Church of Our Lady. Thus the Temple Gift was conceived.

'Half a century before I became an English barrister, Helmuth James Count von Moltke, like myself a Rechtsanwalt or attorney practising in Berlin, was called to the Bar in the Inner Temple Hall in 1938. His mother was of Scottish descent, the daughter of Sir James Rose Innes, Chief Justice of South Africa and an Inner Templar. His father was German, the heir of Silesian Kreisau estate situated in modern Poland. Helmuth James was one of the far too few to give his moral convictions priority over his duty to show allegiance to his government, a government that through its behaviour had lost its claim to loyalty… A lawyer conscripted into the legal functions of the German army, he openly contradicted the lawless views of some of his Nazi superiors. He organised meetings with like-minded friends and colleagues, anticipating the defeat of Nazi Germany and planning Germany's post-war political leadership. He was arrested and incarcerated, then tried, sentenced to death and executed, in January 1945. He left a widow and two sons, then aged five and eight. Freya von Moltke, a widow now for more than fifty-six years, earlier this year gave her consent to name our Foundation's scholarship after her murdered husband. Thus the Temple Gift was given a moral patronage of the highest distinction.'

Part of the Temple Gift was a small organ that seems to have found many friends among organists and listeners. It is the successor of an organ which used to be played by Handel and was destroyed, together with the Temple Church, in 1941. Another part of the Gift was the stone benches outside the Temple Church in Church Court, dedicated in October 2003 by Master Schiemann, then Treasurer, with the following words: 'Behind us is the site of the Lamb Building destroyed by enemy action. Thus also was much destroyed in Berlin where some of us grew up. I can not say with Wilfred Owen, "I am the enemy you killed my friend". But my father was one such. In front of us are benches to mark a fervent wish for peace. Whether you walk from east to west or from west to east, whether you speak English or German, these benches will bring that fervent wish to mind. The inscription behind us speaks of the past. May the inscription before us speak of the future.'

personality

THE LADY AND THE LAW

One of England's foremost legal personalities, Baroness Elizabeth Butler-Sloss is known for her no-nonsense yet humanitarian approach to high-profile, emotionally-charged cases. Recently appointed to preside over the inquest into the death of the Princess of Wales, **Diana Khoo** met up with her for a quick chat when she visited Kuala Lumpur to deliver a public lecture organized by the ASEAN Law Association of Malaysia and the Malaysian Inner Temple Alumni.

photos **DANNY LEE AT PICTURE DESIGNER**

It is hard to imagine the Rt. Hon. Baroness Elizabeth Butler-Sloss involved in controversial and emotionally-charged cases featuring notorious individuals like the two child killers who'd murdered baby James Bulger in Liverpool in 1993 as there is a sweet grandmotherly innocence about her. But look past the silvery coiff and demure frock and you can't help but notice her piercing blue eyes, sharp-as-a-pin wit and engaging personality. One of Britain's most-respected names in the judicial world, Lady Butler-Sloss was recently in Kuala Lumpur to deliver a public lecture organized by the ASEAN Law Association of Malaysia and the Malaysian Inner Temple Alumni. In legal practice from 1955 to 1970, Lady Butler-Sloss was appointed a judge of the High Court in 1979 and in 1988 became the first woman judge to be appointed to the Court of Appeal as well as being President of the Family Division from 1999 to 2005. The indomitable seventy-two year old has also given up her brief attempt at retirement to don her robes once again as she assumes control of the inquest hearings into the deaths of the late Diana, Princess of Wales and her lover, Dodi Al-Fayed, in the infamous 1997 Paris car accident, replacing royal coroner Michael Burgess who took himself off the case in July this year.

DESTINED FOR LAW

Born into a distinguished legal family, Lady Butler-Sloss's father, Justice Havers, was also a High Court judge while her brother, Lord Havers, was a former Lord Chancellor. She is also married to barrister Joseph Butler-Sloss, who was judge of the High Court of Kenya in the mid 80s. "She certainly comes from a very distinguished family of judges and lawyers," observes Tay Beng Chai, Managing Partner of Tay & Partners. "She's certainly amazing and, without a doubt, has been a trailblazer for many women in the UK and beyond." Trailblazer certainly seems to be the apt word. Called to the Bar (Inner Temple) in 1955, she has had a career most women in those days could only dream of. "I

96

The Inner Temple has strong Malaysian links. This article in Peak *magazine followed Master Butler-Sloss's visit to Kuala Lumpur to deliver a lecture.*

Tamzin Brown, who travelled to Mumbai in 2006 as a Pegasus scholar.

I am proud of being a member of the Honourable Society of the Inner Temple. My most memorable and fantastic experience was when I spent a few days with His Honour Judge Coningsby at Croydon law courts. I started work preparing the case in his room full of heavy legal books. We read the witness statements from both the plaintiff and the defendant. The judge guided me though what to do, the legal books to read, the principal civil procedures in practice and case law in the similar cases. I then went with His Honour into the court room, sitting by his side and listening to the prosecuting and defending counsel, which was very exciting for me – my first real life day in court. Call night was grand too, first in the Church and then the party in the garden – much better than an ordinary graduation ceremony.

FLORENCE ONYEJEKWE

It is a matter of great honour for me to be a member and part of the Honourable Society of the Inner Temple since 1995. I spent quality time at the Inn, I learnt a lot from my colleagues and seniors and I am presently practising at Peshawar High Court, Pakistan. I also remained as the city Nazim/Mayor for a period of four years in the Devolution plan.

HAROON BILOUR

I will always look back fondly at my brief but eventful time in London after I began the BVC in September 2004. I recall excellent lecture nights, endless wine and sushi, beef stroganoff, boasting to my friends from other Inns about the incredible selection of cakes at the dessert table. Inner Temple was good for me; it provided a collegiate and communal experience, compared with the commercialised, impersonal and conveyor-belt type experience that education in modern universities often is. I encountered nothing but friendly advice, good service and warm smiles in the Inn, whether it was from the porters, the Benchers or the staff. Our Library is a proper library too; it smells like a library and it inspires one to think. It is also remarkably comfortable, which unfortunately inspires one to fall asleep…

So many things about the culture of Inner Temple are special: the dedication of the Benchers and members who dine with the students, the effectiveness of the Inn's staff and in particular the Education and Training Department which I strongly believe is the best of all the Inns.

SENG BOON CHAN

I am particularly keen to celebrate Inner Templars who made a significant impact on the United States' adoption of English Law principles and practices. HM Queen Elizabeth, addressing a joint session of the US Congress, described the British Parliament and the US Congress as the 'twin pillars of civilisation'. Underlying this is of course the historical legacy of the Inner Temple, among the few institutions responsible for feeding the minds and nurturing the experience of those many individuals who, collectively, uphold the law, protect and defend our rights and promote freedom here, there and everywhere.

GEORGE MOORE

I joined the Inner Temple when I was reading Law at Trinity Hall, Cambridge, from where I graduated in 1948. Unfortunately at the time the Inner Temple Hall had not been rebuilt so dining was suspended; we simply had to sign a book corresponding to the number of times we would normally have dined. This was not such a serious omission for me, having been exposed to three years of dining in hall at Cambridge, but others missed an important part of studying the law.

As a West Indian I decided that I did not want to practise in England, so took a job in Canada. My visits to England were therefore short and intermittent, and it was not until about twelve years ago that I had the opportunity to visit the Inner Temple and see the rebuilt Hall. I invited a young American lawyer, who had never dined in an Inn, to join me in Hall – a first experience for both of us!

WILLIAM S WALKER

When I was helping to organise a dance in Niblett Hall, I tried desperately to hire a piano, but had no luck. Then I was lucky enough to find one for sale for the princely sum of £3 and promptly bought it. Transport to the Hall cost me £5, and when I returned to my home in West Africa at the end of my studies I simply left it there. Several years later, during a holiday in London, I went to visit the Inner Temple and by chance met Miss Morris, the Sub-Treasurer's secretary. Her first words to me were 'Mr Anthony, your piano is still in the Niblett Hall.'

FARID ANTHONY

International Exchanges and Scholarships

Master Southwell

The Inn has long been involved in bringing to the Bar of England and Wales students from many parts of the world, but particularly from the Commonwealth. This international link was to be reinforced when, in 1987, Lord Goff of Chieveley was asked by the Inn to take the lead in an appeal for funds for scholarships. With his customary vision he saw that the best way of proceeding was to provide money for those young lawyers who wished to come to this country to work with our barristers, and for our young barristers to have the experience of working in other countries, particularly in the USA and the Commonwealth. To realise this vision, Master Goff, Stephen Tomlinson QC and I devised a scheme to establish a new type of international scholarship, to be known as the Pegasus Scholarship, which would be available to several newly qualified barristers each year. With immense generosity members of the Inn, particularly Benchers, subscribed to the scheme, which was established under the chairmanship of Master Goff, and the vice-chairmanship of Stephen Tomlinson, who was in charge of day to day administration.

Five judges: Lord Goff of Chieveley is second left. The others are Sir Richard Scott (left), Lord Woolf (centre), Sir Stephen Brown (second right) and Lord Mackay of Clashfern (right).

Master Goff established good relations with a number of countries including New Zealand through Master Robin Cooke, then President of the New Zealand Court of Appeal, and later Lord Cooke of Thorndon, a Lord of Appeal in Ordinary. He also established an excellent link with the American Inns of Court Foundation. As a result, since the 1980s, we have been able to send a large number of young barristers to New Zealand, Australia, USA, Singapore, Hong Kong, the European Court of Justice, the European Court of Human Rights and many other destinations.

The benefits of the scheme can perhaps be illustrated by the experience of one young Inner Templar, Nicholas Lavender. He went as a Pegasus Scholar through the American Inns of Court to New Orleans, where he worked with a partner in an excellent Louisiana law firm. Early in his three months' stay he went with the partner to the court for an interlocutory hearing. When he was introduced to the judge in court, the judge insisted that the English barrister should address the court on the case. This Nicholas Lavender did, and the judge expressed approval of the clarity of the English barrister (and of his accent). He could have had no better experience away from his normal base in commercial chambers in London.

Over the same period we have welcomed as our guests numerous incoming Pegasus Scholars from many of the countries in the Commonwealth and from the USA. They have been among the brightest and most able young lawyers of their time. Some have come through the aegis of the Cambridge Commonwealth Trust founded and run successfully by Dr Anil Seal, others through the American Inns of Court and others directly. We have established recently the New Zealand Pegasus Scholarships bringing from that country some of their ablest young lawyers. I took over from Lord Goff as chairman and have been succeeded by Julian Flaux QC.

As a means of enabling young barristers to have the vital experience of seeing practice abroad, the Pegasus Scholarships have been a real success. Initially the outgoing scholarships were confined to barristers of the Inner Temple, but it was always Lord Goff's and our aim that they should be available to all barristers who were members of any of the four Inns of Court. That was achieved some years ago and we have had the benefit of representatives of all four Inns sitting on our management committee, including Sir John Mummery, a Lord Justice of Appeal and former Treasurer of Gray's Inn.

Another international exchange scheme, the Paris Bar Exchange, was initiated by Gray's Inn under the direction of Sir John Mummery and Michael Brooke QC (now His Honour Judge Michael Brooke QC). This enables young British barristers and avocats from Paris to undertake a short exchange similar in kind to the Pegasus Scholarships, enriching both. I remember particularly the criticisms of our judicial review system which a young Paris avocat expressed to me, and her lucidity and competence, which she thought had been strengthened by seeing our Bar and our judiciary in action.

Lord Goff's aims are being achieved in two ways by the Pegasus Scholarships and the Paris Bar Exchange. In the 1980s we were concerned by what seemed to us to be the insularity of our Bar, and we were determined to do our utmost to break it down by means of exchange scholarships, and slowly persuading our barristers to cite the case law of other countries, whether in the Commonwealth or more recently in Europe. In both these respects the Bar and the judiciary have been enriched, and it is to his vision that we owe a considerable debt.

INN TO THE FUTURE

INN TO THE FUTURE

Master May

Charles Lamb was born on 10 February 1775 in Crown Office Row. He spent the first seven years of his life in the Temple. His father, John Lamb, was clerk and confidential servant to Samuel Salt, who had chambers there, and who was a Bencher of Inner Temple from 1782 until his death in 1792. Crown Office Row was Charles Lamb's childhood home. His Elia essay 'The Old Benchers of the Inner Temple', regarded by a Victorian editor, Alfred Ainger, as 'one of the most varied and beautiful pieces of prose that English literature can boast', is a loosely woven tapestry of recollections from childhood of what must have seemed to him to have included crusty old men, Benchers of the Inn in the last years of the eighteenth century. The Inn was to him:

> *... the most elegant spot in the metropolis. What a transition for a countryman visiting London for the first time – passing from the crowded Strand or Fleet Street, by unexpected avenues, into its magnificent ample squares, its classic green recesses!*

He regretted the passing of sun-dials in favour of clocks. He delighted in fountains, fast vanishing. 'Why not, then, gratify children by letting them stand? Lawyers, I suppose, were children once.'

One of the old Benchers portrayed in the essay was the Hon Daines Barrington KC, Treasurer in 1785. When the account of his year's Treasurership came to be audited, the following singular charge was unanimously disallowed by the Bench: 'Item, disbursed Mr Allen, the gardener, twenty shillings for stuff to poison the sparrows, by my orders.' Daines Barrington is remembered as one of the correspondents of Gilbert White, naturalist of Selborne. The shield bearing his coat of arms may be seen today on the right-hand wall of Inner Temple Hall near the Bench, marking his term of office as Reader in 1784. Samuel Salt likewise has his shield there as Reader in 1787.

Inner Temple was already a centuries-old institution when Charles Lamb was a child. It was even so when King James I on 13 August 1608 granted the Royal Charter, jointly with Middle

Crown Office Row before the Second World War.

Crown Office Row as rebuilt.

Temple, which this book celebrates. The Inn has matured a further two and a quarter centuries since Lamb's childhood. But maturity has not diminished its vigour. Today's Crown Office Row was rebuilt after its destruction in the Second World War, as were the main Treasury buildings, including the Hall, the Parliament Chamber and the magnificent Library. The Inn remains a most elegant spot in the metropolis with a number of fine listed buildings and as ample an open space garden as any in central London east of Trafalgar Square.

Yet venerable antiquity, historic buildings and a cloud of tradition do not obscure the present modern institution. The King James Charter commands the Inn to have and hold the property which the Charter grants to 'serve for the accommodation and education of those studying and following the profession of [law]'; and requires the Inn, with Middle Temple, to maintain the Temple Church in perpetuity and to provide the Master of the Temple with a house and stipend. In the modern world, the Inn remains dedicated to performing these duties in an entirely modern and progressive way.

Daines Barrington's Reader's shield in the Hall.

The maintenance of the Temple Church, including its magnificent choir and superb musical achievements, is enthusiastically undertaken with Middle Temple and faithfully performed. But the Inn's main vision for the future looks to its students of whatever nationality; to their education and qualification as barristers; to their continuing education and fellowship as barristers, wherever they practise, after they are called to the Bar; and to the maintenance thereby of professional integrity and the rule of law in this jurisdiction and worldwide. The Inn also, and importantly, strives to maintain contact and fellowship with those of its many members who do not go on to practise at the independent Bar and who may not continue as professional lawyers.

But lofty vision requires practical application. In formal terms, the Inn will continue to admit students and, when they are duly qualified, call them to the Bar. It will continue to provide and foster the now obligatory continuing professional development of those who practise as barristers. It will continue to maintain and foster relationships with its members in many other jurisdictions with common law traditions and is proud when so many of its members attain high and important offices and positions in their own jurisdictions.

In practical terms, the modern law student working to come to the Bar faces the twin challenge of expense and competitive entry into a profession which cannot accommodate everyone and where some outworn barriers are perceived to exist. On these crucially important matters, Inner Temple embraces without qualification the policy of the Bar as a whole that talent alone must be the criterion for entry into and practise at the Bar. No Inn of Court is able to regulate so as to control the market forces which currently mean that there are more students aspiring to become barristers than the profession as a whole can sustain in practise. The main market force which dictates the number of barristers that the profession can sustain is the quantity of professional work which those who pay for it are prepared and able to afford. The Inn can, however, and does use its resources to the end that those with talent, whoever they are, are enabled to afford the cost of training and thereby of entry into the profession, and that such other barriers as may exist are overcome.

The Inn's resources in this respect are its property and its members and staff. The Inn's property, including the car parking space, is its main source of income. All of the property that can be is let to professional or residential tenants. The product of this enables the Inn to make scholarship, bursary and other awards to students. In the year in which this is written, these awards will for the first time exceed £1m. These awards are made to those with the talent to become barristers who truly need the money to be able to undertake the Bar Vocational Course or other necessary qualification to become a barrister.

The Inn's resources embodied in its members and staff are massively important in all departments. If the Estates Department may be seen as that which manages and maintains the property which produces a majority of the income, all other departments in one way or another interrelate and foster relations with the members of the Inn and in particular its students. If the Education and Training Department, the Library, the Registry, the main office and those who administer scholarships are obviously prominent with the students, so in truth is every one of the Inn's compact and dedicated staff.

All these departments are under the aegis and direction of committees and subcommittees of the Inn's Benchers and barristers; and the critical point is that all these are gratuitous volunteers. The same goes for scores of other Benchers and members of the Inn who sponsor students, helping them find their feet, or participating in a tutorial or pastoral capacity in the various and varied educational activities. This resource of voluntary duty is one which the Inn's vision for the future must take the greatest care to nurture and preserve. For upon it ultimately rests one of the means whereby the rule of law will be maintained – that is, by the maintenance of a properly educated, independent Bar, whose every member understands and fearlessly performs their twin duties to their clients, whoever they may be, and to the courts in which they appear. Thus in substance has every student member of the Inn been duly instructed upon their call to the Bar for upwards of 450 years.

Since maintaining the Inn's income to enable it to make awards to talented students for their education depends on maintaining its property, the vision for the future has to be long term and has to look to progressive modernisation and rebuilding. Because many of the buildings are elderly, the income they produce is at the price of high maintenance costs. Because many of the buildings are listed, there is a limit to the extent to which modernisation may be permitted or structurally possible. Strategically, the Inn needs to look to make the best long term use for income of those of its buildings which it must, and wants to, preserve; and it must, when it may, construct sensitively designed new buildings suitable for use by the modern Bar. The Inn is not, of course, a commercial property company. But it is obliged by its Charter and general charitable objects to manage its property for the benefit of its students and for the continuing professional education of its members. The long term vision may be obscured by today's need to clear leaves from an inaccessible gutter at roof level in Paper Buildings, for instance. But the long term need must be to continue to have buildings fit to be used for modern purposes. That has to mean building some new buildings – building for the future.

No doubt, if a child were born today in Crown Office Row to live there for its first seven years, as Charles Lamb did, that child would see today's Benchers of the Inner Temple as old and perhaps crusty. If I may presume to speak for my fellow Benchers and from a further point along life's perspective, we do not see ourselves quite like that; and certainly today's Governing Benchers are not by modern standards old. The institution itself, for all that it has been in existence as a professional home of barristers for many centuries, is neither old nor crusty. It is a modern institution, looking firmly to the future, cherishing its students who themselves will, I am confident, cherish the Inn's future students, towards the maintenance of the rule of law.

Master May with students.

Opposite: Through Mitre Court archway.

NON RESIDENTS
MUST NOT
BRING DOGS
INTO THE INN

ACKNOWLEDGMENTS

This book does not include footnotes or references, though a few of the original pieces included them; the full texts with references can be consulted in the Inner Temple Archives. A short list of Further Reading is given below, where can be found titles cited by some of the authors as well as more general material. The interview with Joanne Brown (p 123), conducted by Ros Anderson, first appeared in the 2 September 2006 edition of the *Guardian Weekend.*

Huge thanks are due to the many authors and contributors who delivered their pieces to a very tight deadline, as well as to the members of the Editorial Board, chaired by the Sub-Treasurer, Patrick Maddams, who oversaw the planning, writing and production stages of the book. Members of the Treasury Office staff offered unstinting help, in particular Kate Peters whose expertise with the illustrations was invaluable. Charlotte Bircher, Deputy Sub-Treasurer at the outset, saw the project on its way, and her successor, Yeshim Harris, was equally supportive. In addition to those whose mention above and those names appear in the book as authors – Master Baker, Michael Frost, the Rev Robin Griffith-Jones, Dr Clare Rider – other Editorial Board and staff members who were involved were Margaret Clay, Alex Hall-Taylor and Jacqueline Fenton.

The staff at Third Millennium Information were their usual professional selves: Chris Fagg as the publisher, Susan Pugsley as designer, Bonnie Murray as production manager, Michael Jackson as marketing manager and Neil Burkey who managed the database. Many thanks are due to their unflappable approach and their high standards.

PICTURE ACKNOWLEDGMENTS
Illustrations in this book have been drawn from a number of copyright sources. Every effort has been made to trace and contact copyright holders of images reproduced here; we will be glad to correct any unintentional errors or omissions in any future editions of this book.

Please note No image in this book may be reproduced in any media format whatsoever without written permission of the publishers, Third Millennium Information Ltd, 3–5 Benjamin St, EC1M 5QL, acting on behalf of the copyright holders. All enquiries as to images in this book should be directed to Third Millennium Information Ltd, who undertake to direct them to the appropriate copyright holders.

Special photography for this book was supplied by Yael Schmidt (photographer in chief), with additional images from Julian Andrews, Adrian Blunt, Ian Bavington Jones, Mark Mather, Kate Peters, Philippe Terrance and Matthew Wilson.

Prints and engravings reproduced in this book come from the collection of Master Baker.

Archive photographs: National Monuments Record, English Heritage (p 65); Getty Images (pp 168, 169).

Paintings: Chaucer's *Manciple* from Ellesmere Manuscript EL26 C9 f203r (p 17) is reproduced by courtesy of the Huntington Library, Art Collections and Botanical Gardens, San Marino, California; Richard Wilson's *Crown Office Row after the Fire of 4 January 1737* (p 65) is reproduced by courtesy of Tate Britain (copyright Tate, London 2006); van der Meulen's *Robert Dudley, Earl of Leicester* (p 150) is reproduced by permission of the Trustees of the Wallace Collection, London.

FURTHER READING

Baker, J H, *The Third University of England* (Selden Society Lecture) (1990)

Baker, J H, *Readers and Readings in the Inns of Court and Chancery* (2000)

Baker, J H, *An Inner Temple Miscellany* (2004)

Baker, J H, *Legal Education in London 1250–1850* (Selden Society Lecture) (2007)

Blunt, Adrian, 'Historical Manuscripts in the Inner Temple Library', *Law Librarian*, **23(2)** (1992), 57–9

Calendar of the Inner Temple Records, A, 8 vols, three in typescript (1896–1992)

Corner, G R, *Observations on Four Illuminations representing the Courts of Chancery, King's Bench, Common Pleas and Exchequer, at Westminster, from a Ms of the time of King Henry VI* (1865)

Davies, J Conway, *Catalogue of Manuscripts in the Library of the Honourable Society of the Inner Temple*, 3 vols (1972)

Dugdale, W, *Origines Juridiciales* (3rd edn, 1680)

Hart, E A P, *The Hall of the Inner Temple* (1952)

Inner Temple Yearbook, The (1987–)

Ker, N R, *Medieval Manuscripts in British Libraries*, 1 (1969)

Knight, David, 'The Battle of the Organs, the Smith organ at the Temple and its organist', *British Institute of Organ Studies Journal*, **21** (1997), 77

Lamb, Charles, 'The Old Benchers of the Inner Temple', *Essays of Elia* (1823)

Lemmings, D, *Gentlemen and Barristers: the Inns of Court and the English Bar 1680-1730* (1990)

Lewer, David, *A Spiritual Song* (1961)

Lewer, David, and Dark, Robert, *The Temple Church in London* (1997)

MacKinnon, Sir Frank, *Inner Temple Papers*, (1948, reprinted 2003)

Prest, W R, *The Inns of Court under Elizabeth I and the early Stuarts*, 1590–1640 (1972)

Richardson, W C, *A History of the Inns of Court* (1978)

Readings and Moots at the Inns of Court in the Fifteenth Century, Selden Society, **71** (1954); 105 (1990)

Report of the Commissioners appointed to Inquire into the Arrangements in the Inns of Court and Inns of Chancery, for promoting the Study of the Law and Jurisprudence (1855)

Silsoe, Lord, *The Peculiarities of the Temple* (1972)

Wienpahl, R W, *Music at the Inns of Court during the Reigns of Elizabeth, James and Charles* (1979)

Williamson, J B, *History of the Temple* (1924)

INDEX OF SUBSCRIBERS

This book has been made possible through the generosity of the following:

Razman Abdul Rahim
The Rt Hon Lord Abernethy
Nadia Ahmad
K Zaman Ali
Phillip Aliker
Margaret E Allen
Ludwik Allerhand
Sir John Alliott
Zaid A Almihdar
Anthony Anderson QC
Leopold J Antelme
Mr Farid R Anthony
Her Honour Judge Shirley Anwyl QC
Howard W Aplin
Mrs Irene Arbuthnott
R Douglas Armstrong
Professor Charles Arnold-Baker OBE
Miss Anjali Arvinkumar Narshi
Winston Asante
Peter M. Ashman
Nicholas Asprey
Mr Jody Atkinson
Shamsul-Bahrain
Kaare Bangert
David Barker QC
His Honour Judge William Barnett QC
Nicholas Barraclough
Charles N Barton
Eric Baskind
His Honour Paul Batterbury TD DL
Mrs Caroline Beasley-Murray
C Beasley-Murray
Nicholas Beddard
Sir Roy Beldam
G J Bennett
John Beveridge QC
Catherine Helen Bexson
Haroon Bashir Bilour
Inigo Bing
Peter Birkett QC
Sarah Julia Bishop
George Richard Blackburn
Susan Blake
Nopadol Boonyai
Sir William Boulton Bt Kt CBE TD
Les Filles de Paul M Bourassa
(Madeline, Elisabeth et Catherine)
Ian Bourne QC
Martin Bowley QC
Sir Jeffrey Bowman
Jeanne Bradbury (née Pratt)
David Bradshaw
Kate Branigan QC
Ms Daire Brehan
Chris Bridger
Dennis Broadway
S E Brodie QC
James Bromley-Chellenor
Sir Henry Brooke
Helen Lady Broughton
His Honour Judge R Brown
Joanne Brown
Stephen Brown
Mrs C Bruce
Adrian Brunner QC
Mr M J Budworth
Barbara R Bunker
His Honour Judge Burford QC
Anthony Bushell
Lady Butler-Sloss
Peter Butt
His Honour Neil Butter CBE QC
Dr Ann Canham
G R Canner
C J Caradog-Morgan
Sue Carr QC
Michele Carroll
Her Honour Judge Case
Miss Julie D Catt
Rt Hon Sir John Chadwick
Abraham Chan
Seng Boon Chang
Alexandra Chandanou
Jacqueline Chang Li Ch'ing
Puan Sri Grace Chang
Brian Wong Chao Wai
Dr David Chapman-Jones
Tim Charlton QC
Mr S Chelvan
Huan Cheng QC SC
Matthias Chang Wen Chieh
Christopher Chilton
Samson Chee Tsu Chin
Han Choi
Iain Christie
Louisa Cieciora
Philip Circus
Baroness Clark of Calton
Ms Marian Cleghorn
Mr Richard J Clews
Shane Clifford
Mr Christopher Coghlan
Terence Coghlan QC
Richard Colbey
Dercella Iona Cole
John Cole
His Honour Judge Nicholas Coleman
Russell Coleman
Andrew Collender QC
Dr Michael Collins
Sir Michael Connell
Anthony Connerty
Mr Stephen Connor
Jeremy Consitt
Adam Constable
Sir Colin Corness
Jean-Paul Costa
Miss Caroline Cowan
Mrs Justice Laura Cox
John M Coyne
C E Crace
Aubrey Craig
Mrs Muriel Craig

Sir Frederick Crawford
Dr Stephen Cretney
His Honour Judge Critchlow
Kristina H L Croft
Karen C Culbard
The Rt Hon Headley Cunningham QC
Jo Cunningham
Sir Richard Curtis
Advocates Roger Dadd and Mary Ferbrache
Caoimhe S Daly
Michael d'Arcy
D G St E Dasilva
Peter Davidson
Jennifer Lila Dean
John Deby QC
Baroness Deech of Cumnor
Estelle A Dehon
Barry Delaney
Tina Denby
Paul Denham
His Honour Judge Denyer QC
Richard Dew
Robin de Wilde QC
Miss Julia Dias
James Dingemans QC
Kate Dixon
Alice Dobbie
Dominic Dos-Remedios
Anthony Douglas-Hamilton
B T Dove-Edwin
Norma Dove-Edwin
The Hon Justice Garry Downes AM
Lorna Marie Dubois
Sean Duncan
The Rt Hon Sir Robin Dunn MC
T C Dutton
Nigel Eagers
Peter Eastwood
Paul Conrad Eia
Helen G Ellis
Hon Justice Lloyd B Ellis
J Anthony Ellison
Michael Elsom
Anthony Engel
Stephen Eyre
Edward Fan
Magda Faraday-Stupples MS
Eleanor Marie Fargin
Geoffrey Farmiloe
Mr Mario M Farquharson
David Farrell QC
Brenda Farthing
Bruce Farthing
Judge Esmond Faulks
Judge Martin L C Feldman
Mr Biagio Rocco Vittorio Feliciello
Guy Fetherstonhaugh QC
Sir Richard Field
Elisabeth Fisher
John D S Fitz-Gerald
Christopher Floyd QC

Sir Thayne Forbes
Ian Foster
Gordon Rowland Fraser
Henry William Fullman
Professor Charles Garraway CBE
His Honour Judge Gaskell
Charles George QC
Mr Jagadish Chandra Ghosh
Leena Ghosh
Orlando Gibbons
Peter Giles
Patrick Goodall
Jonathan A Goodman
Dr Charles Goodson-Wickes DL
Ian Grainger
Judge J B Greaves
Mrs Barbara Greenrod
Mrs Peter Grey
Martin Griffiths QC
Peter Griffiths
Patrick Ground QC
Matthew Groves
Adam Aubrey Guest
Peter Guimarens
Dr Pehr Gyllenhammar
Paul L Hainsworth
Robin, Caroline, Arabella, Indie and Fleur Halstead
Kenneth Hamer
Christopher Hames
The Rt Hon Lord Hamilton, President of the Court of Session in Scotland
E Hamilton QC
Leone Hamilton
A R Hammerton
His Honour R E Hammerton
Mrs J C Hanretty
Malcolm Hardwick QC
Henry B Hargrave
Judge Charles Harris QC
Joseph William Hart
Omi Hatashin
Philip Havers QC
Mr Hilary R Haydon
Angela Hayley
Volker G Heinz
Miss L McL Henderson
R A Henderson QC
Julianne Hicks
Professor The Worshipful Chancellor Mark Hill
His Honour Derek Hill-Smith
Miss Elizabeth Hindmarsh
Charl B Hirschfeld
Sir David Hirst
His Honour Judge Hodge QC
P E Hogarth-Blood
Elisa Holmes
Ms Jessica Homer-Waugh
Paul J Hopkins
Roger Hopkins
Jennifer Horne-Roberts

Cyril Horsford CVO
Dr Mark SW Hoyle
EW Hughes
His Honour Judge Iain Hughes QC
Judith Hughes QC
Michael Humphries QC
Dermott Hynes
Roy William Insole
Edward and Jill Jacobs
Sir Brian Jenkins
Lim Jit Boo
Nicholas P Johnson
Sean Jones
Mr Pramod K Joshi
Jack G M Joyce
Ahsan Kahlon
Neil Kaplan CBE QC
Mr Binoy Karia
Tom Kark
Sir David Keene
Nicholas Kei Cheong Chan
James D Keir QC
Reynold Oswald Kelman
Michael Kew
Dr Ghulam Sabir Khan
Shona Khan
Abu Hasan Kibla
Lisa R Kiff
Margaret Killerby
Henry King
Neil King QC
Karen B Kneller
Henry Knorpel CB QC
Ranjan M Kumar
Shourav Lahiri
H C D Laing
Ian M Laing
Josh Lait
Mrs Peter Langdon-Davies
Gordon Langley
Nicholas Lavender
Sir Ivan Lawrence QC
Rt Hon Sir John Laws
His Honour Judge Michael Lawson QC
Philip Lawson
Miss Sara L J Lawson
Sir Godfray Le Quesne QC
Guy Lemon
Sydney Levine
Tony See Yee Lim
Ian Lim Teck Soon
David E W Linghorn-Baker
Mr Justice Tom Linson
P A Little CBE
The Rt Hon The Lord Lloyd of Berwick
His Honour Humphrey Lloyd QC
Rhiannon Lloyd
Mark Lomas QC
David Loveday
Dorian Lovell-Pank QC
Mr John Lowe

Michele Lusack
Lord Lyell of Markyate PL QC
Ross MacDiarmid
Lord Mackay of Clashfern
Patrick Maddams
David Maddison
Rajendra Mahto
J R Main
Heather Maizels
Simon Jeremy Mallett
Robert M J Manning
Katerina Markoullis
Ross Marland
J W Marrin QC
Gay Martin
Philip Roger Martin
Thelma Lynne Martin
Mike Mason
David Massam
Mr and Mrs M H Matthewson
Bruce Mauleverer
Sir Anthony T K May
Rohinten D Mazda
Mr Louis C Mazel
Adam Peter McCartney
Peter McCartney
Robert McCracken QC
Dermot McDermott
Vera G McEwan
Henry McHale
Jackie McKie
Jamie McLeod Smith
Professor Gerard McMeel
J McPhillamy Adams
His Honour James Mendl
M Meredith Hardy
Hannah Kathryn Mettam
Michael Michell
Master Milford
Andrew Miller
David C Mitchell
Christopher Moger QC
Julie Mogridge
Ms Nisha Mohamed
Nazar Mohammad JP
His Honour E F Monier-Williams
Philip Moor QC
George C J Moore
Peter Morris
Sheriff N M P Morrison QC
Malcolm Morse
Christopher Morton
Mr Philip Moser
Jonathan Henry Metson Moss
The Hon Richard Nall-Cain
Mr Sunil Paul Nannar
Murelidaran Navaratnam
Mr Justice Robert T-N Ndoping
William F Neburagho
Andreas Neocleous
Jacqueline Newman
Lauretta Newman
Paul Nicholls
Mr Andrew Nickolls
Philip Nicol-Gent
Christine Noone
G Norman
Sir Peter North
Mr Adrian Noviss
Edward Nugee TD QC
His Honour Judge Oliver-Jones QC
Michael B O'Maoileoin
Heather O'Neill
Dr Colin Y C Ong
Elizabeth Ong
Mrs Florence Daisy Onyejekwe
P T Oon
Sir Peter Openshaw DL and
Dame Caroline Swift DBE
His Honour Denis Orde
Georgina Orde
Christopher Owen
Robert Owen
Erkut Ozer
Claire J Paczko
His Honour Judge Paget QC
Cliona Papazian
D J T Parry
Simon Parry
Jeffrey Pegden QC
Mr Justice Penry-Davey
Roger Perrot
Peter S T Petts
Murray Pickering QC
Fionn Peter Alexander Pilbrow
Mark Platts-Mills
Jane Plumptre
James Pond
Hayleigh Poole
Raymond Potter CB
Miss Michelle Powell
Edward A G Prentice
James Price QC
Louise Price
Edwin Prince
Anthony Prosser
W Wesley Pue
J A F Purchas
Robin Purchas QC
Edward Quigg
Christopher Quinlan
Dr The Hon Navinchandra Ramgoolam
The Hon Mr Justice Jack
Paul S M Reed
Matthew Reeve
Joseph Refalo
Robert B S Reid
Stephen Reynolds
Robert Rhodes QC
Jonathan B G Rich
Jeremy Richardson QC
J G Rider
The Rt Hon Sir Bernard Rix
Vivian Robinson QC
Hollie A Robson-Marchant
Kenneth Edward Rogers
Michael R Rogers OBE
James Matthews Rowley
William Salomon
Richard Salter QC
Ana Elizabeth Samuel
Alexander Benjamin William Sandiforth
Neil A Sandys
Catriona Sangster
Sir Konrad Schiemann
Stephen Sedley
Nigel Seed QC
Oliver Sells QC
R Raman Sethu
Miss J Seymour
Thomas Seymour
Colin Shaw
Mark Sheldon CBE
Sarah Alexandra Shellard
The Hon Simon Sheller AD QC
Sarah Sheriff
Benjamin A Shorten
Marion Simmons QC
Anthony Simpson TD
His Honour Judge P R Simpson
Biliwi Singh
Andrew Skinner
Suzanne Smales (née Marsen)
George R R B Smedley
Leonorah P D Smith
Cornelius Smith
David Smith and Jennifer Smith (née Chegwyn)
Amelia Smithers
Miss Noushin Sorayyapour
Richard Southwell QC
Mr Peter D Sparkes
Robin Spon-Smith
George A R Spyrou
Paul Sreenan SC
Jennifer-Marian Sanford
Piers Stansfield
George Staple CB QC
Miss Louise Steel
Mr M T Steiger
Alison Stewart
Charles Peter Stewart
Alastair Stewart-Richardson
Evan Stone QC
His Honour Judge Stone QC
Jeremy B Storey QC
The Hon Philip L Storr
J A G Stoton
Helena Strathdene
Annemarie Strong
Sir Jeremy and Lady Sullivan
D D H Sullivan QC
Mr Justice Sumner
Mark Sutherland Williams

INDEX OF NAMES

Authors or contributors are in **bold**, those appearing in pictures are in *italics*.

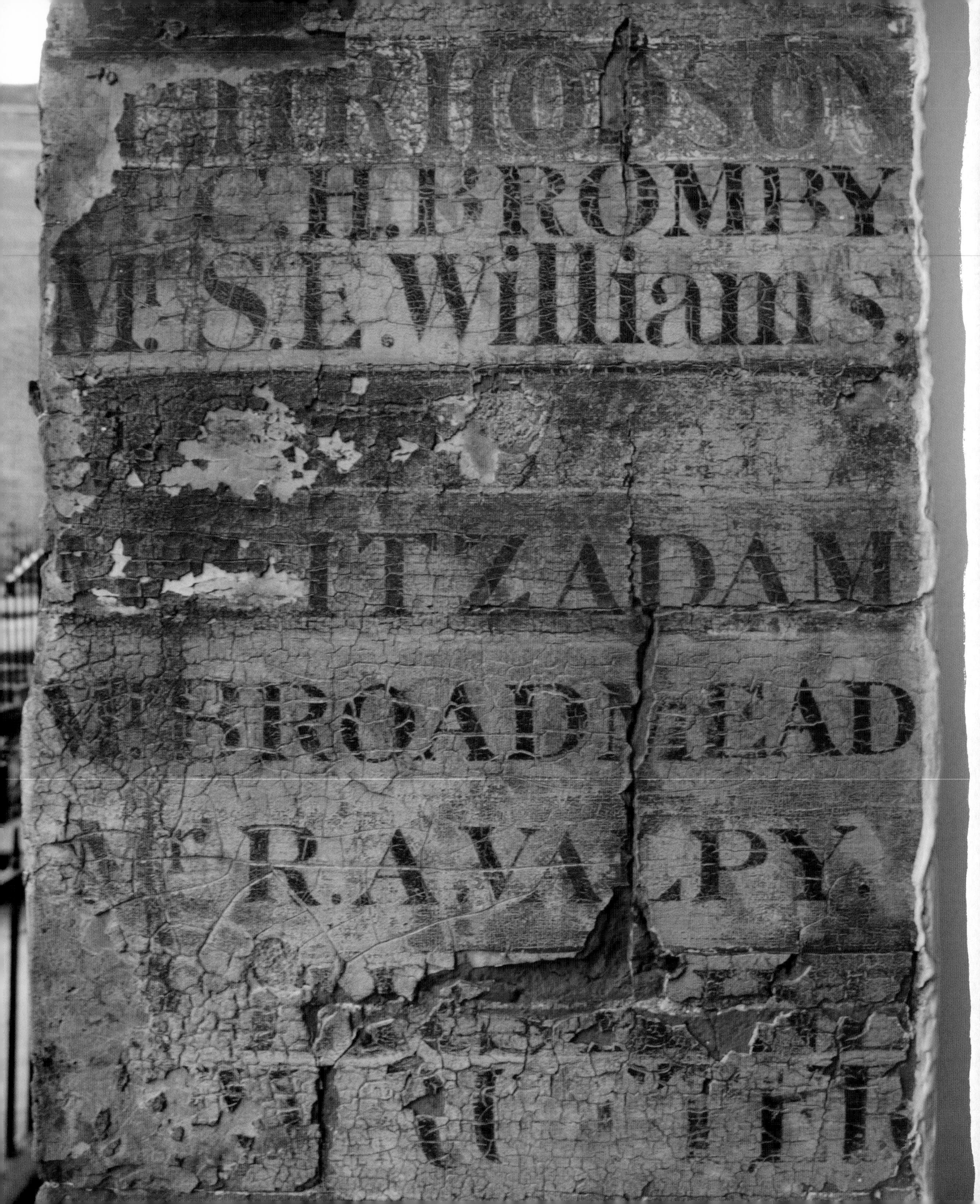
Mr S. E. Williams
ITZADAM

Reference.

k 19. Crown Court.	l 91. Black Eagle Alley.
„ 20. Spread Eagle C^t.	„ 92. Red Cross Alley.
„ 21. Slaughter House Y^d.	„ 93. Three Kings Alley.
„ 24. Blue Anchor Court.	„ 94. Royal Oak Alley.
„ 25. Star Court.	„ 95. White Horse Court.
„ 29. Flying Horse Court.	„ 96. Cross Keys Alley.
„ 30. Bull Head Court.	„ 99. Greyhound Court.
„ 33. Hen & Chicken C^t.	m 1. Sugar Loaf Alley.
„ 35. Falcon Court.	„ 2. Cressers Court.
„ 36. Hercules Pillars Al.	„ 3. Cloath Workers C^t.
„ 39. Passing Alley.	„ 4. Crown Court.
„ 40. Ram Alley.	B 97. Serjeants Inn.
„ 41. Bolt & Tun Court.	„ 98. Bolt and Tun Inn.
„ 42. Boar's Head Court.	„ 99. Black Horse Inn.
„ 45. Essex Court.	75. Dutchy Liberty.
„ 46. Ashen Tree Court.	76. St Dunstan in the W.
„ 49. Brides Alley.	77. White Fryer's Precinct.

The limit of the Great Fire of London thus ~~~

The boundary of the City of London .. ooo

Scale 100 feet to 1 Inch.

B 97

k 19

k 20

k 29

k 30

k 31

FLEET STREET

THE STRAND

...HER ROW

k 21

k 25

k 36

k 35

k 39

194

193

192

191

135

196

73

Hare Court

MIDDLE TEMPLE LANE

Vine Court

Pump Court

Essex Court

Brick Court

Essex House

Elme Court

the Hall Court

Benchers Garden

Middle Temple Hall

...ILFORD